POLICE REFORM

Building Integrity

POLICE REFORM

Building Integrity

Editors

Tim Prenzler and Janet Ransley

HAWKINS PRESS
2002

Published in Sydney by:
Hawkins Press
A division of The Federation Press
PO Box 45, Annandale, NSW, 2038
71 John St, Leichhardt, NSW, 2040
Ph (02) 9552 2200 Fax (02) 9552 1681
E-mail: info@federationpress.com.au
Website: http://www.federationpress.com.au

National Library of Australia
Cataloguing-in-Publication entry

Police reform: building integrity.

Bibliography.
Includes index.
ISBN 1 867606 715 2

1. Police corruption – Prevention. 2. Police corruption –
Australia – Prevention. 3. Police ethics. 4. Police
Ethics – Australia. 5. Police administration. 6. Police administration –
Australia. I. Prenzler, Tim. II. Ransley, Janet.

364.1323

Typeset by The Federation Press, Leichhardt, NSW.
Printed by Shannon Books Pty Ltd, Bayswater VIC.

Contents

INNOVATIONS IN CREATING
ETHICAL POLICE DEPARTMENTS

Preface

At the time of writing this preface, police misconduct issues remained firmly in the headlines. In our home State of Queensland, Australia, two young detectives went to jail for trading in amphetamines. In Western Australia, a Royal Commission began investigations amidst sensational claims from a former detective that he and a senior colleague had fabricated evidence and beaten a suspect in a major fraud case 20 years earlier. In Tasmania, the Industrial Court was hearing an appeal from an officer dubbed 'Sergeant Sleaze' – dismissed after encouraging heavy drinking amongst young police and engaging in a sex act in a public place. In Victoria, there were fears that tainted evidence from drug squad detectives would lead to the release from jail of organised crime figures. But these issues were not confined to Australia. The following is a small selection of media reports on police misconduct from around the world for two months of 2002.[1]

Mexico begins to wade through morass of police corruption – Many of Mexico City's citizens think their biggest law enforcement problem is the police. Thousands of uniformed officers do double duty as criminals: petty thieves, armed robbers, extortionists and, on occasion, killers.[2]

Russian president calls for crackdown on police corruption – The president clearly realises ... the overlap between organised crime and state bureaucracy... 'We must resolutely get rid of officers who have converted their service into a form of business'.[3]

Afghan chief faces huge task – Charged with reforming a bankrupt police force rife with corruption, Afghanistan's new interior minister promised to resign after seven months if he failed in his task.[4]

Report on police corruption more woe for Blair – Prime Minister Tony Blair's beleaguered administration has suffered another setback with the disclosure of an internal report charging that the war against crime in Britain is being damaged by corrupt police ... (who)

---

1   <http://global.factiva.com>, accessed 13 July.
2   *New York Times*, 17 June, p 3.
3   Russian Centre TV, 31 May.
4   *Akron Beacon Journal*, 22 June.

pass on police secrets to the underworld, resulting in failed operations, intimidation of witnesses and the exposure of informants.[5]

This book is about the recurring problem of police corruption, and contemporary efforts to find effective strategies to maximise ethical conduct. It draws on international experience, using Australia as a major source. In the last 15 years, Australian policing has been of significant interest globally because of the combination of advanced democratic processes, exposés of serious police corruption, and extensive – sometimes radical – experimentation with prevention strategies. The book provides an overview of developments and issues in police integrity control, with close attention to special problem areas and to innovations in establishing and maintaining best practice.

Police Reform: Building Integrity is directed towards all stakeholders in police conduct: police managers, professional standards branch personnel, general duties officers, recruits, civilian oversight agencies, civil libertarians, politicians, police studies scholars and students, and the general public. The book brings together the latest research on types of police misconduct in a form that is readily accessible to a wide range of readers; with short, clearly focused, chapters on specialist topics. It balances diagnostic and theoretical explanations of police behaviour with a series of expositions of specific practical strategies for preventing misconduct and creating ethical departments.

The first set of chapters is combined under the heading *Challenges to Reform*. Chapter 1, 'Corruption and Reform: Global Trends and Theoretical Perspectives', sets the international context for the book. It describes the universal problem of police corruption and its discovery in different countries through a variety of mechanisms, especially commissions of inquiry. Different types of misconduct are categorised, along with explanations focused on the police task environment and the traditional organisational culture of police. The chapter concludes with a comprehensive summary of strategies developed to detect and prevent corruption.

The second chapter, 'Miscarriages of Justice', examines how the fabrication of evidence is frequently a core feature of corrupt police cultures, but often neglected in efforts to reform the criminal justice system. Famous cases of wrongful conviction are examined, including the 'Guildford Four' and 'Birmingham Six' cases. The chapter on

---

5   *Washington Post*, 18 June.

'Public Order Policing' tackles a perennial issue currently attracting widespread attention following extreme violence between police and protestors in anti-globalisation protests. This chapter analyses the dynamics of police-citizen conflict and enlarges on principles developed by progressive police departments for managing public demonstrations in an optimally non-confrontational fashion. 'Race Relations' develops the theme of conflict between police and Indigenous people, emphasising the enormous challenge posed by this problem for modern ideas of community policing. A variety of positive initiatives are reviewed, including the introduction of Indigenous liaison officers and the incorporation of principles of tribal justice into criminal justice processes. The chapter, 'Sex Discrimination', argues that discrimination and harassment are forms of internal corruption which have been neglected by corruption inquiries. The extent of the problem is outlined, along with the links between traditional corruption and the male-dominated nature of policing. The new dispensation of gender equity in policing is assessed in terms of practical methods for supporting women. The final chapter in this section, 'The Politics of Reform', shows how the interactions between police chiefs, politicians, union leaders and the media – especially in the context of 'law-and-order' politics – significantly influence the extent to which blueprints for reform are implemented. Emphasis is placed on the need to 'de-politicise' police restructuring and on the important role of an independent anti-corruption body in managing the change process.

The section of the book, titled 'Innovations in Creating Ethical Police Departments', provides the key focus of the book with a series of reports on corruption prevention strategies that have universal application. Some of the strategies examined have been used for decades with contemporary refinements to improve their efficacy. Others are more recent, and some are highly controversial. 'Monitoring Integrity' demonstrates the utility of social science methods for assessing levels of organisational commitment to ethical standards and for monitoring changes over time in standards of police conduct. This information is needed to determine whether existing integrity controls are effective and to highlight areas that warrant further attention. 'Alternative Strategies for Resolving Complaints' begins by demonstrating how formal investigations into complaints typically result in low substantiation rates and high dissatisfaction rates amongst complainants. The imposition of formal sanctions may also have limited benefits in deterring future misconduct. Consequently, increasing use is being made of alternative methods for dealing with the large numbers of complaints against police, such as informal resolution, mediation, conferencing and managerial resolution.

The chapter on 'Complaint Profiling and Early Warning Systems' introduces an extremely promising approach to misconduct prevention receiving widespread attention by police departments around the world. Complaints against police frequently form patterns centred on particular individuals or units. These complaints can be difficult to substantiate by traditional investigative techniques, but are often indicative of real behaviour problems amenable to forms of intervention such as counselling, retraining and enhanced supervision. The next chapter, 'Changing Police Procedures', then focuses on solutions to miscarriages of justice and denial of fair legal process through better training and use of technology such as video and audiotaping.

Simulated corruption opportunities have been used at times with spectacular success to expose officers suspected of corruption. The chapter on 'Integrity Testing' uses deterrence theory to advocate the more systematic use of random testing to prevent misconduct. 'Civil Litigation' reports on a major policing issue internationally; as police are increasingly being sued for a range of abuses of citizens' rights. The chapter analyses recent cases and shows how police can learn from these in developing effective risk management strategies. 'Independent Investigation of Complaints' analyses a trend towards external watchdog agencies having a greater role in hands on investigations of complaints and disciplinary decisions. This is a controversial development, but the process can make a major contribution to overcoming the problem of bias when police investigate police. The chapter, 'Predicting Misconduct Before Hiring Police', reports on the use of increasingly sophisticated psychological tests to guide recruiters in screening out applicants who are at-risk of attracting large numbers of complaints and developing other behavioural problems in the pressure cooker environment of front-line policing. The final chapter, 'Situational Corruption Prevention', reports on a diagnostic study which applied the principles of situational crime prevention techniques to police corruption cases. The analysis identified a number of factors in police procedures that can be addressed to reduce corruption opportunities.

In putting this book together we are conscious that the corruption issue can be used to unfairly stereotype all police as corrupt. However, we recognise that many police are untainted by malpractice. We are also highly conscious of the essential service police provide, and the frequently difficult and dangerous circumstances in which they carry out their task of protecting the public and bringing offenders to justice. Our hope is that an objective understanding of the nature and causes of police misconduct, and application of the lessons for prevention, will contribute to an environment in which honest and conscientious police are able to do their work unhindered by corrupt colleagues and with strong public respect and support.

Tim Prenzler and Janet Ransley
October 2002

Contributors

David Baker is a Senior Lecturer in criminology and criminal justice, School of Political and Social Inquiry, at Monash University, Melbourne. Previously he was a communication skills lecturer at the Victoria Police Academy. He has published numerous studies on Industrial relations, labour history, politics and policing. Public order policing and comparative and historical policing are his main research interests.

Michael Barnes is Head of the School of Justice Studies, Queensland University of Technology, Brisbane. Prior to joining QUT Michael spent nine years with the Queensland Criminal Justice Commission, for the last seven as chief officer of the complaints section.

Meredith Bassett is a sworn member of the Australian Federal Police. Initially working in community policing, she is currently an analyst with the Risk Analysis and Intelligence Team within Professional Standards at AFP Headquarters in Canberra.

David Brereton is Director of the Centre for Social Responsibility in Mining at the University of Queensland, Brisbane. Before that he was Director of the Research and Prevention Division of the Queensland Criminal Justice Commission.

Tess Newton Cain was a Lecturer in law at the University of the South Pacific between 1997 and 2001. During that time she worked with the Australian Federal Police in the development and delivery of courses in the management of serious crime by law enforcement agents in the region. She now operates her own business advisory service, BIZassist, in Vanuatu.

Andrew Ede is a Senior Research Officer in Law and Justice Policy in the Queensland Department of Premier and Cabinet in Brisbane. Before this he was a research officer at the Queensland Crime and Misconduct Commission.

Jenny Fleming is Lecturer in the School of Industrial Relations, Griffith University, Brisbane. Her research interests include State politics, and the politics of criminal justice and police unionism. She is the co-editor of *Motivating Ministers to Morality* (2001).

Ross Homel is Head of the School of Criminology and Criminal Justice, Griffith University; and Deputy Director of the Key Centre for Ethics, Law, Justice and Governance. His research interests include the prevention of crime, violence, corruption, and traffic injuries; the effects of legal sanctions on criminal behaviour; and statistical methods in the social sciences.

Michelle Karas is an industrial-organisational psychologist with sixteen years experience in the design and application of person and job assessment methods and applied research in public and private sector settings. She is currently a psychologist at the Australian Federal Police Headquarters.

Colleen Lewis is a Senior Lecturer in criminal justice and criminology, School of Political and Social Inquiry, Monash University. She is co-editor of *Civilian Oversight of Policing: Governance, Democracy and Human Rights* (2000) and author of *Complaints Against Police: The Politics of Reform* (1999).

Jude McCulloch is a Lecturer in Police Studies at Deakin University, Geelong. She worked for many years as a community lawyer and has written widely on policing issues, including deadly force, policing public protests, and new police weapons. She has recently published *Blue Army: Paramilitary Policing in Australia* (2001).

Tim Prenzler is a Senior Lecturer in the School of Criminology and Criminal Justice, Griffith University; and coordinator of the policing program in the Key Centre for Ethics, Law, Justice and Governance. His research interests include civilian oversight of police, the history of women police, and the development and regulation of the security industry.

Janet Ransley is a Lecturer in the School of Criminology and Criminal Justice at Griffith University. Her main research interests are in the areas of governmental, political and corporate wrongdoing, police reform, and regulation.

Rick Sarre is an Associate Professor in the School of International Business, University of South Australia, Adelaide; where he teaches law and criminal justice and convenes the Legal and Business Regulation Research Group. He has published widely on many aspects of criminal justice policy and practice, and recently co-edited *Considering Crime and Justice: Realities and Responses* (2000).

Syd Sparrow is a Lecturer in the Unaipon School, University of South Australia. This school was established in 1996 from an amalgamation of the Aboriginal Studies and Teacher Education Centre and the School of Aboriginal and Islander Administration. A lawyer, Syd was formerly the Director of the Aboriginal Legal Rights Movement in Adelaide.

CHALLENGES TO REFORM

1

Corruption and Reform: Global Trends and Theoretical Perspectives

Tim Prenzler

In the closing pages of Josef Heller's famous novel *Catch-22* the main character Yossarian is wandering through the slums of Rome when he comes across a scene in which a police officer is struggling with a hysterical man. 'Police! Help! Police!' the man calls as he is dragged away. Yossarian is at first confused and thinks the man is calling for assistance from other police standing by. However, he quickly realises the words carry a double meaning:

> Yossarian smiled wryly at the futile and ridiculous cry for aid, then saw with a start that the words were ambiguous, realised with alarm that they were not, perhaps, intended as a call for police but as a heroic warning from the grave by a doomed friend to everyone who was *not* a policeman with a club and a gun and a mob of other police with clubs and guns to back him up. 'Help! Police!' the man had cried, and he could have been shouting of danger. Yossarian responded to the thought by slipping away stealthily from the police (Heller 1977: 439).

The idea that people should fear police makes for a despairing scenario. When police over-reach their authority or attack innocent citizens, there is a powerful sense that there is nowhere else for vulnerable people to turn. Thus the scholar Maurice Punch claims that '(Police) deviance elicits a special feeling of betrayal. In a sense, they are doubly condemned; that is, not just for the infringement itself but even more for the breach of trust involved' (1985: 8). How is it that police sometimes change roles – from protectors to criminals – and how can this occur in mature democracies? What are the nature and causes of police corruption? How extensive is it? Can anything be done to prevent it? These questions are the concern of this chapter.

Defining corruption

Discussion and analysis of police corruption includes a great deal of variation and overlap in terminology. The word 'corruption' can be used broadly – along with common terms such as 'misconduct' and 'deviance' – to cover any behaviour by police that is considered illegal or unethical. However, 'corruption' also has a very specific usage referring to soliciting or accepting a bribe. An example would be a police officer accepting money from a drug dealer in return for not charging the dealer with trafficking. This specific usage is sometimes extended to include any misuse of a police officer's position for a personal benefit. In this view, an officer who steals cash or goods from a crime scene would be accused of 'corruption'. It is possible in such a case that the officer would be charged either with the criminal offence of stealing or with a criminal offence of acting corruptly or both. Alternatively, the officer might be charged criminally with stealing and then dismissed from the department for acting corruptly. However, if the officer committed an offence *off-duty* – such as stealing from a shop – they might be charged criminally and then dismissed for bringing their office into disrepute. An obvious issue here is the extent to which the offence is related to the officer's employment. For example, should an officer who commits a minor crime off-duty be dismissed from the department? Normally, the high standards expected of public law enforcement officials mean that their off-duty behaviour is considered to reflect their capacity to perform effectively on-duty.

The above examples are provided to give an indication of the different ways of approaching the definition and prosecution of police misconduct. Indeed, scholars have created different typologies that attempt to differentiate between different types of police misbehaviour. Police departments and civilian oversight agencies that monitor police conduct also have their own categories for the purposes of investigating and sanctioning misconduct. These are often embodied in statute law. In one of the better known typologies, Barker (1983: 31) separated 'police deviance' into two categories of 'corruption' and 'misconduct', as shown in Table 1.1.

'Corruption of Authority', according to Barker, includes free meals and discounts. 'Kickbacks' are benefits received for referring calls to particular tow truck drivers or other service providers. 'Shakedowns' involve forcibly taking money from offenders. 'Internal Payoffs' includes the sale of holidays, work assignments or similar items from one officer to another. 'Other Violations' include speeding

Table 1.1: Typology of 'Police Occupational Deviance' - Barker, 1983

Corruption (Involves a material reward or gain)	Misconduct (No material reward or gain)
Corruption of Authority	Police Perjury
Opportunistic Thefts	Police Brutality
Shakedowns	Sex on Duty
Protection of Illegal Activities	Drinking on Duty
Traffic Fix	Sleeping on Duty
Misdemeanour Fix	Other violations
Kickbacks	
Felony Fix	
Direct Criminal Activities	
Internal Payoffs	

in police vehicles and shopping while on duty (Barker 1983: 32). Inevitably though, quite different typologies are possible and there is probably little point trying to control the natural tendency for people to use terms broadly and interchangeably.

The following is a four-part typology of police corruption and misconduct that readers are invited to consider (adapted from Prenzler, in press).

1. **Classic corruption**, in the sense of 'bribery' or 'graft', involves an officer receiving a personal benefit for not doing their duty. This may be *organised*, as in a 'protection racket' where police receive a regular fee from a brothel or gambling den for not raiding and prosecuting the premises. Alternatively, it may be *opportunistic* and irregular, such as a traffic officer accepting a bribe offered by a motorist stopped for speeding. Some critics describe gifts and discounts (gratuities) as 'petty corruption' because they may involve an expectation of favourable treatment (Sigler and Dees 1988). Classic corruption may also include police obtaining a benefit from theft of goods in custody, re-selling seized drugs or selling confidential information.

2. **Process corruption** involves the fabrication of evidence and other forms of perverting the course of justice. The victims of this type of corruption may be innocent or guilty of crimes, but police pursue a conviction in court through fraudulent means. Process corruption is sometimes referred to as 'bricking', 'fitting up' or 'verballing' (putting words in the mouths of the accused or of witnesses). Process corruption usually involves lying in the witness box, withholding contrary evidence or coercing suspects into

making confessions. It can also occur in the investigation phase, when intelligence is obtained by illegal searches or wiretaps, or when suspects are not informed of their rights or are denied legal advice.

3. **Brutality** or 'excessive force' covers the full range of forms of unjustified violence related to a police officer's work. This can extend from excessive frisking through serious assault to murder. Verbal abuse and threats of violence can also be included in this category. Normally, only the use of 'reasonable' or 'proportionate' force is permitted when police arrest suspects, stop fights, direct people, break into premises or act in defence. Most jurisdictions prohibit actions such as shooting fleeing suspects or frisking people at random.

4. **Miscellaneous misconduct** covers remaining types of deviance – sometimes grouped together in typologies as 'misconduct' or 'disciplinary offences'. These can include harassment, discriminatory law enforcement, incivility, inaction, drug abuse and intoxication, abuse of sick leave, dangerous high-speed vehicle pursuits, misuse of confidential information, abuse of strip searching, racist or sexist slurs, and neglect of detainees. It also covers forms of *internal corruption* or misconduct such as sexual harassment, and discrimination in assignment and promotion. It could also include criminal offences and unethical behaviour committed off-duty but deemed to reflect adversely on the officer's work (such as drunk driving, assault and abusive language).

A more positive way of identifying corruption and misconduct is by measuring conduct against a formal ethical standard. Consistent with the 'discovery' of police corruption since the 1960s, police organisations have refined and extended their professional codes of conduct (Kleinig 1996). There is now a strong consensus at the official level in most democracies about core principles that should guide and direct police decision-making. Perhaps the best expression of this consensus is the *Law Enforcement Code of Conduct*, developed by the International Association of Chiefs of Police (IACP 2001). The code addresses specific ethical issues, enjoining such positions as protection of confidential information, rejection of bribes and gratuities, and co-operation with lawful agencies. The code also sets out general principles of ethical policing. The most significant and encompassing of these is the requirement to enforce the law and assist the public equitably, without discrimination. In the words of the IACP code:

A police officer shall perform all duties impartially, without favour or affection or ill will and without regard to status, sex, race, religion, political belief or aspiration. All citizens will be treated equally with courtesy, consideration and dignity (2001: 1).

In terms of the exercise of police powers, threats and force should be used 'only after discussion, negotiation and persuasion have been found to be inappropriate or ineffective' (IACP 2001: 1, 2).

Measuring corruption

Knowledge about police misconduct comes from a number of sources. Commissions of inquiry have been the most important. These usually consist of an independent team of lawyers and investigators headed by a judge or senior legal officer. There is a long history of failure on the part of such inquiries to either expose corruption or to affect permanent reforms that would prevent recurrences (Lewis 1999). However, this failure has usually resulted from limited terms of reference or inadequate powers and resources. It is mainly in the last three decades of the 20th century that public pressure and political maturity have led to the establishment of properly equipped inquiries. The success of modern inquiries has been based on the use of carefully selected investigators, reasonable time limits for completion, broad jurisdiction on matters to be pursued, and power to demand answers to questions. The capacity to use covert surveillance and 'stings' (simulated misconduct opportunities) has also been important (Wood 1997). A key weapon is the ability to 'turn' corrupt officers to become witnesses, usually through offers of indemnities from prosecution. Often the initial impetus for an inquiry comes from pressure on governments when investigative journalists and courageous police whistleblowers combine forces to provide compelling newspaper exposés.

The 'Knapp Commission' in New York City from 1970 to 1972 best marks the turning point in modern consciousness about police misconduct (Knapp 1972). People around the world became familiar with the bureaucratically organised sub-culture of corruption in the NYPD through the dramatised books and films *Serpico* (Maas 1973) and *Prince of the City* (Daley 1978). The extensive, almost universal, corrupt practices in the NYPD at the time were based on the exploitation of routine police functions such as prosecution of traffic violations and illegal gambling. Police abused their authority to create a system of extortionate gratuities from restaurant and other business owners. Law enforcement was highly selective, as Robert Daley recounts of detectives in the Special Investigating Unit in the NYPD:

> They chose their own targets and roamed New York at will. Someone once called them the Princes of the City, for they operated with the impunity, and sometimes with the arrogance, of Renaissance princes. They could enforce any law or not enforce it, arrest anyone or accord freedom. They were immune to arrest themselves (1978: 6).

Since the Knapp Commission, many other jurisdictions have undergone similar painful exposés of corruption. These inquiries and associated scandals have varied in the problems they reveal, as the following examples show.

- The 1981 Scarman Inquiry into the Metropolitan Police in London, following the Brixton riots, focused on police harassment and racism (Scarman 1986).

- The MacPherson Inquiry into racism followed the inadequate investigation by Met officers of the murder of a black man (MacPherson 1999).

- The 1991 Christopher Commission in Los Angeles was focused on brutality. It followed the infamous police bashing of Rodney King, revealed through a citizen's videorecording (Christopher 1991).

- The large-scale Wood Commission in the Australian State of New South Wales (1994-97) was more in the mould of Knapp, uncovering diverse forms of misconduct, 'pockets' of serious misconduct, and a hard core of organised graft centred around vice operations (Wood 1997).

- The 1989 Fitzgerald Inquiry in Queensland, Australia, revealed serious vertical corruption, with the police commissioner being jailed for 14 years for acceptance of corrupt payments from a gambling and prostitution protection racket. Other allegations included fabrication of evidence, opportunistic corruption and sex discrimination (Fitzgerald 1989).

- The Mollen Commission in New York City in 1994 uncovered small but extreme forms of police deviance involving exploitation of the drug trade (Mollen 1994).

- The 'Rampart Scandal' in Los Angeles in 1997-98 involved serious crimes by a small number of officers including armed robbery, theft of drugs, assaults on detainees and fabrication of evidence (Board of Inquiry 2000).

- The United States Federal Bureau of Investigation (FBI) came into disrepute following a raid against a religious sect at Waco in 1993 in which 80 people died, as well as the 1997 scandal over the integrity of forensic procedures in its main crime laboratory (Hoffman 1997).

Along with inquiries, other factors have contributed to a growing awareness about police abuses. The period from the 1960s to the 1980s saw large demonstrations over issues such as the Vietnam War, conscription, racism and the environment. In many cases these protests were brutally suppressed by police, often in full view of television news cameras (see Chapter 3). Many people who would ordinarily have little contact with police began to see them as the enemy. Conflict was exacerbated by the growing social acceptance of drug use and police targeting of minor drug users. Public trust in police was further eroded by revelations of miscarriages of justice stemming from process corruption, including suppression of evidence favourable to the defendants. The most notorious cases occurred in Britain in the 1980s when groups such as the 'Guildford Four' and 'Birmingham Six' were wrongfully convicted of terrorist bombings (see Chapter 2).

International human rights groups are another source of knowledge about police abuses. Following a review of excessive force cases in 14 major cities in the United States, the 1998 report by Human Rights Watch, *Shielded from Justice*, described police brutality as 'one of the most serious, enduring, and divisive human rights violations in the United States' (1998: 1). It is not surprising then that non-democratic countries, or those with less developed democratic institutions, typically have entrenched police malpractice. For example, much of the sexual exploitation of women and children in impoverished nations occurs under police protection. In a number of countries, police still serve a dual function of general criminal law enforcement and repressive protection of dictatorial regimes through the routine use of torture, summary execution, fabricated prosecutions and suppression of demonstrations. Hence the continued currency of the term 'police state'.

The 1980s and 1990s saw enormous changes in the world in terms of democratisation and its effects on policing. With the collapse of the Soviet Union in the 1980s many new democracies were born. These countries faced severe challenges as they moved from social and economic systems based on communist dictatorship to ones based on democracy and managed capitalism. After the initial round of changes to the political system and the economy, a major challenge for refinement of government accountability is reform of police. The same challenge has occurred in Central and South America as mainly right-wing dictatorships became democracies. The police forces of these countries, like their post-communist counterparts, carry a heavy legacy of secrecy and violence, and are often intensely resistant to moves to make them more accountable. In a recent review of police integrity issues in Latin America, Kinney (1999: 5) reported on surveys that found 'an extraordinary 91 per cent of Venezuelans and 96 per cent of Argentines believed their police forces are corrupt'.

Crises in policing and attendant media attention tend to shift between jurisdictions and between countries as scandals or changing politics put the spotlight on different police forces. There has been a great deal of interest, for example, in cultural change within the previously racist police force of South Africa following the removal of apartheid (Melville 1999). The pro-English Protestant-dominated Royal Ulster Constabulary (RUC) in Northern Ireland is also currently going through a major reform process to make it more accountable and more representative of the community it serves. At times corrupt police become so complacent that they go too far and pressure for change becomes almost impossible to evade, following public outcry over repeated incidents of violence or other abuses. Typically, the change process is driven by a detailed inquiry report and accompanying set of recommendations, such as the recent report on the RUC by the Independent Commission on Policing (1999). Subsequent to the 1972 Knapp inquiry, the misconduct event that has drawn the most attention internationally and highlighted the issue of police brutality was the above mentioned bashing of Afro-American Rodney King by Los Angeles Police officers. The covert video footage of King, lying prone and defenseless and repeatedly kicked by one group of officers while another group stood by and watched, was shown on news bulletins around the world. The subsequent acquittal of the officers by an all white jury caused a major riot in Los Angeles. The potentially catastrophic effects of police malpractice and public outrage are captured in Chief Bernard Parks' description:

> On April 3, 1992, the City of Los Angeles was enveloped in a riot in response to the 'not guilty' verdicts in the trial of Los Angeles Police Department officers accused of unlawfully beating Rodney King. Six days later, when the fires were finally extinguished and the smoke had cleared, 54 people had been killed, more than 2,000 injured, in excess of 800 structures were burned, and the profile of police work in the

City of Los Angeles and the United States was forever changed. The 1992 riots in the City of Los Angeles were arguably the most devastating civil disturbance in the history of the United States (Parks and Smith, 1999: 1).

The findings of numerous inquiries have been the primary sources of knowledge about police corruption. However, commissions of inquiry are increasingly being supported by social science research using observational studies, surveys and interviews to assess the nature and extent of corruption. For example, Barker (1991) used an anonymous survey to ask officers in a city police department about their perceptions of corruption. He found respondents estimated that 40 per cent of officers had engaged in excessive force against a prisoner, 23 per cent had committed perjury, eight per cent had drunk alcohol on duty, 31 per cent had sex on duty, and 39 per cent had slept on duty. A survey conducted for the New South Wales Royal Commission found an interesting discrepancy between serving officers – 33 per cent of whom claimed to have 'personally encountered corruption' – and resigned officers – 60 per cent of whom claimed to have encountered corruption (AIC 1996: 130). Other researchers, such as Skolnick ([1966] 1994), made telling observations of routine misconduct by melting into the background as they accompanied police at work. Police are often very candid about corruption in anonymous interviews (Graef 1990). Additionally, increasing use is being made of ethics surveys to identify attitudes that may support corrupt behaviour (Klockars, Ivkovich, Harver and Haberfeld 2000) (see Chapter 7).

So, how extensive is police corruption? The New York City Knapp Commission report explicitly attacked what it termed the 'rotten apple' theory of isolated individual corruption, supporting instead a concept of what is now called 'systemic corruption' (see below). The rotten apple theory claims that corruption involves only a few officers who are guilty of moral failure, while the organisational 'barrel' remains sound. Many police chiefs, politicians and police unions have used this stock argument to defend the status quo and their own role in failing to prevent corruption. It is certainly the case that individual cases of corruption occur, or that misconduct is limited to a small group of officers. Nonetheless, most modern inquiries have identified widespread misconduct. This is why corruption is often described by scholars as 'endemic' or 'pervasive' in policing (Newburn 1997). At the same time, it must be kept in mind that corruption levels can vary substantially between departments, as well as varying within departments over time and across different internal sections. Police corruption is highly fluid, and a challenge for scholarship is to explain why some police departments operate for many decades with very few scandals or allegations of corruption.

This section concludes by comparing findings from two of the worst cases of police corruption in modern democracies: the Knapp Commission in New York City (1970-72) and the Wood Royal Commission in New South Wales (1994-97). The quotations in Table 1.2 show many of the common features and the potential extremes of police corruption. In addition to those listed in the table, references were made in both reports to the sale of confidential information, interference with investigations of police, 'kickbacks' from tow truck operators, and internal corruption in overtime and sickness benefits. However, there were also some significant differences. In New York in the 1960s police had very wide responsibilities, with resulting corruption in building construction, liquor regulations and parking. The Knapp report also noted a significant trade within the department for preferred assignments. The Wood report also identified cover-ups of drunk-driving accidents involving police, and neglect by police of the activities of paedophiles.

Table 1.2: Comparison of statements from the Knapp Inquiry in New York City and the Wood Inquiry in New South Wales

Knapp, 1972	Wood, 1997
General	
Police corruption was found to be an extensive, Department-wide phenomenon, indulged in to some degree by a sizeable majority of those on the force (61).	A state of systematic and entrenched corruption existed within the Service (84) … the Royal Commission disclosed a very serious state of corruption that was widespread and of long-standing origin (161).
Process corruption	
The Commission was told about numerous kinds of payoffs which affected the outcome of court cases. The most common court-related payoffs were those made to policemen to change their testimony so that a case was dismissed or the defendant acquitted (187).	In almost every segment of the evidence called, the issue of process corruption reared its head, comprising variously: perjury, planting of evidence, verbals in the forms of unsigned records of interview and note book confessions… assaults and pressure to induce confessions … (and) tampering with the product of electronic interception (84).

Vice

Organised crime is the single biggest source of police corruption, through its control of the city's gambling, narcotics, loansharking, and illegal sex-related enterprises... all of which the Department considers mob-run (68) ... The collection of tribute by police from gamblers has traditionally been extremely well organised and has persisted in virtually unchanged form for years (71).	The protection of clubs and vice operators was at Kings Cross conducted on much the same basis as that for the drug suppliers. Key members of the group involved in 'the laugh' and various Kings Cross identities admitted to the regular payment of corrupt monies for these purposes (123).

Drugs

Corruption in narcotics law enforcement has grown in recent years to the point where high-ranking police officials acknowledge it to be the most serious problem facing the department [including] '(K)eeping money and/or narcotics confiscated at the time of an arrest or raid. Selling narcotics to addicts-informants in exchange for stolen goods' (91).	There was an overwhelming body of evidence suggesting the existence of close relationships between police and those involved in the supply of drugs ... a controlled environment was created (119-20)... Perhaps most disturbing of all was the extent to which police admitted to being directly involved in the supply of cocaine, heroin and cannabis. (133)

Gratuities

By far the most widespread form of misconduct the Commission found was the acceptance by police officers of gratuities in the form of free meals, free goods, and cash payments (170).	There was abundant evidence of the ready availability of various forms of gratuities ranging from small amounts of money to free liquor, meals and sexual services (95).

Drinking on duty

In the course of its investigation into bars, Commission investigators could not help but observe numerous police officers imbibing free drinks – both on duty and off... Three patrol sergeants in the Nineteenth Precinct regularly spent their entire tours going from one bar to another. While the behaviour of patrolmen was less extreme, there was plenty of drinking on duty (176).	The abuse of alcohol was graphically described by many of the detectives who assisted the Royal Commission... drinking on duty, and covering for police affected by alcohol while on duty, was an entrenched and expected practice (98).

Opportunistic corruption

An extortion attempt by police officers is sometimes the end product of careful surveillance of a target (98) ... Most often a police officer seeking to score simply keeps for himself all or part of the money and drugs confiscated during a raid or arrest (99).	In a disturbingly large number of cases, the Royal Commission received complaints of money and property having been stolen by police in the course of routine police work. Theft and extortion from criminals had become regular features of policing in some sections (114).

Explaining corruption

Systemic theories about the causes of police corruption devolve primarily into 'structural' and 'cultural' explanations.

Structural perspectives

A structural (or structural-functional) perspective focuses on the nature of police work – or the 'task environment' (Bennett 1984). In this view, corruption opportunities derive directly from the police law enforcement function. Police work involves frequent contact with criminals who are motivated to trade money and other benefits for immunity from prosecution. Patrol officers and detectives enjoy very low levels of supervision and high levels of discretion that give them wide scope to bend or break laws and evade detection (Barker 1983). This demand-and-supply scenario applies to any illegal behaviour coming to police attention, and may result in corruption in limited forms with individuals acting opportunistically. The scenario has also led to acute problems of intergenerational corruption networks spanning decades, particularly where there is a high demand for illegal commerce in drugs, liquor, prostitution, abortion and gambling, or information held on police databases. Hence, corruption is a major unintended consequence of well-intentioned efforts to prohibit 'vice'. A structural approach also explains variations in deviance related to specific tasks. Patrol officers, for example, may be more likely to engage in brutality, whereas detectives may be more prone to fabricate evidence. Officers in licensing or vice squads are more likely to engage in organised corruption. Traffic officers are more likely to engage in opportunistic corruption.

A structural perspective is also useful for explaining process corruption. Pressure to fabricate evidence comes from a number of sources including political and community pressure to bring offenders to justice – particularly for more terrifying or repugnant crimes (see Chapter 2). This can be exacerbated by the use of crime 'clearance rates' as a police performance measure. Corrupt process may also follow from police frustration with due process constraints such as the right to silence or the high standard of proof in criminal cases. This has given rise to the concept of the 'Dirty Harry syndrome', based on the methods of a Hollywood screen detective who feels compelled to break the law to protect innocent citizens from predatory criminals. Similarly, police brutality is influenced by perceived or actual pressures for summary punishment associated with cynicism about defendant safeguards and sentencing policies. It can also be argued that brutality follows from the fact that police are given an impossible task of controlling crimes caused by social factors such as unemployment and poverty. Officers who feel powerless may be tempted to exceed their powers and use threats, harassment and beatings to deter criminal behaviour. Police are therefore 'structured' into often highly provocative conflict situations in which they are also subject to frequent insults and assaults from members of the public.

A structural perspective can include a 'political context theory' of police corruption. This applies when politicians are themselves part of protection rackets and receive pay offs from police, or when politicians fail to exercise proper accountability over police. In some corruption situations politicians will turn a blind eye to police deviance in return for police support and for police action against political enemies (Fitzgerald 1989). Police unions have been notoriously defensive of corrupt colleagues and can exercise considerable influence over politicians to ignore misconduct. Up until the last few decades, even the most sophisticated democracies have relied on a 'minimalist model' of police accountability (Prenzler and Ronken 2002). This approach was essentially passive, trusting police to keep their house in order, and relying on internal command processes and the criminal courts to detect and punish corruption.

Cultural perspectives

The second main area of theory concerns the concept of organisational culture (Crank 1998). The distinctiveness of the police occupational subculture is easily overstated. Many other occupations have problems of corruption, unethical practices and protective solidarity. However, attention to 'culture' – to attitudes, practices, traditions and unwritten codes of practice – is useful for understanding processes through which misconduct is facilitated and reinforced. Secrecy and solidarity are central to cultural perspectives on police misconduct, and the most extreme expression of this is the persecution of police whistleblowers. The concept of a police subculture includes the 'slippery slope' theory of corruption. In this view, rookie officers are first encouraged to accept gratuities and then through peer pressure and threats are gradually socialised into participating in more and more serious types of corruption (Sherman 1977).

Police subcultures of corruption have also developed from recruitment and training processes that produced a narrow conformist type of officer. Recruitment in many countries has been almost exclusively from amongst poorly educated lower class males. In racially-divided societies police were often predominantly or exclusively white. Training was often perfunctory, focused on law, fitness and physical control techniques. It is little wonder that police developed a socially-isolated 'macho' culture that encouraged violence and disdain for civil rights. Many aspects of the traditional or negative police subculture are closely associated with structural-functional influences, such as the need for confidentiality to protect sensitive operations or the camaraderie deriving from the stress and danger of police work. The problem occurs when these positive values mutate and become reinforcers of unethical practices. The common problem of racism is similarly closely related to conflict between police and minority groups in the arena of street crime (see Chapter 3). But brutality and discriminatory policing also follow from the 'cultural' dimension of ethnically biased police recruitment, use of racist and sexist jokes and stereotypes, and inadequate training in cultural sensitivity.

Preventing corruption

The decades following the Knapp Commission report have seen a sharpened consciousness about abuses in policing and a consequent search for effective prevention strategies. It follows from both structural and cultural perspectives that strong and permanent measures are needed to guard against the many pressures for policing to slide into deviance. Table 1.3 below sets out a way of conceptualising the links between diagnoses of the causes of corruption and approaches to prevention.

Table 1.3: Theory and practice in police corruption prevention

Theoretical orientation	Approach to prevention
Structural	Situational
	Law enforcement
Cultural	Human resource management

Situational approaches

One corollary of a structural approach to police deviance is to modify the task environment to reduce the opportunities for corruption. This follows the same approach as situational crime prevention (Clarke 1998) in attempting to modify environmental variables to make corruption impossible or more difficult (see Chapter 15). Although the crime control function of policing makes radical changes to the task environment quite difficult, some well known strategies include legalisation or decriminalisation of vice – to remove targets – and the introduction of tape recording of interviews with suspects – as a form of formal surveillance.

Law enforcement approaches

One aim of situational prevention is to increase potential offenders' perceptions of the probability of being caught and punished. Hence there is a close link with a 'get tough' law enforcement approach to police corruption. The aim is either to deter officers from engaging in corruption because of heightened expectations of being caught or, as a last resort, to incapacitate corrupt officers by removing them from the department. Some more controversial strategies in this category include integrity tests, informants and the investigation of complaints by independent agencies (see below).

Human resource management approaches

Prevention initiatives deriving from cultural perspectives include recruitment strategies aimed at creating more points of resistance to group pressures – what could be called a 'functional divisiveness' (Henry 1994: 167). Women appear to be more resistant to corruption, act less aggressively and are more capable in diffusing conflict (see Chapter 5). In addition, more attention is being given to ethical assessments in recruitment, as well as psychological testing to screen out people who may have a predisposition towards violence or crime. Training initiatives include more attention to ethics, communication skills and cultural sensitivity. These strategies are designed to develop officers who have internalised high ethical standards and are resistant to misconduct opportunities. Human resource management strategies can also be closely linked to deterrence and opportunity reducing strategies. For example, many jurisdictions have introduced compulsory reporting of misconduct in an effort to break down the code of silence. Many police departments now train specialist negotiators who can take over from patrol officers and apply their skills in diffusing violence in siege situations. More sophisticated physical restraint techniques have been developed to minimise harm in situations where force is unavoidable.

Specific strategies

The following section summarises 25 prevention strategies employed to fight police corruption (adapted from Prenzler and Ronken 2002; see also Newburn 1997). Some are controversial – such as random integrity testing – and are not necessarily advocated here. However, any advanced democracy committed to minimising police corruption would have the majority of these strategies in place. Many of them can be implemented by police themselves or by an oversight agency or by the two working together. Some are directed at identifying and stopping corrupt behaviour, but most are 'proactive' in that they are concerned with preventing the initial development of corruption.

1. **Internal affairs departments** provide a specialist unit dedicated to maintaining organisational integrity. Internal affairs departments ensure a degree of independence, consistency in the rigour of investigations and application of rules, and they allow for a central repository of intelligence and complaints data that can inform proactive prevention strategies.

2. **Independent civilian oversight agencies** are one of the most distinctive developments of the post-Knapp period (Goldsmith, 1991). These agencies – such as the Civilian Complaint Review Board in New York City and the Police Complaints Authority in England and Wales – are designed to circumvent the strong tendency for police to protect their own and cover up misconduct. They can operate across a spectrum of powers, varying between relatively weak reviews of police disciplinary decisions through to independent investigations and sanctioning (see Chapter 13).

3. **Overt recording devices** are used in areas at-risk for misconduct such as interviews with suspects and in police detention facilities (see Chapter 10).

4. **Covert high technology surveillance** has been used to overcome problems of lack of witnesses or lack of supervision capacity by secretly recording conversations and actions that may involve misconduct.

5. **Targeted integrity testing** is used in cases where traditional investigative methods fail to produce sufficient evidence for a conviction against individuals or groups strongly suspected of corruption. Simulated corruption opportunities are created similar to the type of suspected corruption (for example, theft from a

crime scene). The officers' responses are monitored, usually by hidden cameras (see Chapter 11).

6. **Randomised integrity testing** is designed to provide a more comprehensive and objective source of detection and deterrence through the random assignment of simulated monitored misconduct opportunities (see Chapter 11).

7. **Drug and alcohol testing** has been introduced in response to inquiry findings about police use of illicit drugs and drinking on duty. Tests can be random or targeted and are conducted by breathalyser for alcohol, and by urine test for drugs.

8. **Quality assurance tests** could be classified under 'targeted' and 'randomised integrity tests' (above). However, they can also be classified separately as a lower level activity. They are focused on conduct standards to do with 'customer service', such as how station attendants answer inquiries (from ethnic minorities for example).

9. **Internal informants** report behaviour and information kept secret within police informal networks. Advertising the presence of these spies can aid deterrence.

10. **Complaints profiling** can identify patterns of misconduct (see Chapter 9). Complaints may not be proven, but when they increase in number and pertain to similar behaviours they may indicate a real problem (such as sexual harassment of motorists by a traffic officer). Complaints profiling can be done on organisational units (such as individual police stations or detective squads) or on individual officers. Tailor-made interventions can include re-training, counselling or improved supervision.

11. **Supervisor accountability** involves reviews of line managers' performance that take into account behaviour problems occurring under their command, with results clearly linked to promotion or continuation of command.

12. **Integrity reviews** should occur in all progression decisions. Recruitment processes include ethics tests and psychological tests (Chapter 14) as well as independent referee reports. As personnel move through training and are deployed and promoted, the diversity of integrity assessment sources can be expanded to include integrity test results and complaints profiles.

13. **Mandatory reporting** of observed or rumoured misconduct is designed to challenge the code of silence and is enforceable if unreported misconduct comes to light.

14. **Whistleblower protection** includes provision of safe houses, penalties for persecuting informants, and forms of support such as counselling.

15. **Compulsory rotation in corruption-prone sections** is designed to prevent police exploiting corruption opportunities over the long term (for example, by developing bonds with organised crime figures or establishing corruption networks).

16. **Asset and financial reviews**, targeted or random, may provide evidence of officers living beyond their means or at-risk of succumbing to corruption opportunities (for example, excessive spending on gambling).

17. **Surveys of police** can be used as a way of anonymously gauging officers' perceptions of levels and types of misconduct. Ethics surveys can identify predisposing attitudes toward misconduct.

18. **Surveys of the public** can identify perceptions of police conduct. Surveys or interviews with sub-groups having direct contact with police, such as detainees, can also assess personal experiences with police.

19. **Personnel diversification** is aimed at breaking down the culture of solidarity through civilianisation and recruitment of people from diverse ethnic backgrounds and older, more educated, people, as well as more women.

20. **Comprehensive ethics training** communicates and reinforces messages about organisational commitment to integrity through-out an officer's career and through the numerous specialisations within policing. Ethics training should clarify departmental expectations about officer conduct (summarised in codes of conduct) and assist in managing ethical dilemmas (for example, how to reject offers of gratuities without causing offence).

21. **Inquisitorial methods** and a civil standard of proof are usually adopted in police disciplinary hearings, judicial inquiries and external tribunal hearings. This is in response to failed prose-cutions of police in criminal courts where a higher standard of proof applies. The emphasis should be on fact-finding and removal of unsuitable officers. A fair appeals system is needed to balance any surrender of the right to silence.

22. **Complaint resolution** includes forms of mediation involving complainants and the subject officer or police managers (Chapter 8). Resolution is designed to balance the need to avoid covering up misconduct with the need to respond efficiently to (a) the large numbers of complaints that hold little hard evidence of misbehaviour and (b) relatively minor behavioural matters. Complaint resolution can function diagnostically as a misconduct strategy when integrated with complaints profiling.

23. **Monitoring and regulation of police procedures** in areas such as informant relations and securing of drug exhibits can clarify processes and reduce opportunities for corruption. Access controls can also be used to prevent unauthorised use of information held on computer databases. This can be achieved with passwords, log-in windows that require a reason for accessing information, time outs (so information does not stay on a police officer's screen for someone else to see), separation of more sensitive databases (such as for protected witnesses), and recording of all log-ins and attempted log-ins.

24. **Decriminalising vice** needs to be undertaken by politicians, but police should be lobbying to reduce their involvement in areas of traditional market-driven corruption (such as prostitution and drugs) or to change the nature of their involvement. Examples of the latter include the regulation of legal brothels and diversion to treatment programs with drug offenders.

25. **Risk analysis** involves the use of complaints data and other intelligence to identify areas of police work which are corruption prone and which may be amenable to interventions such as tightened regulations, rotation or overt surveillance.

Conclusion

It is now an accepted tenet of police studies that the nature of police work makes it an extreme high-risk occupation for misconduct. Revelations of corruption and excessive force have been so frequent and widespread that accountable governments can no longer trust police to keep their own house in order. The numerous pressures and opportunities for corruption in policing, and the diverse forms of possible misconduct, mean that constant vigilance is required to protect democratic liberties and prevent police abusing their authority.

Acknowledgement

Parts of this chapter will appear in the article 'Police: Brutality and Corruption' in *Encyclopedia of Criminology*, Chicago and London, Fitzroy Dearborn Publishers, 2003, forthcoming. The author wishes to thank Fitzroy Dearborn and Lorraine Murray for permission to use this material.

References

AIC, 1996, *Analysis of Material Derived from a Survey Undertaken by the Royal Commission into the NSW Police*, Australian Institute of Criminology.

Barker, T, 1983, 'Rookie Police Officers' Perceptions of Police Occupational Deviance', *Police Studies* 6(2), 30-38.

Barker, T, 1991, 'An Empirical Study of Police Deviance Other Than Corruption', in T Barker and D Carter (eds), *Police Deviance*, Anderson.

Bennett, R, 1984, 'Becoming Blue: A Longitudinal Study of Police Recruit Occupational Socialisation', *Journal of Police Science and Administration* 12(1), 47-58.

Christopher, W, 1991, *Report of the Independent Commission on the Los Angeles Police Department*, Independent Commission on the LAPD.

Clarke, R, 1998, *Situational Crime Prevention: Successful Case Studies*, Harrow and Heston.

Crank, J, 1998, *Understanding Police Culture*, Anderson.

Daley, R, 1978, *Prince of the City*, Houghton Mifflin.

Fitzgerald, G, 1989, Report of a Commission of Inquiry Pursuant to Orders in Council, Goprint.

Goldsmith, A (ed), 1991, Complaints Against the Police: The Trend to External Review, Clarendon Press.

Graef, R, 1990, *Talking Blues: The Police in Their Own Words*, Fontana.

Heller, J, 1977, *Catch-22*, Corgi.

Henry, V, 1994, 'Police Corruption: Tradition and Evolution', in K Bryett and C Lewis (eds), *Un-Peeling Tradition: Contemporary Policing*, Macmillan.

Hoffman, J, 1997, 'Fighting Corruption: The US Department of Justice Looks at Integrity and Ethics in Policing', *Law and Order* 45(3), 87-92.

Human Rights Watch, 1998, Shielded from Justice: Police Brutality and Accountability in the United States, Human Rights Watch.

IACP, 2001, 'Law Enforcement Code of Conduct', International Association of Chiefs of Police, <http://www.theiacp.org/> accessed 3 March 2002.

Independent Commission on Policing, 1999, *A New Beginning: Policing in Northern Ireland*, Independent Commission on Policing.

Kinney, M, 1999, 'Latin America: Reform Moves Slowly in Countries Noted for Corruption and Abuse', *Crime and Justice International: Worldwide News and Trends* 15(25), 5-6, 30.

Kleinig, J, 1996, *The Ethics of Policing*, Cambridge University Press.

Klockars, C, Ivkovich, S, Harver, W and Haberfeld, M, 2000, *The Measurement of Police Integrity*, Washington DC, National Institute of Justice, Research in Brief, May.

Knapp, W, 1972, *The Knapp Commission Report on Police Corruption*, George Braziller.

Lewis, C, 1999, *Complaints Against Police: The Politics of Reform*, Hawkins Press.

Board of Inquiry, 2000, *Board of Inquiry into the Rampart Corruption Incident: Final Report*, Los Angeles Police Department.

Maas, P, 1973, *Serpico*, Viking Press.

MacPherson, W, 1999, *The Stephen Lawrence Inquiry: Report of an Inquiry by Sir William MacPherson of Cluny*, Her Majesty's Stationery Office.

Melville, N, 1999, *The Taming of the Blue: Regulating Police Misconduct in South Africa*, Human Sciences Research Council.

Mollen, M, 1994, *Commission Report, Commission to Investigate Allegations of Police Corruption and the Anti-Corruption Procedures of the Police Department (New York City)*.

Newburn, T, 1997, *Understanding and Preventing Police Corruption*, Home Office.

Parks, B and Smith, A, 1999, 'The 1992 Los Angeles Riots: Lessons Learned, Changes Made', <http://www.lapdonline.org/> accessed 3 July 2002.

Prenzler, T, 2003 (forthcoming), 'Police: Brutality and Corruption', in R Wright (ed), *Encyclopedia of Criminology*, Fitzroy Dearborn.

Prenzler, T and Ronken, C, 2002, 'A Survey of Innovations in the Development and Maintenance of Ethical Standards in Australian Policing', *Police Practice and Research: An International Journal* 3(3), in press.

Punch, M, 1985, *Conduct Unbecoming: The Social Construction of Police Deviance and Control*, Tavistock.

Scarman, Lord, 1986, *Scarman Report*, Penguin.

Sherman, L, 1977, 'Police Corruption Control: Environmental Context versus Organisational Policy', in D Bayley (ed), *Police and Society*, Sage.

Sigler, R and Dees, T, 1988, 'Public Perceptions of Petty Corruption in Law Enforcement', *Journal of Police Science and Administration* 16(1), 14-20.

Skolnick, J, 1994, *Justice Without Trial: Law Enforcement in Democratic Society*, Macmillan.

Wood, J, 1997, *Royal Commission into the New South Wales Police Service: Final Report*, Government Printer.

2

Miscarriages of Justice

Janet Ransley

The inquiries into police corruption discussed in Chapter 1 prove without doubt that on occasion police tell lies, coerce or fabricate confessions, withhold contrary evidence or obtain evidence by illegal means. Many of the strategies discussed later in this book aim at identifying and preventing this misconduct. But preventing corruption is only one side of the equation – what about redress for those who have suffered as a result of this behaviour? And are there lessons from miscarriages of justice for the strengthening of police integrity?

This chapter examines what is meant by miscarriages of justice and their relationship with police misconduct, how and why miscarriages occur, how the legal system responds to them and why this has proved inadequate. The chapter concludes by looking at some new responses to miscarriages, but argues that reforms need a supportive political and cultural climate to succeed.

Defining miscarriages of justice

Conventional conceptions of miscarriages of justice depict innocent people wrongly convicted of serious crimes and imprisoned (Hogg 1991). The many notorious examples include the Guildford Four, Maguire Seven and Birmingham Six in Britain (Walker and Starmer 1999), and the Chamberlains, Tim Anderson and Alexander McLeod-Lindsay in Australia (Carrington, Dever, Hogg, Bargen and Lohrey 1991a). However, a broader conception sees a miscarriage whenever there is a failure to achieve justice, which includes not only wrongful conviction, but also failures to prosecute those responsible for crimes, and unjust laws or inhumane punishments (Nobles and Schiff 2000). On this conception, miscarriages occur when the state:

- breaches the rights of suspects, defendants or convicts through deficient processes (including the fabrication or manipulation of evidence), or the laws applied to them (because they target minorities or deny human rights), or because there is no factual justification for their treatment (because of wrong or fabricated identifications, or faulty forensic evidence); or

- adversely treats suspects, defendants or convicts, disproportionately with the need to protect the rights of others (because trivial conduct is harshly treated); or

- fails to protect the rights of others from wrongdoers or from state law itself, such as police not intervening to protect minority victims (Walker 1999).

While most public attention is on miscarriages in serious criminal trials, the great bulk of miscarriages probably occur at a lower level, in the routine processing of over 95 per cent of criminal cases before Magistrates Courts (Bottomley and Parker 1997). Defendants whose guilty pleas arise from a lack of legal advice or resources, or plea-bargaining, also represent potential miscarriages of justice, but are much less likely to attract attention than those wrongfully imprisoned for murder. Miscarriages, therefore, can occur at any stage of the criminal justice process, from law-making through street policing practices, investigations, court processes and custodial practices. But as the focus of this book is police misconduct, the rest of this chapter concerns those types of miscarriage most likely to involve police.

Miscarriages of justice are significant for two main reasons: first, because in a liberal legal system individual rights and autonomy are paramount. The liberal state protects individual rights through conventions such as the right to be presumed innocent, requiring the prosecution to prove guilt, the beyond reasonable doubt standard of proof, and the right to a trial by jury. Miscarriages undermine these individual rights, potentially affecting an individual's enjoyment of liberty, privacy, family life, secure financial status and perhaps even the right to life (Walker 1999). Miscarriages have caused people to be wrongly imprisoned for long periods (17 years for the Birmingham Six, eight years for Tim Anderson). In Britain, Timothy Evans was executed then posthumously pardoned, and serious doubts have also been raised about the conviction of Ronald Ryan, the last man executed in Australia (Wilson 1991).

But miscarriages of justice have a second, broader impact. They highlight deficiencies in the criminal justice system, and when the system appears unable or unwilling to rectify its mistakes, the miscarriages lead to a failure in public confidence or even a 'crisis in criminal justice' (Walker 1999: 45). Such a crisis occurred in Britain in the late 1980s and early 1990s, with a succession of convictions overturned amid great public concern, leading to the establishment of the Runciman Royal Commission. Repeated miscarriages indicate a system unwilling to consider its mistakes and provide a focal point for reformers appealing to moral outrage among the community (Nobles and Schiff 2000).

Despite the occasional crisis, there has been relatively little interest in miscarriages among criminal justice policymakers and scholars (Wilson 1991; Rapp 2000). This lack of interest may arise because criminal justice and legal professionals are unwilling to examine their own mistakes. There can also be a lack of sympathy with the victims of miscarriages, because of their perceived connection with terrorism, or because they are already 'known to police' (Hogg 1991) or are members of minority groups. All of these factors can help justify the treatment of the convicted as a necessary departure from normal standards. Thus Tim Anderson was labelled a terrorist, and was associated with the Ananda Marga, emphasising his marginal standing and justifying abnormal treatment by police (discussed further below).

Miscarriages also reflect a tendency for police investigators to develop a theory as to responsibility for a crime, and then to exclude all other avenues for investigation (Dixon 1999). This may occur by not following up other potential avenues of investigation, or by active manipulation of evidence to support the theory. Tunnel vision is ensured by police reluctance to admit their initial presumptions were wrong. 'Noble cause' perceptions of police misconduct help justify this manipulation, because while police view the accused as guilty, they perceive bureaucratic rules or lack of resources as preventing the gathering of enough evidence to actually prove guilt.

There is also a relative lack of concern for miscarriages of justice because they are seen as the rare and even tolerable mistakes of a system that is fundamentally fair. In a policy climate where the war against crime is the prime concern, 'the public accepts a few miscarriages in order to win the war' (Wilson 1991: 2). One view is that existing processes are validated both because proven miscarriages of justice are relatively rare, and because recent prominent miscarriages have been identified and overturned. This view might be tenable if all or even most miscarriages are eventually discovered and redressed through the normal processes of the legal system, but the evidence suggest that in fact many more miscarriages occur than are ever detected (Kirby 1991).

This lack of detection makes it difficult to know how many miscarriages do occur. For every notorious case there are unknown numbers of wrongful plea bargains in the lower courts. Even with serious crimes, for many convicted people the financial and emotional costs necessary to generate a review are too high. As a result, there is no systematic evidence on how many miscarriages occur. United States research shows that since the reinstatement of the death penalty in 1973, 92 people sentenced to death have been exonerated, almost entirely by the use of DNA testing (Rapp 2000). A survey for the Runciman Commission found two per cent of convictions in the British Crown Court each year were viewed by judges as 'problematic', with defence lawyers putting the figure at 17 per cent per year, or about 2000 convictions annually (Walker 1999). Similar data are not available for Australia, for reasons including the lack of relevant research and the fragmentation of the criminal jurisdiction, but there is no reason to suspect a different pattern.

Miscarriages of justice then, are not isolated, regrettable errors in the otherwise smooth and fair administration of criminal justice, but a systemic, under-researched, unresolved problem. They have untold impact on the rights and lives of individuals, but also undermine the legitimacy of the legal system. Additionally, an often overlooked side effect of imprisoning people for crimes they have not committed is that the real offenders remain undetected, unpunished and perhaps re-offending.

Causes of miscarriages of justice

Examples where convictions have been overturned illustrate some key causes of miscarriages of justice. Frank Button, a Queensland Aboriginal man, was convicted of the rape of a 13-year-old girl, and spent ten months in custody prior to the quashing of his conviction. His appeal succeeded because DNA evidence conclusively proved he had not committed the crime and identified the real perpetrator. That evidence was not available at the trial because investigators had decided not to test the bedding on which the offence occurred, as any evidence obtained could not prove that Button committed the crime. The fact that it could exclude him as the perpetrator was apparently not considered important! Other evidence contributing to Button's conviction included identification by the victim in her second statement to police in a reversal of the identification evidence she had given in her first statement the previous day, and an alleged confession by Button to a nephew, which was denied by the nephew at trial. Police made no effort to gather evidence contrary to their perception of Button's guilt, and perhaps, as alleged by defence lawyers, influenced the victim into a false identification and the nephew into fabricated evidence of a confession (Nolan and Koch 2001). The trial did not detect these errors and the jury made its decision on incomplete evidence. Despite this, and although he may not agree, Frank Button was lucky – his lawyers continued acting for him after his conviction, and physical evidence in the form of the bedding still existed in police custody and yielded viable DNA. His lawyers then framed a claim that succeeded within the confines of the rules of appeal.

Less fortunate was Stephen Downing, convicted of murder in Britain in February 1974 when he was 17 and sentenced to life imprisonment. He had discovered and called police to where the victim lay dying in a cemetery where he worked as a gardener. The prosecution relied on forensic evidence that blood on his clothing could only be explained by his being the killer, rather than from him holding the victim as she died, and on his admissions in a police interview, during which he had not been informed he was under arrest, and was denied access to a solicitor, although he had a reading age of only 11 at the time. Downing's appeal was rejected in October 1974 and he served 18 years in prison, denied parole because he refused to admit his guilt (CCRC 2000). He was released in January 2002 after a further review found the forensic evidence to be unreliable, and the confession to have involved substantial and significant breaches of police rules on the questioning of suspects. It was also claimed that police did not pursue witness evidence that cast doubt on Downing's guilt. None of these errors were detected at the trial or the original appeal, and the new evidence for the review was uncovered largely by a local newspaper editor who ran a media campaign with Downing's parents (Vasager 2002).

A third example involves Tim Anderson, the subject of two separate miscarriages. In 1978 a bomb killed three people outside the Sydney Hilton Hotel where a regional Commonwealth Heads of Government meeting was being held. Police and security services identified as likely culprits local members of Ananda Marga, a spiritual group whose members had protested against the Indian Prime Minister's visit for the meeting. Police recruited an informant to infiltrate the group, and on his evidence Anderson and two colleagues were arrested, not for the bombing, but on charges that they had conspired to murder a prominent neo-Nazi. They were tried, tried again after the first jury was hung, convicted and sentenced to 16 years' jail. In both trials, the prosecution was allowed to introduce evidence and cross-examine the accused regarding the Hilton bombing, even though they had not been charged for that offence. Supreme Court and High Court appeals against the convictions failed. After a public campaign a judicial inquiry was appointed to examine the convictions. The inquiry recommended pardons, but exonerated police from any wrongdoing, placing all blame on their now discredited informant. Anderson and his colleagues were freed in May 1985 (Carrington et al 1991b; Anderson 1992).

In May 1989, Anderson was again arrested, this time charged with murder arising from the Hilton bombing. The charges were based on confessions allegedly made by Anderson to another prisoner while he had been in custody. This prisoner later received an indemnity for other offences, based partly on his evidence against Anderson. After Anderson's arrest, a former member of Ananda Marga, Evan Pederick, confessed to having committed the crime with Anderson. The priest to whom he first told his story did not believe him, and neither it seems did the Queensland police to whom he next confessed, who listened to his story then drove him home, asking his wife if he did this often! His evidence was central to Anderson's conviction, despite the flaws in his story that emerged during the trial. Pederick's reasons for making a false confession are not clear, but the police and prosecution accepted his story because it fitted their preconceived notions of Anderson's involvement. They chose not to verify aspects of his story that could be checked, and ignored bits that did not fit their version of events (Carrington et al 1991b). In doing this they were aided by the media, which uncritically reported police theories as evidence, and painted Anderson and other Ananda Margiis as deviants (Pugliese 1991). Police granted certain journalists privileged access to Crown witnesses or photo opportunities, and were rewarded with uncritical reporting of the trial. The media had in fact been referring to Anderson as the Hilton Bomber for years prior to his conviction, including throughout the period of the earlier trials on the conspiracy charges. Not only was much of this reporting prejudicial to a fair trial, it was also 'hopelessly wrong and ... never properly corrected' (Hogg 1991: 207). Far from correcting these errors, prior to the trial the prosecutor unsuccessfully applied to have a bail condition imposed on Anderson to prevent him from making public comments or encouraging other people to disseminate material or views concerning the case (Anderson 1992). Anderson's appeal in May 1991 overturned the verdict as unsafe and unsatisfactory, largely because of prosecutorial errors and unfairness in the presentation of Pederick's evidence.

The prejudicial representation of defendants has been prominent in other Australian miscarriages. In 1989, Harry Blackburn was paraded before invited media at his arrest and identified as the serial rapist sought by police, despite there being no evidence to connect him with the crimes (Hogg 1991). The media presentation of Lindy Chamberlain as unnaturally lacking in grief over the death of her daughter contributed to perceptions of her guilt (Wilson 1991). The media have also played central roles in campaigns to expose miscarriages (as in the Irish, Chamberlain and Downing cases). This dual media role results in part from its symbiotic relationship with the criminal justice system (Hogg 1991) with police dependent on the media for public support and assistance, and the media looking to police for newsworthy stories. This leads to institutionalised relationships, with it being in the interests of neither organisation to criticise or even analytically consider the processes and conduct of the other. These institutionalised relationships break down where the police become the story, as in cases of corruption or misconduct, but are reinforced where the crime and its punishment are the story. In a cultural 'war on crime' police and media act together to protect criminal justice processes. The legal system and the media are engaged in fundamentally different and disparate discourses and are seeking differing versions of the truth (Nobles and Schiff 2000). Legal 'truth' is concerned with the disposition of cases and finality, while for the media 'truth' is about its presentation of what happened. These discourses rest on competing underlying values – finality versus newsworthiness.

The cases discussed above indicate key factors leading to miscarriages, including:

- unreliable confessions, obtained through police pressure, mental instability or other incapacity (as in the Downing case);

- the fabrication of evidence, whether by police as 'verballed' confessions, or by unreliable informants, particularly those in prison or facing charges themselves (the fabricated confession by Frank Button to a nephew; unreliable informants in the Anderson trials);

- unreliable evidence, such as suspect witness identifications or dubious forensic evidence (the victim identification of Button, unreliable forensic evidence in the Downing case);

- the concealing of evidence by police, prosecutors or forensic scientists (the decision not to test bedding in the Button case);

- incompetent investigations or focus on police theories, excluding alternative inquiries (the exclusion of other witnesses in the Downing case; the construction of police theories of Anderson's guilt);

- the conduct of the trial including judicial or prosecutorial unfairness (prosecutor's conduct in the Anderson murder trial); and

- prejudicial representation of the defendant by police or the media (in the Anderson case).

(adapted from Wilson 1991; Hogg 1991; Brown, Farrier and Weisbrot 1996; Wood 1997; Walker 1999)

While police corruption is not responsible for all miscarriages, at various times it may be a significant cause. Separate inquiries into police misconduct in Queensland in 1989 and New South Wales in 1997 both considered the entrenched corruption discovered was likely to have caused serious miscarriages. The Queensland inquiry reported 'police and former police have admitted instances of it [verballing]' and recommended a review of convictions of alleged victims (the recommendation was not implemented) (Fitzgerald 1989: 332). The corrupt activities of the West Midlands Police Serious Crime Squad in Britain led to the quashing of some convictions obtained by the squad (Walker 1999). The Los Angeles Police in the Ramparts district went beyond verballing to the planting of drugs and other attempts to frame suspected gang members, and led to hundreds of reviews of convictions still being processed through the courts. So far, the Los Angeles City Council has paid about 35 million dollars in compensation to victims (McGreevy 2002: B-3).

The underlying cause for these types of miscarriage is that police have little accountability for their investigative and evidence-gathering processes. This lack of accountability suggests a deeper problem with criminal justice, namely the adversarial system itself, with its focus on an idealised contest between two equally armed sides, rather than on discovering the truth. This leads to faults including self-serving investigative processes, unequal resources between prosecution and defence, strict and artificial rules of evidence and limited use of experts (Walker 1999). These criticisms of the adversarial process have in turn led to arguments for a move to a more inquisitorial system, with Bell (1999) arguing that the French version of inquisitorial justice has three important strategies for preventing miscarriages. First, it has judicial supervision throughout the investigation to act as a check on police. Secondly, it makes use of court-appointed, independent expert witnesses in the giving of forensic evidence, and thirdly, it relies on a single written case file containing all relevant evidence and to which the defence has open access during the investigation, minimising the dangers of both non-disclosure and manipulation of evidence.

The legal system's response to miscarriages of justice

The problem with miscarriages of justice is not just that they occur, but that the legal system tends to be unable or unwilling to rectify them on an individual basis, and unwilling to review procedures that facilitate them. The appeals system is seen as a crucial check, but various factors prevent it from detecting and overturning miscarriages, including that:

- there are relatively few appeals, due to a lack of financial, legal and emotional resources on the part of the convicted;

- most appeals are confined to investigating alleged errors of law (such as the judicial exclusion or admission of evidence, or defining of offences or the burden of proof to juries), rather than a reconsideration of the evidence or the investigation;

- restrictions generally prevent the presentation of fresh evidence unless it was not reasonably obtainable at the time of the trial, and also would have raised a significant possibility of the jury acquitting;

- many police investigative decisions in the pre-trial process which produce the facts presented to the jury (such as which witness statements to pursue and which forensic evidence to collect) are not formally recorded or disclosed, and are therefore not reviewable;

- aspects of the trial may contribute to wrongful convictions but generally cannot be corrected on appeal, such as the dynamics of cross-examination favouring experienced, plausible witnesses, and the influence of the judge in summing up;

- restrictions generally prevent appeals on the basis of an incompetent or tactically wrong defence;

- appeal courts are generally reluctant to overturn the findings of juries and tend to see appellants as guilty unless they prove their innocence; and

- appeal courts lack and independent investigative capacity to re-open issues of fact

(adapted from Wood 1997; Wilson 1991; Hogg 1991; Brown et al 1996).

In Britain the Runciman Commission led to changes aimed at overcoming some of these barriers to appeal. Walker (1999) concludes these reforms have had little effect partly because of excessive deference to the jury system, but also because of the continuing need for systemic changes to judicial appointments and training to reflect broader, less insular views of the criminal justice system, and to produce a judiciary more prepared to entertain claims of miscarriage.

If reforms to the appeal system have not worked as an avenue for correcting miscarriages, until recently, the only other avenue (and still the only way in all Australian States but New South Wales), was the right to petition the Attorney-General, or in Britain the Home Secretary, to initiate a review. This usually occurred after the discovery of fresh evidence, not available at the original appeal. The response to the petition was within the discretion of the relevant minister, and could include rejecting it, referring the matter back to the relevant court of appeal for fresh consideration, or especially in Australia, setting up a royal commission or judicial inquiry to examine the new evidence and make recommendations. The main problem with the petition process is that it is essentially political, with the review being requested of a government minister and its outcome entirely dependent on his or her discretion. The prospects of success are strongly linked to the extent of the media and public campaign mounted in its support, and the policy of the government at the time in relation to criminal justice. Thus in 1987, the British Home Secretary refused to initiate reviews in the Maguire and Guildford Four cases on the basis that no new evidence cast doubt on the convictions. By 1991, each case had been referred back to the Court of

Appeal and the convictions overturned. The reversal of the decision not to review was caused by mounting media and public pressure on the government rather than the uncovering of any further new evidence (Rozenberg 1992).

The advantage of review inquiries is that they are not confined by the technical rules governing appeals, and can re-examine both the facts and the investigative process to try to arrive at the truth. As such they represent a partial importation of the inquisitorial process into the common law system. Their disadvantage is that they can only make recommendations, either for a referral back to the appeal court, or to the Attorney-General for a pardon.

Alternative approaches

Recognition of the deficiencies in appeal and post-appeal review processes has led to the development of alternative models. In Australia, the first was in New South Wales, where in 1993 Pt 13A was inserted into the *Crimes Act* 1900 (NSW). This deals with the post-appeal review of convictions, and resulted from a series of miscarriage cases that failed to be corrected on appeal (Brown et al 1996). The provisions enable petitions for review to be referred to an inquiry by a judge, to the Court of Criminal Appeal as a new appeal or for an opinion on any point. Section 474C sets out the grounds on which the Governor or Minister may refuse to deal with or defer a petition. Subsequent amendments in 1996 reformed the process further, providing for an application for an inquiry to be made direct to the Supreme Court, thereby avoiding executive government altogether (see s 474D-E). Inquiry judges are given all the powers and immunities of a royal commission, must submit a written report, and may themselves refer the matter back to the Court of Criminal Appeal for review of the conviction or sentence.

This approach has advantages over the traditional procedure including the possibility of excluding the executive from the review and thereby at least partly de-politicising it; the setting of statutory guidelines for dealing with petitions; and the conferring of inquisitorial investigative powers on reviewing inquiries. Some disadvantages remain. Despite their powers, inquiries cannot conduct thorough investigations unless they are properly and independently resourced. Additionally, given that inquiries must be conducted by judges, many of the broader problems in the appeals process discussed above, such as judicial attitudes to jury verdicts and judicial training, may simply be transposed to the new system. Finally, many of the problems in initiating reviews are not addressed by the new system, such as the difficulties for most convicted people in accessing ongoing legal advice and in obtaining new evidence to support their petitions.

The Royal Commission into the New South Wales Police considered whether an independent body should be established to review convictions but subject to recommendations about resources and legal aid, concluded that the current system provides 'substantial opportunity for any applicant armed with fresh evidence' to have their conviction reviewed on its merits (Wood 1997: 447-50). The flaw in this argument is that it fails to recognise the need for systemic, independent reinvestigation of suspect cases to uncover the necessary fresh evidence, particularly when corruption inquiries have revealed the high probability of miscarriages having occurred (Brown 1997). Placing this burden on the applicant makes use of the review process unattainable for most wrongfully convicted people who lack the necessary resources.

The other main approach to reform is the model now adopted in Britain of an independent review agency. The Criminal Cases Review Commission (CCRC) was recommended by the Runciman Commission and implemented in the *Criminal Appeal Act* 1995 (UK). The CCRC largely assumes the previous role of the Home Secretary, to receive applications for review, investigate them and if appropriate refer them to the Court of Appeal for consideration (CCRC 2001). As in the New South Wales process, there is statutory guidance for the exercise of the discretion to investigate and refer, although Taylor and Mansfield (1999) argue that the criteria differ little in real terms from those previously used to advise the Home Secretary. Despite this, the record of the CCRC to date seems promising – as at 31 March 2001, of 2900 applications, 124 were referred to the Court of Appeal, which had determined 63. In 48 of these cases convictions were quashed or sentences modified, with 15 trial verdicts upheld (CCRC 2001). This success rate seems to indicate a preparedness by the court to take seriously the findings of the CCRC.

Despite this, and while the reforms undoubtedly remove the executive from the direct review process, the outcome of reviews is still dependent on the Court of Appeal. Taylor and Mansfield argue that the 'single most important change must therefore be to ensure that the Court of Appeal is more receptive to cases of potential injustice' (1999: 245). They also point to the composition of the CCRC as chosen by the Home Secretary, 'heavily weighed towards the prosecuting authorities' rather than those with expertise in uncovering miscarriages of justice, and largely reflective of the 'white, male, middle class background that is so often a feature of judicial institutions' (235). Potential reforms including giving the CCRC power to make recommendations to the court, with the court being required to justify any departures from those recommendations, having appointments to the CCRC made by a Parliamentary Select Committee, and strengthening its investigative capacity with seconded police officers and lawyers. Again the ready availability of legal aid is a critical issue. Perhaps the largest obstacle facing the CCRC is that of resources and its outstanding caseload. As at 31 March 2001, this stood at 1100, with the CCRC estimating that it would not finish processing the backlog until 2004 (CCRC 2001). Such delays may be too long for applicants serving unjust prison sentences.

Victims of miscarriages

While the new approaches just discussed address some of the problems in achieving review of miscarriages, they do not address one of the main problems facing victims – obtaining compensation for their wrongful conviction and imprisonment. The traditional approach to compensation has been either that victims must pursue civil remedies, which is both difficult and expensive, or seek ex gratia payments from governments. Ex gratia payments are entirely at the discretion of government, are generally determined in secret and according to no set criteria. In Britain fewer than ten per cent of such claims succeeded, with most successful claims being for relatively small amounts (Taylor and Wood 1999). Additionally, such payments tend to be both long delayed and inconsistent; for example in Australia former senior police officer Harry Blackburn received almost $1 million despite never being convicted and serving no time in prison, Lindy Chamberlain received $1 million for three-and-a-half years in jail, but Tim Anderson and his colleagues received $100,000 each for over seven years' jail (Anderson 1997). Furthermore, ex gratia payments are generally made only where conventional appeals have failed, but convictions are subsequently overturned.

An alternative approach is a statutory compensation scheme, as introduced in Britain in 1988. However, applications must still be made to the Home Secretary, cannot involve cases overturned in a normal appeal, and judicial interpretations of the Act have confined its scope narrowly. While the scheme has resulted in larger payments than under the ex gratia scheme, they still do not match civil damages awards in wrongful imprisonment cases. Additionally, there is no formal apology or rehabilitation program offered to people released after wrongful incarceration (Taylor and Wood 1999).

Conclusion

This discussion of the features and causes of, and responses to, miscarriages suggests two strands of continuing concern. The first is the need for reform of police investigative and evidence gathering processes to improve accountability. Secondly, the legal system also needs reform to ensure that its inevitable mistakes are detected and rectified. The British CCRC is one step in this process, but harder issues like judicial culture remain unaddressed. Furthermore, any reforms remain subject to the prevailing political culture, which influences government decision-making and resource allocation. A climate where elections are fought on 'tough on crime' policies does not encourage protection of the rights of suspects. In this climate, reform will continue to be slow.

References

Anderson, T, 1992, *Take Two: the Criminal Justice System Revisited*, Bantam Books.

Anderson, T, 1997, 'Miscarriages of Justice: Background on Compensation for NSW Victims', <http://www.breakout.net.au/ju/JstAct/miscarrback. html> accessed 15 January 2002.

Bell, J, 1999, 'The French Pre-Trial System', in C Walker and K Starmer (eds), *Miscarriages of Justice: a Review of Justice in Error*, Blackstone Press.

Bottomley S and Parker S, 1997, Law in Context, 2nd edn, Federation Press.

Brown, D, Farrier, D and Weisbrot D, 1996, *Criminal Laws* (2nd edn), Federation Press.

Brown, D, 1997, 'Many Other Players in the Game of Criminal Justice', *Sydney Morning Herald*, 16 May, p 13.

Carrington, K, Dever, M, Hogg, R, Bargen, J and Lohrey, A (eds), 1991a, *Travesty! Miscarriages of Justice*, Academics for Justice.

Carrington K, Dever, M, Hogg, R, Bargen, J and Lohrey, A, 1991b, 'The Conviction of Timothy Edward Anderson over the Hilton Bombing: Verdict Unsafe' in K Carrington, et al (eds), *Travesty! Miscarriages of Justice*, Academics for Justice.

CCRC (Criminal Cases Review Commission), 2000, 'Commission Refers Conviction of Stephen Leslie Downing to Court of Appeal', 14 November, <http://www.ccrc.gov.uk/latestnews/pr141100.html> accessed 17 January 2002.

CCRC, 2001, Annual Report 2000-01, <http://www.ccrc.gov.uk/latestnews/pr141100.html> accessed 17 January 2002.

Dixon, D, 1999, 'Police Investigative Procedures' in C Walker and K Starmer (eds), *Miscarriages of Justice: a Review of Justice in Error*, Blackstone Press.

Fitzgerald, G, 1989, *Report of a Commission of Inquiry Pursuant to Orders in Council*, Goprint.

Hogg, R, 1991, 'Identifying and Reforming the Problems of the Justice System' in K Carrington, et al (eds), *Travesty! Miscarriages of Justice*, Academics for Justice.

Kirby, M, 1991, 'Miscarriages of Justice – Our Lamentable Failure?' *Commonwealth Law Bulletin* July: 1040, 1049.

McGreevy, P, 2002, 'LA Settles 7 Rampart Cases', *Los Angeles Times* 20 February, B-3.

Nobles, R and Schiff D, 2000, *Understanding Miscarriages of Justice: Law, the Media and the Inevitability of Crisis*, Oxford University Press.

Nolan, J and Koch T, 2001, 'Testing Justice', *The Courier-Mail*, 16 April, p28.

Pugliese J, 1991, 'The Rhetoric of Criminality: The Print Media and the Hilton Bombing Case' in K Carrington, et al (eds), *Travesty! Miscarriages of Justice*, Academics for Justice.

Rapp, G, 2000, 'DNA's Dark Side', *Yale Law Journal* 110: 163-171.

Wood, J, 1997, *Royal Commission into the New South Wales Police Service: Final Report*, Government Printer.

Rozenberg, J, 1992, 'Miscarriages of Justice', in E Stockdale and S Casales (eds) *Criminal Justice under Stress*, Blackstone.

Taylor N and Mansfield M, 1999, 'Post-Conviction Procedures' in C Walker and K Starmer (eds), *Miscarriages of Justice: a Review of Justice in Error*, Blackstone Press.

Taylor N and Wood J, 1999, 'Victims of Miscarriages of Justice' in C Walker and K Starmer (eds), *Miscarriages of Justice: a Review of Justice in Error*, Blackstone Press.

Vasager, J, 2002, End of a Nightmare, The Guardian, 16 January, <http://www.guardian.co.uk/Print/0,3858,4336235,00.html>accessed 17 January 2002.

Walker, C, 1999, 'The Agenda of Miscarriages of Justice', 'Miscarriages of Justice in Principle and Practice' and 'The Judiciary' in Walker C and Starmer K (eds), *Miscarriages of Justice: a Review of Justice in Error*, Blackstone Press.

Walker, C and Starmer, K, (eds), 1999, *Miscarriages of Justice: a Review of Justice in Error*, Blackstone Press.

Wilson, P, 1991, 'Miscarriages of Justice in Serious Criminal Cases in Australia' in K Carrington, et al (eds), *Travesty! Miscarriages of Justice*, Academics for Justice.

3

Public Order Policing

David Baker

The policing of public protest is uncertain, unpredictable and volatile. Public protest can take diverse and changing forms – political, industrial, festive, sporting, environmental – and each form of dissent exhibits its own dynamism and potential for violent confrontation. Debate about the shifting nature of policing public disorder has considerably influenced the standing of policing in different eras and presented challenges for integrity and accountability (Reiner 1997). Police are charged with the sometimes incompatible functions of enforcing the law and maintaining public order. Police capacity to make sound, strategic choices when handling potentially hostile protests and blockades tests police doctrines of independence, impartiality and use of minimal force.

This chapter analyses police responses to public demonstrations in terms of political independence and the historical problem of excessive force. The chapter also examines an emerging approach to handling public dissent that focuses on minimising violence and balancing the rights of companies, governments and the general public with those of workers and special interest groups. A case study is made comparing the relatively successful policing of the 1998 Australian waterfront dispute with the less successful policing of the anti-globalisation protests of recent years.

Traditional policing of industrial confrontation

Historically, in periods of bitter industrial strife, police have usually not stood in the middle as neutral arbiters of the law but have served employer and government demands for decisive action. Employers have customarily relied on the apparatus of the state in the form of the police to make their plants accessible, to protect staff and strikebreakers, and to safeguard business productivity. Since the establishment of modern police in the early 19th century they have been subject to allegations of ruling class control, especially in the suppression of working class movements and industrial union activities (Reiner 1992: 11-56). The baton charge has been the symbol of police public order might. Historically, it was the main coercive instrument of crowd dispersal, and potentially a source of escalating violence (della Porta and Reiter 1998: 2). In Australia, police were ruthless in the suppression of shearers in the Great Strikes of the 1890s and the stevedores in the late 1920s. Public order theory indicates how the state's force, in the form of aggressive and heavy-handed policing, can escalate the tensions and potential violence of industrial conflict (Waddington 1992). Unionists have perceived police as the agent making it possible for the capitalist employer to continue production by the use of 'scab' (non-striking or replacement) labour – the enemy of the unionised workforce. Almost invariably such confrontations are weighted in the favour of police with their modern armoury of guns, rubber bullets, tear gas, riot shields and helmets, horses, water canon, armoured personnel carriers and surveillance helicopters.

The history of the policing of industrial disputes and political protest in totalitarian regimes elicits a cacophony of violence and death. Protests and strikes were viewed as a threat to the state's ruling elites and were ruthlessly repressed. In the mid-1980s in South Africa, the funerals of black activists, including union organisers, provoked violent political demonstrations. The South African Police regularly selected to confront black protesters. If they failed to disperse, CS smoke or birdshot or ultimately high-velocity rifles were used (Waddington 1998: 135). The new capitalist economies emerging from the dismantling of the Soviet Union face challenges in transforming from militaristic, authoritarian and often brutal policing regimes accountable only to the ruling elites to police agencies theoretically now dependent on the consent of the people for their legitimacy. However, reliance on surveillance, informants and undercover agents is still widely practised and directly impinges on private lives and group activism (Shelley 1999).

Democratic societies have also witnessed demonising of strikers and subsequent ruthless policing. British Prime Minister Margaret Thatcher's labelling of the coal-miners as 'the enemy within' and the Conservative Government's pursuit of a criminal rather than a civil strategy to defeat the National Union of Miners rationalised harsh repression of picketers during the coal strike of 1984-85. The arrest of

11,000 miners, but not one police officer, highlighted the effectiveness of this criminalisation process. Within two years, ordinary uniformed police were transformed into riot squads with all the paraphernalia of hard-line policing (Alderson 1997).

Although there has been no formulated policy of repression against strikers, whenever major conflict between worker and police occurred on the Australian industrial front, police actions were usually swift, uncompromising and ruthless. Though not consistent throughout history, police actions at specific times and during specific conflicts attempted to suppress picket activities, left-wing agitation and unemployment dissent (Baker 2001). Police have perceived protesters, especially ringleaders, as 'trouble'. Disorder was seen as stemming from the actions and provocations of radical extremists – providing the modern justification for selective and forceful police actions of arrest and dispersion, thereby intensifying strikers' perceptions of injustice. The failure of government to hold police accountable for alleged excesses, violence and brutality while controlling disputation has been a common characteristic of Australia's industrial history. A few notable examples follow.

- On 2 February 1912 - 'Black Baton Friday' - about 15,000 demonstrators in Brisbane were confronted by the police and special constables who were armed with rifles and bayonets. Batons were used freely against the marchers. Mounted police, mustered from around the State, dispersed the demonstrators (Johnston 1992: 185-187).

- On 2 November 1928 constables fired approximately 100 bullets at fleeing stevedores at Port Melbourne. An eye-witness account described how an unarmed stevedore, Alan Whittaker, 'got shot right through the back of his neck. The bullet came out through his mouth' (in Lowenstein and Hills 1982: 64). The stevedores went 'berserk' and showered the police with blue metal. The Hogan Labour Government, like the police department, refused to investigate the shootings; the daily press supported police actions (Baker 2001).

- In Queensland, the illegal march of unionists, known as 'the 1948 St. Patrick's Day bash', resulted in numerous arrests, raids on union offices, the hospitalisation of several demonstrators and the bashing of Fred Patterson, a member of the Queensland Parliament (Blackmur 1993).

The quandary remains whether police aggression in such confrontations was designed to appropriately disperse the gatherings or whether it was designed to teach the workers a disciplinary lesson in social control and class authority. Nonetheless, alleged police coercion of picketers has received little, if any, scrutiny, review or inquiry from state authorities in Australia. For example, authorities refused to investigate police bashings of La Trobe University students during two 1970 anti-Vietnam War marches in Waterdale Road (Melbourne). The *Sunday Observer*, 20 September 1970, quoted the local Inspector: 'They got some baton today and they'll get a lot more in the future'. During the 1971 Springbok tour, Queensland Police were far more adept at arresting anti-apartheid demonstrators than rugby supporters who tackled demonstrators.

Geary (1985) argues that there has been a linear de-escalation of violence between police and striking unionists in 20th century Britain, a theory that was feasible until 1975 but subsequently discredited by police paramilitary-style aggression at Grunwick photographic processing laboratories (1977), the miners' strike (1984-85) and Wapping (1987). Similarly, Taft and Ross (1979: 187-241) argue that violence in American labour-management relations was pervasive from the 1870s to the 1930s and that America experienced the 'most frequent and bloody labour violence' of any industrial nation, but that this has been less frequent since World War II. Brecher (1997: 1) chronicles a much more pessimistic account of repeated and bloody repression of worker dissent 'by company-sponsored violence, local police, state militias, and the US Army and National Guard'. Desperate revolt and direct industrial action spread through working class organisations during the 1930s Depression. Longshoremen clashed repeatedly with police. When, on 3 July 1934, thousands of strikers attacked picket lines, according to *The New York Times*, 'Mounted and foot police swung their clubs and hurled tear-gas bombs, strikers hurled bricks and rocks, battered heads with clubs and railroad spikes and smashed windows' (in Brecher 1997: 169). Police, deputised special police and National Guardsmen fought strikers at the Auto-Lite plant in Toledo, Ohio, in May 1934. New Guardsmen attacked the picket lines and evacuated strike-breakers from the plants, but were driven back by the crowds. The guardsmen, backed by machine gun units, advanced again with bayonets. The third time, the troops were ordered to fire; two strikers were killed and 15 wounded in the single battle (Brecher 1997: 176-178).

Police on many Western university campuses in the 1960s and 1970s encountered widespread student resistance and public protest. In May 1970, the Ohio National Guard, after previously smashing a wildcat teamsters strike, opened fire on anti-Vietnam demonstrators at Kent State University and killed four students who were unconnected to campus violence. No one was indicted for the killing of the unarmed students (Alderson 1998). The pervasive lesson is that close physical contact between police and picketers and protesters demands self-control and discipline from both parties. Because police usually have superior fire power, the prime responsibility for managing conflict lies with them.

Modern trends in public order policing

The lack of accountability of public order policing was a key feature of worker-police relations, and protests generally, until at least the 1970s. From that time, the introduction of mobile television cameras began to make both police and protesters more sensitive to the adverse publicity that violence can create. The mere presence of journalists at public events and rallies in some countries appears to tame police 'toughness' (della Porta and Reiter 1998: 18). The increasing sophistication of police public order planning and training has emerged from better-educated, management-trained and media-savvy police leaders and union organisers with greater knowledge of civil rights. The creation of police internal investigation units and civilian review agencies has enhanced the accountability of police and the desirability of police-protester communications.

During relatively peaceful times police find that discretion is a better method of preserving the peace and maintaining legitimacy in the eyes of the populace than prosecuting the law to its fullest. When large numbers are gathered in protest or blockade, police are unable to move and arrest all people who are technically breaking a law. The prudent police approach is often to forego arrests (or pursue a minimum arrest policy) and to preserve the peace. This outcome has not been so much the result of specific policing policy but rather the approach of those police on the spot who value the course of minimum intervention (Reiner, 1997).

When times have been unsettled and militant, policing has been inclined to follow a more legalistic and aggressive approach. Lofthouse (1997) argues that in 'times of crisis, repression, through the application of force by the police, is the norm'. Despite an apparently more tolerant approach and the rhetoric of minimum confrontation with marginalised groups in modern society, hard-line policing of dissent did not cease with the massive anti-Vietnam moratoriums or anti-apartheid marches that occurred in many western democracies in the 1970s. The 13 December 1993 police baton charge at Richmond Secondary College (Melbourne) illustrates how confrontation and suppression remain possible against even passive picketing. The Victorian Trades Hall Council and the Victorian Secondary Teachers' Association endorsed the picket; such authorisation usually constitutes official recognition of the picket by police. However, 177 members of the newly established Force Response Unit conducted a military-orchestrated baton charge of approximately 40 unarmed picketers at the former school. Deputy Ombudsman Perry's inquiry (1994: 78) concluded that police employed 'unreasonable actions and excessive force', especially when prodding picketers with batons.

Despite 'setbacks' of the RSC type, della Porta and Reiter (1998: 2) contend that in western democratic countries, there has been a widespread trend in recent years towards softer, more tolerant, flexible, preventive, selective and less coercive styles of policing protest. Many of these countries and regions have historically been noted for militarised and armed policing — brutal, repressive, confrontational and rigid. Formalised negotiated management between police leaders and protest organisers has lessened the extent of coercive policing intervention through an emphasis on peace-keeping rather than rigid law enforcement. In 1997, German police showed tolerance in monitoring organised and prolonged protests against trains laden with nuclear waste travelling across the country. Not all western democratic police forces have adhered to negotiated management strategies. Ericson and Doyle (1999) detail how the Royal Canadian Mounted Police in 1997 reneged on a negotiated accord with student protesters prior to the Asia Pacific Economic Cooperation summit at the University of British Columbia. Police, employing preventive arrests, censorship and violent dispersion, rejected protest rights of political expression in favour of 'security concerns'. Nonetheless, contemporary policing of public disorder is generally characterised by under-enforcement of the law, complex procedures of negotiation and large-scale gathering of prevention-oriented information and intelligence (Kratcoski, Verma and Das 2001; Waddington 1994 and 2001).

Evolutionary police strategies for handling industrial conflict: The challenge of policing the 1998 national waterfront dispute

The primary source of improved public order policing is to advance formal cooperation between the parties. As a result of violent clashes between police and the Builders Labourers Federation in the 1980s, Victoria Police and the Victorian Trades Hall Council (VTHC) established professional protocol arrangements to deal with potentially volatile situations. Victoria Police established the position of Industrial Disputation Officer to liaise with employer, unions and government in order to provide practical and pragmatic advice to operational police about industrial law and 'desirable procedures for the policing of picket lines' in terms of available numbers, location, timing, acceptable behaviour and control contingencies. In accord with policing philosophy, the Australian Council of Trade Unions (ACTU) executive developed a reciprocal union policy in relation to authorised strikes and pickets to avoid confrontation by contact being established 'at the earliest opportunity, between union officials and local Police to establish the nature of the dispute, the role of Police and to identify representatives from the union(s) with whom the police can liaise' (*ACTU/VTHC memorandum* 1994).

Police and Trades Hall Councils co-operate in relation to notification of rallies, boundaries, routes and acceptable picketing practices. Neither union leaders nor police want injured members or the stigma of violence associated with negative publicity. But if police are called to a dispute, either major or minor, they 'take control of it' (Winther 2001). Police prefer an identifiable group to constrain and contain because unknown picketers, outsiders, can elicit an unexpected police response (Kahn, Lewis, Livock and Wiles 1983: 86-91). Although there are no laws specifically prohibiting picketing and protests, 'they are subject to the laws necessary for the maintenance of public order' such as traffic violations, assault, obstruction, trespass, besetting, harassment, intimidation, failing to obey a lawful police order (*Police Gazette*, 1997: paragraphs 42 and 23).

The 1998 Australian waterfront dispute, a large-scale national conflict, revealed the effectiveness of community union protest and the desirability of negotiation, compromise and formal protocol between the union movement and non-confrontational State police in order to maintain peaceful protest (Baker 1999). On 7 April 1998 Patrick Stevedoring sacked its entire unionised workforce of 1,400 full-time and 600 part-time workers. The ingredients of a prolonged and bitter national dispute existed in a federal government headstrong for both waterfront reform and the demise of the Maritime Union of Australia (MUA), a stevedoring company prepared to sack its entire workforce and a powerful union prepared to fight for its survival. However, the volatility and unpredictability of the five month 'War on the Wharves' did not culminate in full-scale pitched battle between picketers and police. The reinstatement order of Justice North (21 April), which directed Patrick Stevedoring to re-employ its MUA workers and which was upheld by the full bench of the Federal Court (23 April) and the High Court (4 May), determined the course of events.

Throughout the dispute, the MUA, various Trade Hall Councils (THCs) and ACTU officials advocated and generally maintained a peaceful, disciplined and law-abiding protest determined to gain significant sections of community support. In response, police normally adhered to a peace-keeping and non-interventionist philosophy as opposed to the rigid law enforcement of arraigning summary offences, that are basically minor charges (Winther 1998). The Victoria Police Chief Commissioner's instructions (Police Gazette 1997: para 30) state that minor offences (those common to picketing) should be 'ignored in the interests of containing the overall situation' in public order situations and not deplete police personnel numbers by conducting arrests. The seeds of the police and union cooperation, based on communication and negotiated management of potential conflict scenarios, had been nurturing for about a decade.

At the beginning of the picketing, the Victoria Police Industrial Disputation Officer explained to the union negotiating team the legal requirements as they pertained to the State, indicated standards of acceptable behaviour, and identified police responsibilities (Nation, 1998). Daily meetings between police, MUA and Victorian Trade Hall Council (VTHC) negotiators were conducted at Police Headquarters, and close consultations took place on days of great industrial volatility. A special mobile telephone listing of key personnel was kept by both police and union negotiators (Winther 1998). Victoria Police viewed the consultation as an extension of its Project Beacon training, seeking non-violent strategies to control potentially dangerous situations emphasising 'safety first' rather than a culture of 'risk-taking' (Victoria Police 1997: 4, 59-60). In a reciprocal arrangement, MUA officials pledged that they would maintain control of the 'peaceful assembly'. Specific unwritten guarantees on trust were given by both police and union negotiators. In Victoria, MUA officials made commitments of no violence, only routine yelling at change-overs of non-union labour; police agreed not to employ shields, batons and horses to intimidate protesters. According to Chief Inspector Winther, MUA marshals were 'completely successful' in organising and sustaining 'a peaceful community protest'. The MUA's John Higgins had 'no criticism whatsoever' of the police role. In most States, union leaders imposed bans on swearing, racial abuse and alcohol (*West Australian*, 13 April 1998: 4).

The potential for conflict was most pronounced at East Swanson Dock, Melbourne, which became the focus of mass picketing. On 17 April, police notified the union negotiators that they would be removing the picket line because it was blocking vehicle access to the port. They informed the negotiators that there would be no riot shields, no truncheons, no excessive physical force and that horses would not lead the operation. In return, the unions agreed to safeguard women and children: there would be no violence, only passive resistance (Higgins 1998). Near dawn on Saturday, 18 April, 1000 police confronted a determined opposition from 4000 MUA members and supporters, later augmented by 2000 construction workers. Strategically, the lack of open space at the dock limited police ability to manoeuvre the throng of people. Police, legally empowered to arrest, move and detain, used discretionary powers not to arrest protesters on trespass laws.

Intense discussions occurred between police and union orga-nisers in order to maintain the peace. In anticipation of court outcomes in relation to the legality of the Patrick sackings and the alleged government involvement in contravention of its own 1996 *Workplace Relations Act* (Cth), a truce ensued between police and picketers in which 'both parties were true to their word' (Winther 1998). Police promised that no trucks would convey freight from the docks and they would not attempt to move union pickets (Foley 1998: 2). When this peace agreement expired, police resumed talks rather than attempt to break the pickets. Some discussions were 'heated': the physical blockades, obstructions to freedom of movement on the port, were sources of bickering between union and police negotiators and of frustration to the employer.

Although the MUA's 'community assembly' was technically an obstruction, senior Victoria Police, including Chief Commissioner Comrie, acted upon operational police discretion to avoid bloodshed on the streets. If full-scale pitched battle between picketers and police ensued, Comrie feared 'serious injury and even loss of life to a number of people' (3LO Terry Laider program, 17 March 1999). By contrast, in Western Australia, police played a more aggressive, interventionist and legalistic role, although violence was still largely avoided. In accord with traditional police acquiescence to employer requests to remove pickets, 120 police, including the tactical response group and the independent patrol group attired in riot gear, used batons to disperse a union protest at Fremantle on 16 April (*West Australian*, 17 April 1998: 1, 7). The sortie of the riot police was a 'tactical blunder' which tarnished the police image at a time when policing rhetoric extolled the importance of developing community links (Cooke 1998). State police forces elsewhere avoided such forays.

In an unprecedented and significant initiative, State police commissioners at their annual conference in Melbourne on 21 April issued a statement advocating a 'negotiated' and 'non-violent' resolution of the maritime dispute. Conscious of the 'complex and emotive' nature of the dispute, the commissioners stressed that police would act as necessary to deal with unlawful blockades, but reaffirmed 'their strong desire that the maritime dispute is settled through negotiations and the legal processes rather than violent conflict' (Millett 1998: 1). The police commissioners advocated to all ranks the low-key, non-confrontational, approach instead of coercive tactics: 'Physical contact on the wharves is likely to lead to violence and perhaps serious injury to participants and police' (*Courier Mail*, 23 April 1998).

Criticism from employer and conservative politicians focused on the police's inaction against the MUA assemblies. Victoria Police Command, exhibiting independence from political pressure, ensured that police members were not manipulated in the dispute. Chief Commissioner Comrie, boasting of a record of managing disputes with 'minimal violence', refused to enter 'battle mode' and be 'pushed into using excessive force' (Hudson and Hall 1998: 5). Patrick's Chairperson Chris Corrigan scorned police inaction in the face of illegal 'community protest', time delaying 'while the police sniff the wind to see who's winning the public relations war before deciding whether to enforce the law' (Corrigan 1999: 16). Corrigan, like the Federal Government, acted upon the traditional assumption that if the employer demands police intervention to clear passage that police will immediately concur without consideration of the consequences.

During the waterfront dispute, police were not enforcing those offences, mainly minor, that relate to picketing, but rather were concerned with the practical and potentially dangerous consequences of enforcing such laws. This low-key strategy necessitated interference to the company's business and transportation of goods and some inconvenience to the general public. According to senior Victoria Police, the lack of arrests, complaints and injuries justified 'a good result' for a hundred days' operation (Winther 2001).

Contrasting the policing of anti-globalisation demonstrations

The advent of 19th century industrial England, accompanied by rioting and spiralling crime levels, gave birth to Peel's 1829 London Metropolitan Police. The globalisation of contemporary capitalism may witness the emergence of a 'new police order', one in which the accountability of public order policing is fundamental. Anti-globalisation protests at the turning of the millennium (Davos, Seattle, Melbourne, Gothenburg and Genoa) have highlighted the problems of maintaining public order in a shrinking world. The global economic trade summits have witnessed the re-emergence of full-scale paramilitary policing reliant upon riot technology, with only limited success in maintaining order. Preparations for the meeting in the medieval city of Genoa, a logistical nightmare, resembled fortification of a walled city in anticipation of an enemy siege. Rubber bullets, stun grenades and water cannon were utilised. After the death of a young demonstrator in Genoa, 150,000 protesters occupied the streets the next day. Police in Athens faced chants of 'Murderers! Murderers!' Police who shot three protesters in Gothenburg are under investigation but are expected to argue that the shootings took place amid life-threatening circumstances. The 2001 Gothenburg and Genoa police shootings raise the spectre of extremist agitators becoming more marginalised and militant and special tactical response units becoming the flagship of police operations at such economic summits. If violence is to be avoided, the challenge lies in the dialogue, precautions and planning arrangements prior to the actual event.

On 12 September 2000, Chief Commissioner Comrie ordered Victoria Police, garbed in full riot-gear for the first time, to use force against the anti-globalisation S11 protest during the World Economic Forum. Despite some preliminary meetings with police over minor issues, S11 organisers did not have the same working relationship with police that the union movement and police utilised to mutual advantage to maintain the peace during the waterfront dispute. S11 appeared to be a loose alliance of diverse interests and agendas, unclear lines of command and fragmented strategies. Meaningful dialogue between S11 and police was much more difficult to achieve and sustain. According to della Porta and Reiter's 1998 European studies, police distinguish between 'good' demonstrators (MUA peaceful assemblies), who are well-organised and strive for comprehensible and rationale ends, and 'bad' demonstrators (S11), whose objectives are mixed and confused and whose actions are disorganised. Despite graphic television footage of police aggression, Ombudsman Barry Perry's investigation concluded that Victoria Police Command was justified in ordering reasonable force (level four force including the use of batons) against S11 blockaders who refused to negotiate. He did, however, acknowledge the likelihood of civil actions against individual police for use of excessive coercion (Hannan 2001: 3).

Unlike the S11 protest, the subsequent May Day and M1 march of 6000 trade unionists and anti-globalisation protesters in Melbourne caused no traffic chaos, no violence and no arrests. Lessons had been heeded from the S11 fracas. Some vandalism occurred and some businesses felt compelled to close for the day. Nonetheless, the police officer in charge of the operation thanked the march organisers in charge of the well-behaved protesters, the community for staying away and the union organisers for a 'disciplined and well-managed march' (*The Age* 2001: 18).

Conclusion

Police discretionary power allows certain capacity for manoeuvre and accord with protesters and picketers. But police retain the capacity to act decisively and forcefully to quell unrest if compromise and negotiation fail. The violence and brutality of historical encounters between police and picketers no longer prevail to the same extent, but excesses can originate from either party. In Western democracies, public order policing is increasingly ambiguous. The trend has been toward a more 'softly softly' cooperative approach but recent years have also witnessed the proliferation of paramilitary squads and riot weaponry (McCulloch 2001). If a repressive approach to dissent is to be avoided, police leaders need to take the initiative to develop detailed policies, specific training, negotiated forward planning and practical preparation for specific public events. This is likely to find a positive response from the more enlightened leaders of modern industrial unions and other groups who have a stake in non-violent protest. The big challenge is for police to make negotiation and other violence minimisation strategies effective when dealing with diffuse, disorganised and violence-prone protesters.

References

ACTU/VTHC memorandum, 1994, May.

Alderson, J, 1998, *Principled Policing*, Waterside Press.

Baker, D, 1999 'Trade Unionism and the Policing Accord: Control and Self-Regulation of Picketing during the 1998 Maritime Dispute', *Labour and Industry*, 9 (3): 123-144.

Baker, D, 2001, 'Barricades and Batons: A Historical Perspective of the Policing of Major Industrial Disorder in Australia', in M Enders and B Dupont (eds), *Policing the Lucky Country*, Federation Press.

Blackmur, D, 1993, *Strikes: Causes, Conduct and Consequences*, Federation Press.

Brecher, J, 1997, *Strikes!*, South End Press.

Corrigan, C, 1999, Speech to the Australian Institute of Company Directors.

della Porta, D and Reiter, H, 1998 *Policing Protest: The Control of Mass Demonstrations in Western Democracies*, University of Minnesota Press.

Editorial, 2001, *The Age*, 3 June, p 18.

Ericson, R and Doyle, A, 1999 'Globalization and the policing of protest: The case of APEC 1997', *British Journal of Sociology* 50(4): 589-608.

Foley, B, 1998 'Police Say Handling of Dispute a Success', *The Australian*, 20 April, p 2.

Geary, R, 1985, *Policing Industrial Disputes*, Cambridge University Press.

Hannan, E, 'Why Some Police Face More Scrutiny on S11', *The Age*, 16 June, p 3.

Hudson, S and Hall, L, 1998, 'Australia: Police Pledge Restraint', *The Australian*, 21 April, p 5.

Johnston, RW, 1992, *The Long Blue Line*, Boolarong.

Kahn, P, Lewis, N, Livock, R and Wiles, P, 1983, *Picketing: Industrial Disputes, Tactics and the Law*, Routledge and Kegan Paul.

Kratcoski, P, Verma, A and Das, D, 2001, 'Policing of Public Order: A World Perspective', *Police Practice and Research: An International Journal* 2(1-2): 109-143.

Lofthouse, M, 1997, 'Policing the Future: the Problem of Legitimation', paper presented at Scarman Centre, University of Leicester, 10 March.

Lowenstein, W and Hills, T, 1982, *Under the Hook: Melbourne Waterside Workers Remember: 1900-1980*, Australian Society for the Study of Labour History, March.

McCulloch, J, 2001, *Blue Army: Paramilitary Policing in Australia*, Melbourne University Press.

Millett, M, 1998, 'PM Tells Police – Clear Docks', *Sydney Morning Herald*, 23 April, p 1.

Perry, B, 1994, *Investigation into Alleged Excessive Force by the Victoria Police against Demonstrators at the Richmond Secondary College on Monday*

13 December 1993 and Investigation into Crowd Control Methods used by the Victoria Police Against Demonstrators outside the Department of Conservation and Natural Resources Headquarters, Victoria Parade, East Melbourne on Thursday 10 February 1994, Ombudsman's Office, Victoria.

Reiner, R, 1992, The Politics of the Police, Wheatsheaf Press.

Reiner, R, 1997, 'The Policing of Mass Demonstration in Contemporary Democracies: Policing, Protest, and Disorder in Britain', European University Institute Working Papers no 2, Badia Fiesolana.

Shelley, L, 1999, 'Post-Socialist Policing: Limitations on Institutional Change', in R Mawby (ed), Policing Across the World: Issues for the Twenty-first Century, UCL Press.

Taft, J, and Ross, P, 1979, 'American Labor Violence: Its Causes, Character and Outcome', in H Graham and E Gurr (eds) Violence in America: Historical and Comparative Perspectives, vol 1, Sage.

Victoria Police, Victoria Police Gazette, 1997, 28 April.

Victoria Police, Victoria Police Manual: Operating Procedures, updated 22 December 1997.

Victoria Police, 1997, Annual Report 1996-1997.

Waddington, D, 1992, Contemporary Issues in Public Disorder: A Comparative and Historical Approach, Routledge.

Waddington, PAJ, 1994, Liberty and Order: Public Order Policing in a Capital City, UCL Press.

Waddington, PAJ, 1998, 'Controlling protest in contemporary historical and comparative perspective' in della Porta, D and Reiter, H, 1998 Policing Protest: The Control of Mass Demonstrations in Western Democracies, University of Minnesota Press.

Waddington, PAJ, 2001, 'Negotiating and Defining 'Public Order'', Police Practice and Research: An International Journal 2(1-2): 3-14.

Interviews

Alderson, John, 1997, former Chief Constable of Devon and Cornwall, 25 February.

Cooke, Tony, 1998, WA Trades and Labour Council Secretary, 30 July.

Higgins, John, 1998, MUA Deputy Secretary and VTHC Vice-President, 28 May and 17 September.

Nation, Daryl, 1998, Acting Superintendent Victoria Police, Forward Commander at Swanson Dock, 2 June.

Winther, John, 1998, 2001, Chief Inspector, Victoria Police Industrial Disputation Officer, 4 June 1998 and 22 May 2001.

4

Race Relations

Rick Sarre and Syd Sparrow

Any review of the history of relationships between police and indigenous peoples the world over usually provides a sorry litany of misunderstanding, conflict, neglect, injury and death. Few countries are immune from racial conflict in policing. If a particular crisis occurs, governments are quick to instigate an inquiry (eg, Scarman, 1982). Invariably, these inquiries recommend a range of imperatives for police policy-makers. Too often, very little changes.

In other words, documenting instances of poor relations is one thing. Acting strategically to bring about effective change is quite another. The failure of the much-vaunted United Kingdom Community Race Relations strategy that followed the publication of the McPherson Inquiry Report into a race-related death and police investigation in 1993 is a case in point (Home Office 1999; Kamira 2001: 78). In view of the public pronouncements made at the time regarding the challenge of police to respond appropriately to racial incidents, it was disappointing, but perhaps not surprising, to find how little had been progressed three years after the publication of Her Majesty's Inspectorate of Constabulary's (HMIC) report *Winning the Race* in 1997:

> The conclusion of findings indicates that progress has been less than satisfactory with many of the recommendations 'side-lined' and few forces placing the issue high on their agendas (Home Office 2000: 7).

Policy-makers in Australia have faced similar tests of will over the past two decades. In their attempts to transform police-indigenous conflicts into workable strategies and effective solutions, police managers have had their share of successes and failures. The material provided in the pages that follow provides some insights into that period.

Indigenous Australians and police

Scientific evidence indicates that occupation of the Australian continent by Indigenous peoples began some 47,000 years ago. Over these millennia, Aboriginal 'lore' developed and thrived. British colonisation changed all of that in a comparatively short period of time. The legacy of 200 years of tension-laden police-Indigenous relations in this country is a massive over-representation of Indigenous Australians in the criminal justice system today.

The breakdown of relations between Indigenous and non-Indigenous Australians began early in the colonial experience (Jennett 2001: 50-51; Kamira 2001: 71-72). An unofficial policy of Aboriginal eradication began to unfold amongst the military peace-keepers in late 18th century New South Wales. The history of this phase of Australia's colonial movement is replete with stories of savagery, waterhole poisonings and shootings (eg, Elder, 1988). It was not unusual for colonial administrators to deploy police in frontier warfare against Indigenous tribes, and as a form of self-defence. Caught up in a world of land theft, attack and reprisal, colonial police, even those who may have harboured some sympathy for native populations, had little option but to carry out their assigned tasks. Eradication activities ended under a policy of protection in the 1880s. Along with policies of assimilation (from the 1930s) and integration (from the 1960s) came the widespread, albeit well-meaning, practice of taking 'half-caste' children from their families and placing them in 'proper' Christian homes, a practice scrutinised by the Human Rights and Equal Opportunity Commission through its Stolen Generation Inquiry (HREOC 1997; Healey 1998; Jennett 2001: 59) and referred to in the report of the Royal Commission into Aboriginal Deaths in Custody (Johnston 1991a: 8).

The links with policing are clear. Police were instructed not only to remove individuals from their families but sometimes entire communities from their tribal lands in order to place them in missions for benevolent reasons or so that Aboriginal land could be used for nuclear weapons testing. The upshot of this becomes immediately apparent:

> For many Aboriginal people the first contact they had with the police was with a paramilitary force of dispossession, dispensing summary justice and on some occasions involved in the indiscriminate massacre of clan and tribal groups (Cunneen 2001: 50).

A breakdown in relationships is not simply an historical legacy. Ongoing suspicion and mutual antagonism is fuelled by contemporary experience as well. Elliott Johnston QC, the Royal Commission report writer for the Royal Commission into Aboriginal Deaths in Custody, commented in 1991:

> [F]ar too much police intervention in the lives of Aboriginal people ... has been arbitrary, discriminatory, racist and violent. There is absolutely no doubt in my mind that the antipathy which so many Aboriginal people have towards police is based not just on historical contact but upon the contemporary experience of contact with many police officers (Johnston 1991b: 195).

Overt racism by police was cited by the Human Rights and Equal Opportunity Commission's National Inquiry into Racist Violence (HREOC 1991: 116), and a controversial documentary 'Cop It Sweet' (ABC 1991) captured racist language and discriminatory policing in Redfern, a suburb of Sydney. In 1992, an amateur video was broadcast of police in eastern Australia with their faces painted and imitating two Aboriginal people who had died in police custody (Cunneen 2001: 147). In Queensland, the death of Daniel Yock in police custody in 1993 (Prenzler 2000), and the lamentable events in 1994 that involved six young Aboriginal boys being driven by police officers to a remote location and then abandoned (Prenzler 1997), highlight the difficulty of removing entrenched attitudes even in a more enlightened age.

Specific manifestations of relationship breakdown

Relationship breakdown is manifested in the 'over-policing' of Indigenous Australians, the choice of arrest over non-arrest options, and the choice of remand in custody over non-custodial remand options. Each of these issues is now discussed.

'Over-policing'

There is strong evidence of 'over-policing' of Indigenous communities in contemporary Australia. Beyond the available observational evidence, it is difficult to demonstrate that police routinely use their discretion to intervene in situations involving Aboriginal people where the same behaviour or situation would be ignored if it involved non-Aboriginal people. However, the substantial contemporary and historical accounts presented in a range of forums, as well as other documentation on adverse police decisions after intervention, lend substantial weight to the conclusion that police discretion is adversely used in this regard (Cunneen 2001: 31).

An example is required. Aboriginal people, because of their close connections to family, will invariably be in the company of other Aboriginal people, often in large numbers. Such gatherings often result in some level of surveillance by police. This surveillance increases markedly where these people are in possession of alcohol, or where the group is made up of young people. Attention to these offences or areas by police, and an absence of workable alternatives to arrest, ensure a self-fulfilling prophecy (Lustgarten 1986: 19).

Talk back radio announcers echo the sentiments of many callers in applauding this level of surveillance (often described as 'zero tolerance' policing) as a way of making the streets safe, (which is comforting to Aboriginal people, too, given that they like to feel safe), but in most circumstances surveillance amounts to little more than police harassment, and may escalate, by mutual provocation, into a series of criminal acts.

> Zero tolerance policing is more likely to increase the level of antagonism between Indigenous people and the police than lead to improved relations. ... In this sense, zero tolerance policing recalls the historical role of police in enforcing an exclusionary social order which kept Indigenous people 'off the streets' for much of the twentieth century (Cunneen 2001: 103).

Generally these criminal acts are not of a serious nature. The sorts of offences targeted might be disorderly behaviour, offensive language, or failing to cease loitering. In most cases no such offence would, on its own, attract an outcome of imprisonment. But when the conflict escalates, what is known as 'the trifecta' may come into play (Jochelson 1997: 4). It works this way. Police allege disorderly conduct, and, as a result, physical resistance is met. An arrest is affected, during which the police struggle with the arrestee. In an instant, the police have three charges (the trifecta) of disorderly conduct, assault and resisting arrest, all arising from the one event. The possibility of an overnight stay in police cells becomes a reality. This is not an uncommon phenomenon, especially when police are dealing with intoxicated persons (Social Justice Commissioner 1996; Sarre 1999).

Aboriginal communities are burdened with very high police-community ratios. In the remote New South Wales town of Walgett, for example, where 18 per cent of residents identified as Indigenous in 1993, Amnesty International (1993: 23) found that there was one police officer per 96 residents, while the average for the rest of the State of New South Wales (where just 1.8 per cent of population are of Aboriginal descent) was one police officer per 459 residents. Disproportionate levels of surveillance, arrest and detention are very likely to follow over-concentrations of police, the report concluded. Furthermore, Amnesty surmised that Aboriginal persons were less likely than non-Aboriginal Australians to have access to legal aid, familial and societal support structures when they confronted the criminal justice system. This situation, concluded the report writers, simply exacerbated the malaise.

Arrest

Available data show that arrest is the preferred police option when bringing Indigenous persons before the courts. Indigenous young people in South Australia, for example, are far more likely than non-Indigenous youth to be brought into the criminal justice process by arrest (Wundersitz 1996: 204). In the Northern Territory, 29 per cent of Aboriginal people coming to court in 1996 did so by way of summons. By comparison, 42 per cent of non-Aboriginal persons coming to court were directed there by summons (Luke and Cunneen 1998: 19). What is disturbing is how little has changed since 1991 notwithstanding the recommendations of the Royal Commission into Aboriginal Deaths in Custody. A key recommendation was as follows:

> 87(a). All Police Services should adopt and apply the principle of arrest being the sanction of last resort in dealing with offenders.

This is not to say that Indigenous people do not commit significant numbers of arrestable offences. But the decision to arrest is contextualised by an occupational culture that defines Indigenous people as a problem group – as trouble-makers, as hostile, as drunken, as unlikely to turn up at court, and so forth (Cunneen 2001: 155). Gale, Bailey-Harris and Wundersitz (1990: 48) argued that the higher rates of violent crime may reflect nothing more than that violence in an Aboriginal community is often an open and public event to which police are readily called. More recently, Alvarez (1998: 117) found that more than 25 per cent of assault victims (at the hands of Indigenous offenders) were police officers themselves. One might also assume that alleged abusive language provides police with the rationale for arrest in circumstances that do not warrant it. The Royal Commissioner in 1991 was concerned enough about this issue to recommend as follows:

86(a). The use of offensive language in circumstances of interventions initiated by police should not normally be occasion for arrest or charge.

There is thus evidence that the activities that influence the choice to arrest are commonly linked to the operational concerns of the agencies responsible for controlling (and producing knowledge about) crime, and the environment in which that crime occurs (Cunneen 2001: 28). Moreover, nearly one-third of the adult Indigenous population of Australia have been arrested in the past five years. Hunter (2001) made a national comparison of Aborigines who are arrested with those who are not. Indigenous Australians who are unemployed, drink alcohol or have been physically attacked or verbally threatened, he found, are much more likely to be arrested by police compared with other Indigenous Australians who are employed or do not drink alcohol or have not been physically attacked or verbally threatened. The research highlights the importance of recognising that offending behaviour is inextricably linked to, and enmeshed with, crime victimisation, substance abuse and poverty. The 'problem', therefore, cannot be addressed by law enforcement alone. It needs to be addressed from an array of welfare and social justice perspectives as well.

Finally, the use of the caution, as an alternative to arrest, is less common for Indigenous Australians than it is for non-Indigenous Australians for reasons that probably relate to higher recidivism rates. This has the effect of 'confirming' a self-fulfilling prophecy (Cunneen 2001: 28). In Victoria, Indigenous young people are significantly less likely to receive a police caution than non-Indigenous young people (11.3 per cent versus 35.6 per cent in 1995/1996) (HREOC 1997: 514), and a similar tale emerges from the data in South Australia (Wundersitz 1996: 20).

Remand in custody

Aboriginal Australians are less likely to get bail upon arrest than non-Indigenous arrestees, essentially because they are more likely to have a record of previous offending (Luke and Cunneen 1998: 20). A more recent study (Wright 1999) confirmed that Aboriginality is significantly associated with the likelihood of being remanded in custody. Wright tracked 4,758 adult defendants whose cases were finalised in 1996 in South Australian magistrates' courts. 25 legal and extra-legal remand-in-custody predictors derived from the court and police data were fed through a multivariate regression analysis. The study concluded that Aboriginality is significantly associated with a custodial outcome, independent of any other variable in the model. This is especially significant given the findings of an Australian remand in custody comparative study that suggests that the role police play in denying bail (including court bail) is a crucial one (Bamford, King and Sarre 1999: 19, 77).

Consider also the evidence of the racial origin of remandees in South Australia and Western Australia (where the attitude is that those charged with assault can expect to be remanded in custody) compared to Victoria (where such an assumption does not prevail). Of Indigenous remandees in South Australia and Western Australia at June 1997, 29 per cent were there with 'assault' as the most serious offence charged. In Victoria there were no Indigenous remandees charged with assault *at all* (Bamford et al 1999: 65). In other words, extra-legal issues were more instrumental in determining justice outcomes than criminal conduct per se. It should come as no surprise, then, that a study by the South Australian Office of Crime Statistics on Aboriginal involvement in the Magistrates Courts in South Australia found that Aboriginal involvement was 10.9 times higher than would be expected on a per capita basis (South Australia 2000: 3).

Where to from here?

Reform is long overdue. As Elliott Johnston QC remarked in reporting the findings of the Royal Commission:

> The challenge for police departments is to accept that there is a basis for Aboriginal resentment and suspicion about police conduct and to consider the Aboriginal perspective when devising policing strategies (Johnston 1991b: 197).

Why has there been so little improvement in the relationships between Indigenous Australians and police? It is not for want of good research and clear recommendations. The answer, seemingly, involves a mixture of poor implementation of these recommendations (RCGRMU 1997) and the presence of justice policy initiatives (including 'zero tolerance') that defy received wisdom (Bernardi 1998: 114). While the numbers of deaths in police lock-ups appear to have been reduced Australia-wide, perhaps because new, clearer guidelines dictate how an Aboriginal person must be treated when first taken into custody, (eg, Council for Aboriginal Reconciliation 1994: 23; McDonald and Cunneen 1997), little has changed on just about every other front, especially in relation to so-called 'public order' offences (Jochelson 1997).

In the section that follows, policy options and challenges for improved police and indigenous relations in a variety of settings are reviewed.

Better police relationships, training schemes and multi-racial recruitment practices

'Professional partnership policing' – where Aboriginal people are given a key role in controlling anti-social behaviour, minor infractions and serious breaches of the law – can be successfully integrated into policing policies (Etter 1993: 11). Training of new recruits in cultural awareness, in order to overcome the police racism that has been documented in the past (eg, HREOC 1991: 116), has been introduced in most Police Services, and, in New South Wales and Queensland, police have adopted the suggestion of the 1991 Royal Commission that new recruits who are to be posted to areas with significant Aboriginal communities spend time in the area before they begin policing duties.

Another initiative has been the establishment of Aboriginal Police Aides or, as they are known in South Australia, 'Aboriginal Community Constables'. Initially created to act as mediators between the Aboriginal community and the police, Aboriginal Police Aides first appeared in rural communities where there had been strained relations with police. The scheme has been expanded to include metropolitan areas. Community Constables now work in mainstream policing activities. While it is recognised that women are too few in number as Aides or Community Constables, especially given the double impact of gender and 'racial' inequalities in policing Indigenous women (Cunneen 2001: 157; Sarre 1996), there have been a number of positive benefits for police and Indigenous communities alike as a result of these partnerships. Moreover, a number of Aides later undergo the training required to become fully-fledged police officers. The recruitment of Indigenous people is in keeping with the spirit of the 1991 Royal Commission (Kamira 2001: 79-81). As more Indigenous people become police officers, it is envisaged that future generations of young Indigenous people will aspire to follow in their footsteps. In that environment, Indigenous peoples will be more an accepted part of police services throughout the country and not merely an object of curiosity or a 'lesser' version of police.

Furthermore, specific training in non-racist attitudes has received some overdue attention by police administrators (Cunneen and McDonald 1997a: 106). However, a study by Wortley and Homel (1995) highlighted that police prejudice is more likely to emanate from police interactions with Indigenous Australians rather than inherently racist attitudes. This finding highlights the need for strategic policy-making that moves well beyond the provision of cultural awareness programs in police training.

Customary law: Indigenous community policing and justice systems

The view of the social anthropologists and international jurists of the colonial period was that Antipodean 'natives' had no system of law of their own (ALRC 1986; Sarre 1997, 2000a). It would never have been thought, as a corollary, that 'natives' would have the ability to look after their own policing needs. There are signs that that view has changed significantly, especially in relation to Indigenous self-policing, 'community' sentencing authorities, and self-administration of Aboriginal communities that are based upon tribal law and customary practice. These include Community Justice Panels in Victoria (Cunneen 2001: 193), and Aboriginal community justice groups (eg, Homel, Lincoln and Herd 1999), especially those at Kowanyama and Palm Island (Chantrill 1998: 176; Cunneen 2001: 195) in a manner not unlike the way in which the government of Canada allows its First Nations communities to establish, in certain circumstances, their own police organisations (Murray 1996: 122).

Initiatives may also include Indigenous-run policing patrols, over one hundred of which operate around Australia (Blagg and Valuri, 2002). One of the best known is the Tangentyere night patrol and social behaviour project in Alice Springs, an operation designed to take drunk and disorderly people into care before police need to be called to arrest them (Cunneen and McDonald 1997b: 80; Tangentyere Council 2001). Similarly structured Aboriginal Community Patrols in Kempsey Shire Council and Deniliquin (amongst others) have been funded since 2001 by the New South Wales Attorney-General's Department's *Indigenous Justice Strategy*.

Decriminalisation of certain offences

If societies are serious about reducing the numbers of Indigenous people entering the criminal justice system, decriminalisation of some 'street' offences should be considered more seriously. For the most part, 'street' offences such as offensive language, being drunk and disorderly and failing to cease loitering are taking up a great deal of police time and, consequently, are clogging the courts. There are more effective ways of dealing with this type of offending. Attention could be given to treating street offences in the same manner as the law deals with certain traffic offences and minor drug offences. Infringement (or 'expiation') notices could be introduced that would provide for 'on the spot' fines to be issued when 'street' offences have been committed. While not a panacea for the identified problems, an expiation approach may contribute towards justice being achieved more expeditiously.

The Nunga court experience in South Australia

Non-appearances at court by Indigenous offenders provide much work for police in tracking down, and arresting, those accused persons who have failed to answer their bail. Non-appearance, then, has two major consequences for police and indigenous relations: offenders are likely to be arrested on warrant, and the likelihood of bail being refused at the next hearing is extremely high. One initiative that has drastically reduced the rate of non-appearances (and therefore rates of arrest) is the 'Nunga Court'. After being trialled successfully in one Adelaide metropolitan summary court as a pilot over the last five years, 'Nunga' courtroom arrangements have been established in three regions in South Australia. These courts sit on a regular basis for Indigenous offenders only (Sarre 2000b: 72). The only stipulation is that defendants must enter a guilty plea to their charges. The environs of the court are adapted to make them less intimidating for the offender with the emphasis being placed on informality. The offender is seated at the bar table rather than standing in the dock. The magistrate sits at eye level with the offender. Next to the magistrate sits an Aboriginal Elder. The magistrate takes advice from him or her as to sentencing options. The Elder is actively involved throughout the process and will often have some prior knowledge of the offender that might be relevant to the sentencing process.

Another feature of the Nunga Court is the involvement of the offender in the process. In mainstream magistrates court cases offenders are passive participants in the case, with a legal practitioner speaking on their behalf. In the Nunga Court, there is direct dialogue between the Magistrate and offenders, despite the presence of legal counsel. This is of especial importance to offenders as they are able to become more involved and accountable for the actions that have brought them before the court. This also makes the administration of justice more relevant to the offenders, as cases are not allowed to drag on indefinitely. A higher rate of appearance by offenders allows the wheels of summary justice to turn more quickly and effectively, and lessens the potential for acrimonious contact between police and accused persons.

Choices of caution, report and summons to ensure a court appearance

There are strategies that can be employed by police that can stop offensive behaviour without the need for arrest. Police can be trained to exercise their discretion not to make an arrest and to issue warnings or cautions to suspects or those observed committing minor offences where the circumstances warrant it. Cautions should be made more accessible and available as an option for police. This does not mean to suggest that all drunkenness or inappropriate language or behaviour in public places is to be condoned. In many cases, however, a stern warning to unruly persons might be just as effective as an arrest in stopping inappropriate behaviour. One recommendation of the Royal Commission is particularly appropriate in this context:

> 81. [L]egislation decriminalizing drunkenness should place a statutory duty upon police to consider and utilize alternatives to the detention of intoxicated persons in police cells.

Another important option available in lieu of arresting an offender is for police officers to exercise their discretion to report and summons an offender. In the usual course, offenders would be issued a summons to attend court on a particular day to answer the charges. It is apparent that this option is often not used by police despite the fact that this type of policing can be an effective way of dealing with inappropriate behaviour. It is conceded that this option may not be reasonable in situations where an offender continues to act inappropriately after police intervention, but it is certainly worthy of greater use as a policing tool. Above all, any idea that reduces the perception and reality of over-policing should be explored, a strategy mirrored in a recommendation of the Royal Commission.

> 88 (a). [Police should, in negotiation with Indigenous community leaders, consider whether] there is over-policing or inappropriate policing of Aboriginal people in any city or regional centre or country town.

Conclusion

There is little doubt that the experiences of Indigenous people in their relationships with police has been, and continues to be, qualitatively different from those of non-Indigenous Australians. This arises in contemporary Australian society primarily through two main factors: a racist and frontier war colonial heritage, and 200 years of social construction of Indigenous peoples as inferior. These constructions continue to provide the context in which police decision-making occurs (Cunneen 2001: 128). The official and unofficial reports prepared in the last decade to address racial disparities in the criminal justice system have made a number of recommendations to correct the malaise. However, many of these have either been ignored or lost in poor implementation practices.

Policy-makers need to consider designing policing strategies that will bring about fewer Aboriginal arrests, eradicate any police racism that may still remain, and make it less likely that officers will seek custodial remands for Indigenous offenders. Furthermore, self-policing and 'Nunga'-style courts in appropriate regions should be explored as part of a broader political agenda that embraces the possibilities of Indigenous self-policing, self-administration of justice and self-determination. This may be a long, even arduous process (Cunneen 2001: 250) and will likely remain a major challenge for governments and Indigenous administrators alike (Jennett 2001: 66). If these issues remain in the forefront of police research and policy-making, however, they promise to improve policing for all Australians.

References

ABC, 1991, *Cop it Sweet*, Jenny Brockie, filmmaker, Australian Broadcasting Corporation.

Alvarez, E, 1998, 'Police Charging in Bourke, 1980-1992', LLM thesis, University of Sydney.

Amnesty International, 1993, *Australia: A Criminal Justice System Weighted Against Aboriginal People*, Amnesty International.

ALRC, 1986, *The Recognition of Aboriginal Customary Laws*, Report No. 31, Australian Law Reform Commission.

Bamford, D, King, S and Sarre, R, 1999, *Remand in Custody in Three Australian Jurisdictions*, Australian Institute of Criminology.

Bernardi, G, 1998, 'Recasting Old Solutions to Old Problems', *Alternative Law Journal* 23(3): 112-116.

Blagg, H and Valuri, G, 2002, *Profiling Night Patrol Services in Australia*, Report of a Research Project for National Crime Prevention and ATSIC.

Chantrill, P, 1998, 'Community Justice in Indigenous Communities in Queensland: Prospects for Keeping Young People out of Detention', *Australian Indigenous Law Reporter* 3(2): 163-179.

Council for Aboriginal Reconciliation, 1994, *Responding to Custody Levels. A Greater Community Response to Addressing the Underlying Causes*, Key Issues Paper No 6, Australian Government Publishing Service (AGPS).

Cunneen, C, 2001, *Conflict, Politics and Crime: Aboriginal Communities and the Police*, Allen and Unwin.

Cunneen, C and McDonald, D, 1997a, 'Indigenous Imprisonment in Australia: An Unresolved Human Rights Issue', *Australian Journal of Human Rights* 3(2): 90-110.

Cunneen, C and McDonald, D, 1997b, *Keeping Aboriginal and Torres Strait Islander People Out of Custody*, Aboriginal and Torres Strait Islander Commission.

Elder, B, 1988, *Blood on the Wattle: Massacres and Maltreatment of Australian Aborigines since 1788*, Child and Associates.

Etter, B, 1993, 'The Police Culture: Overcoming Barriers', *Criminology Australia* 5(2): 8-12.

Gale, F, Bailey-Harris, R and Wundersitz, J, 1990, *Aboriginal Youth and the Criminal Justice System*, Cambridge University Press.

Healey, K (ed), 1998, *The Stolen Generation*, Spinney Press.

Home Office, 1999, *Sir William McPherson Inquiry into the Matters Arising from the Death of Stephen Lawrence on 22 April 1993*, Her Majesty's Stationery Office (HMSO).

Home Office, 2000, *Winning the Race – Revisited, Code of Practice on Reporting and Recording Racist Incidents in Response to Recommendation 15 of the Stephen Lawrence Inquiry Report*, HMSO.

Homel, R, Lincoln, R and Herd, B, 1999, 'Risk and Resilience: Crime and Violence Prevention in Aboriginal Communities', *Australian and New Zealand Journal of Criminology* 32(2): 182-196.

HREOC (Human Rights and Equal Opportunity Commission), 1991, *Report of the National Inquiry into Racist Violence in Australia*, AGPS.

HREOC, 1997, *Bringing Them Home: Report of the National Inquiry into the Separation of Aboriginal and Torres Strait Islander Children from their Families, Final Report*, Author.

Hunter, B, 2001, *Factors Underlying Indigenous Arrest Rates*, NSW Bureau of Crime Statistics and Research and the Australian National University.

Jennett, C, 2001, 'Policing and Indigenous peoples in Australia', in M Enders and B Dupont (eds), *Policing the Lucky Country*, Hawkins Press.

Jochelson, R, 1997, 'Aborigines and Public Order Legislation in New South Wales', *Crime and Justice Bulletin: Contemporary Issues in Crime and Justice*, 34, NSW Bureau of Crime Statistics and Research.

Johnston, E, 1991a, *Royal Commission into Aboriginal Deaths in Custody, National Report, Volume 1*, AGPS.

Johnston, E, 1991b, *Royal Commission into Aboriginal Deaths in Custody, National Report, Volume 2*, AGPS.

Kamira, J, 2001, 'Indigenous Participation in Policing', in M Enders and B Dupont (eds), *Policing the Lucky Country*, Hawkins Press.

Luke, G and Cunneen, C, 1998, *Sentencing Aboriginal People in the Northern Territory: A Statistical Analysis*, North Australian Aboriginal Legal Aid Service.

Lustgarten, L, 1986, *The Governance of Police*, Sweet and Maxwell.

McDonald, D and Cunneen, C, 1997, 'Aboriginal Incarceration and Deaths in Custody: Looking Back and Looking Forward', *Current Issues in Criminal Justice* 9(1): 5-20.

Murray, T, 1996, 'A Comparative Examination of Police Reform in Federal Systems: Canada and Australia', in D Chappell and P Wilson (eds), *Australian Policing: Contemporary Issues*, 2nd edn, Butterworths.

Prenzler, T, 1997, 'The Decay of Reform: Police and Politics in Post-Fitzgerald Queensland', *Queensland Review* 4(2): 13-25.

Prenzler, T, 2000, 'Civilian Oversight of Police: A Test of Capture Theory', *British Journal of Criminology* 40(4): 659-674.

RCGRMU, 1997, *Implementation of the Commonwealth Government Responses to the Recommendations of the Royal Commission into Aboriginal Deaths in Custody Annual Report 1995-1996, Volumes 1 and 2*, Royal Commission Government Response Monitoring Unit, Aboriginal and Torres Straight Islander Commission (ATSIC).

Sarre, R, 1996, 'Aboriginal Australia: Current Criminological Themes', in M Schwartz and D Milovanovic (eds), *Race, Gender and Class in Criminology: The Intersection*, Garland.

Sarre, R, 1997, 'Is there a Role for the Application of Customary Law in Addressing Aboriginal Criminality in Australia?', *Critical Criminology: An International Journal* 8(2): 91-102.

Sarre, R, 1999, 'The Imprisonment of Indigenous Australians: Dilemmas and Challenges for Policy-makers', *The Georgetown Public Policy Review* 4(2): 165-182.

Sarre, R, 2000a, 'Sentencing in Customary or Tribal Settings: An Australian Perspective', *Federal Sentencing Reporter* 13(2): 74-78.

Sarre, R, 2000b, 'Diversionary Programs within the Criminal Justice System and Their Effects on Victims', in M O'Connell (ed), *Victims of Crime – Working Together to Improve Services*, South Australian Institute of Justice Studies.

Scarman, Lord, 1982, *The Scarman Report*, Penguin.

Social Justice Commissioner, 1996, *Indigenous Deaths in Custody 1989 to 1996*, ATSIC.

South Australia, 2000, 'Aboriginal People and the Criminal Justice System', *Information Bulletin*, 13, Attorney-General's Department.

Tangentyere Council, 2001, *Tangentyere Council Remote Area Night Patrol*, Office of the Status of Women, Department of the Prime Minister and Cabinet.

Wortley, R and Homel, R, 1995, 'Police Prejudice as a Function of Training and Outgroup Contact: A Longitudinal Investigation', *Law and Human Behavior* 19(3): 305-317.

Wright, J, 1999, *Blind Justice: An Examination of the Differential Use of Custodial Remands with Aboriginal and Non-Aboriginal Defendants*, MSocSci thesis, University of South Australia.

Wundersitz, J, 1996, 'The South Australian Juvenile Justice System: A Review of Its Operation', Attorney-General's Department.

5

Sex Discrimination

Tim Prenzler

Very few inquiries into policing have made a proper examination of sex discrimination as part of the larger complex of corrupt practices. Consequently, exposés of misconduct have frequently failed to address this serious and extensive problem, and have often missed the interconnections with other forms of misconduct. This is despite the fact that resistance to gender integration appears to be a feature of policing. One study has alleged that:

> The incursion of women into traditionally 'male' occupations has been opposed, resisted, and undermined wherever it has occurred. In few other occupations, however, has their entry been more vigorously fought – on legal, organisational, informal, and interpersonal levels – than in policing (Martin 1980: 79).

This chapter summarises the history of both formal and informal discrimination against women in policing, and discusses corruption as part of the masculine culture of traditional police organisations. The chapter concludes by emphasising the need to overcome the legacy of resistance to women with a range of special measures and intensive oversight to ensure equity in all areas of police work.

The record

Exclusion

The beginning of so-called 'modern policing' is most closely associated with the introduction of the 'New Police' in London in 1829. However, the first officially titled 'police woman' is believed to have been appointed in Stuttgart, Germany, in 1903; followed by an appointee in Los Angeles in 1910 (Owings, 1969). In London in 1914 women formed police volunteer organisations and joined the Metropolitan Police in 1923. In Australia the first women police were appointed in New South Wales in 1915. Other States followed until by 1917 five of the six States had women police.

Modern policing was the exclusive domain of men for roughly half the period of its existence. The vehicle for this discrimination was the law. Generally speaking, statutes described police as men, thereby simply and effectively excluding half the population from member-ship (as occurred in many occupations at the time). The idea of women police was promoted by the 'women police movement', which consisted of women's charitable and political groups who lobbied for a specialist group within the police to deal with women and girls. A major factor in the establishment of the early female police was the desperate labour shortage that resulted from the carnage of World War I (1914-18) and the mass deployment of men to the military (Owings 1969). Women police were appointed in New Zealand during World War II (1939-45).

Containment

The establishment of women police was something of a Pyrrhic victory. They were confined in separate women's sections in tiny numbers, with strict limitations on their functions. Their presence took the steam out of the efforts of the women police movement while their negligible numbers and limited scope meant they had only the most minimal impact on policing. Numbers were also curtailed by the fact that married women and single mothers were usually ineligible for recruitment, and female officers who married had to resign. Like many other women in employment, they were often paid lower wages because their work was considered inferior to that of men and it was assumed they had no family to support (Prenzler 1994).

The 1950s and 1960s saw the beginnings of a gradual break out from this ghetto environment as women entered juvenile aid units and school traffic squads, eventually joining mixed patrol teams in the 1970s (Heidensohn 1992). By the early 1990s women police in the more progressive democracies reached the ten per cent mark and numbers continued to rise, albeit extremely slowly. Even in the 1980s and 1990s women police were often restricted by quotas, by tough height and weight restrictions, by the absence of adequate maternity leave, and by a strong tendency to deploy women into welfare roles. They were usually entirely absent from smaller highly competitive units such as water police or dog squads. The most recent survey in the United States found that in the year 2000 women made up only 13 per cent of police, despite the fact that women constituted 46 per cent of employed persons. In addition, 'coloured women' made up only nine per cent of women police (NCWP 2001). Women were also under-represented in senior ranks; as they are in Australia where women made up 19 per cent of sworn officers but only three per cent of the senior executive service in 2001 (AIC 2001).

Resistance

Anti-discrimination legislation introduced in many countries in the 1970s greatly accelerated the rate of female recruitment. Piecemeal change included the removal of the marriage bar and quotas, disestablishment of women's sections, the creation of mixed patrol teams, and integration into training and seniority lists. However, the legal requirement not to discriminate was often met by intense resistance and diverse strategies of evasion. The initial response was usually to ignore the new laws. For example, in New South Wales police ignored the 1977 *Anti-Discrimination Act* (NSW) until in 1980 a rejected female applicant took the Service to the Anti-discrimination Board challenging the quota system still in place. The Service was directed to remove the quota and agreed to actively encourage women's employment. The marriage bar was lifted in 1981 only after a complaint to the Board (Tynan, 1995). In the United States, revelations of blatant discrimination obliged courts to force affirmative action decrees onto police departments – usually for racial minorities as well as women (NCWP 2001).

The legacy of differing attitudes toward women police on the part of senior managers in the 1990s can be seen in the Australian case in Figure 1. New South Wales (with 21.3%) was the leader in the employment of women police as a result of deliberate efforts in recruitment (Prenzler and Hayes 2000). Queensland (19.7%) had varying policies, but these included some preferential selection in the latter '90s. The figures for South Australia (19.5%) and Tasmania (19.4%) appear to have resulted simply from non-discrimination in recruitment. Victoria (16.4%) and Western Australia (13.2%) were behind, largely because of difficult physical entry tests. Since 2000, Victoria and Western Australia have adopted pro-equity policies following the appointment of new commissioners, including the first female commissioner in Australia in Victoria.

Figure 5.1: Males and Females in State Police Services in Australia, 2001

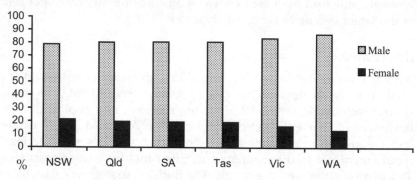

Source: AIC, 2001.

Reversals

In the book *Backlash: The Undeclared War Against American Women*, Faludi (1991) argued that the feminist gains of the 1970s had provoked a major backlash in the 1980s. Faludi's main contention was that there had been a revival of the conservative view that women's place was in the home and she cited statistics on employment, wealth, power and domestic labour to show reversals in women's status in many areas. Some similar reversals of fortune have occurred in policing. One of the most prominent cases was in Queensland in the period covered by Faludi's study (Prenzler, Jones and Ronken 2001). In 1970 a police minister concerned about corruption appointed Commissioner Whitrod to reform the Queensland Police. Whitrod was dissatisfied with the quality of many recruits and began recruiting women. He supported equal pay, removed the bar on married women and adopted a policy of integration. By 1976, sworn female officers and recruits equalled 10 per cent of police – possibly the highest figure in the world at the time. In response to Union alarm over women taking men's jobs, the next commissioner, Lewis, introduced a quota on female recruits, re-instated the marriage bar, pursued a policy of removing lesbian officers, and curtailed the deployment of women. Figure 5.2 shows the effect of these policies in reversing the number of women police. Lewis also shut down Whitrod's anti-corruption unit and allowed corruption to become entrenched in the force.

Figure 5.2: Percentage of Women in Australian Police Forces and in the Queensland Police, 1966-1991

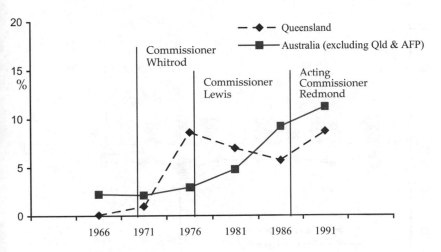

Source: Prenzler et al, 2001: 52.

Such dramatic reversals appear to be rare in police history. Resistance has tended, instead, to be subtle. Obstacle course tests have been a particularly effective method of excluding women, as well as other applicants that did not fit the police stereotype of masculinity. These tests have the appearance of scientific objectivity and gender neutrality, although courts have systematically struck them down as not reflecting job requirements. An imputation made in some cases in the United States was that physical tests were specifically developed to keep out women following the imposition of anti-discrimination legislation (Prenzler, 1996).

Queensland again provides an instructive tale of progress and reversal in the area of physical entry tests. In the early-1990s, professionalisation strategies included non-discriminatory recruitment. Increases in the number of female recruits led to renewed Union alarm, including uncorroborated claims of assaults against policewomen and threats to the safety of policemen. In response, in 1994, a 'physical competency test' was introduced into recruitment. The main effect was to exclude hundreds of female applicants and scores of less agile males in the six years it operated in different forms in defiance of new equity laws. Figure 5.3 shows how the educationally-based

Figure 5.3: Percentages of Female Applicants and Female Recruits per Intake, Queensland Police Service, February 1991 to October 1994

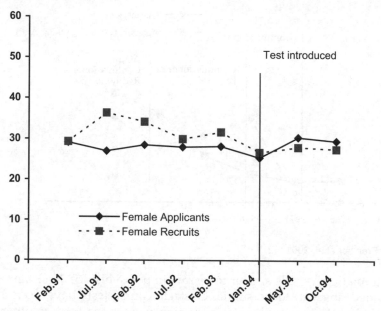

Source: Prenzler, 1996: 318.

recruitment criteria of the initial reform period favoured female applicants and how the physical competency test reversed this trend (Prenzler 1996).

Harassment and discrimination

When women police worked in small numbers in separate sections dealing with women and children they were usually accorded respect by male police. A 'chivalry factor' applied. When formal discrimination was replaced by policies of integration women were exposed to informal discrimination in assignments and promotion. They were also suddenly exposed to the problem of sexual harassment. In patrol cars, on the beat, in stations and offices they became targets of sexual predators who often made their working lives a living hell (Balkin 1988).

Research suggests that about 80 per cent of women police in countries such as Britain, the United States and Australia have experienced some form of harassment (Brown 1998). A survey of women police in New South Wales in the mid-1990s showed that 54 per cent with two years or less service had experienced sexual harassment (Sutton 1996). The types of harassment that can occur, and the way that harassment and discrimination often go together, are highlighted in one of the case studies from a recent Australian report, *Brute Force II: The Continuing Need for Affirmative Action in the Victorian Police Force*:

Senior Constable Narell McKenna took the Victoria Police to the Anti-Discrimination Tribunal because she no longer wanted to tolerate sexist attitudes, discrimination and harassment.

Ms McKenna endured endless demeaning and cruel derogatory comments from her male co-workers when she was stationed at the Bairnsdale police station. Not only was she subjected to constant sexist jokes about a woman's rightful place [in] the home, bedroom and kitchen, she was intrusively fondled, asked for oral sex and dragged kicking and screaming to a police cell. Enduring this type of abuse for two years led Ms McKenna to attempt suicide in 1997 and she still suffers from panic and anxiety attacks.

In trying to gain career advancement Ms McKenna again encountered discrimination. Ms McKenna applied for a four-wheel drive course, even after her fellow co-workers had stated, 'don't bother you won't get on it'. She was unsuccessful. When [she] asked why she was refused Ms McKenna was told it was because she 'was a girl' and it was a 'traditionally male position' ...

Ms McKenna was also denied access to a number of other special duties ... Completion of these special duties is important for career advancement because it proves the officer is responsible and can handle matters. Ms McKenna stated that 'she was not given an opportunity to do this work whereas male members of equal or lower rank were'. When Mr Heesom [her former supervisor] was questioned about restricting Ms McKenna's promotional opportunities, by denying access to special duties, he stated 'I still don't think that there would be one station that would have a female in charge. I don't know that they are quite ready for that yet' ...

The behaviour that Narell McKenna was forced to endure was so outrageous she was awarded an unprecedented amount of $125,000 by the Anti-Discrimination Tribunal.

Disappointingly, rather than accept the finding and work for positive change, Victoria Police chose to appeal this finding. The Supreme Court denied the appeal (FCLCV 1999: 21, 27).

Neglect by inquiries

Sex discrimination and harassment are forms of internal corruption because they involve violation of departmental rules and ethical standards, and they often involve an abuse of position for personal benefit or perceived organisational benefit (see Chapter 1). Given this fact, and the extensive nature of the problem, it is surprising that so few corruption inquires have considered the issue. The landmark Knapp Report into the NYPD reads largely as though women do not exist. Throughout the report police are almost always referred to as 'policemen', 'patrolmen' and 'plainclothesmen' (Knapp 1972). The more recent Mollen Report on the NYPD similarly ignored sex discrimination (1994). The 1994-97 Wood Inquiry occurred at a time when the NSW Police Service was a leading employer of women, although the Service remained extremely male dominated. In describing the traditional police culture, the Wood Report listed 'a machismo culture that permits sexism and glorifies the abuse of alcohol and heterosexual indulgences' (Wood 1997: 31). However, it did not directly address the issues of discrimination and harassment.

One exception to this pattern was the 1989 Fitzgerald Inquiry in Queensland (see also Christopher 1991 83-88, on the LAPD). The Fitzgerald Report identified a problem of sex discrimination in recruitment; although the brief assessment was apparently only included in response to a submission from the Policewomen's Association (Prenzler, et al, 2001). Nonetheless, Figure 5.4 demonstrates the potential for corruption inquiries to impact positively on gender inequalities. The percentage of women in the Queensland Police had been targeted at seven per cent, but quotas were increased during the Fitzgerald Inquiry (1987-89) and were abandoned in 1990 following the Inquiry's recommendation of appointment by merit. The number of female recruits leapt from nine per cent in 1987, when the Inquiry began, to 32 per cent in 1991. The Inquiry also led directly to a change of government and the introduction of State anti-discrimination legislation.

The neglect of sex discrimination by corruption inquiries is surprising because the victims go well beyond the millions of women who failed to obtain careers in policing, and all the female police who have been restricted and harassed. In addition, millions of male and female victims of crime, as well as suspects and offenders, have been denied the benefits of attendance by women police. This applies particularly in terms of the appalling record of male police in their neglect of, or further abuse of, female victims of sexual and domestic

Figure 5 4: Percentages of Female Applicants and Female Recruits, Queensland Police Service, 1988-89 to 1991-92

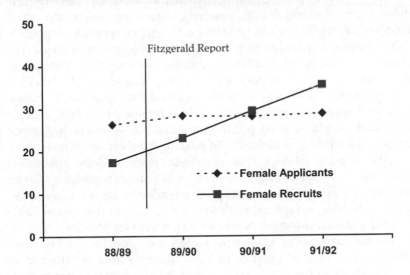

Source: Prenzler, et al, 2001: 55.

assault (Hanmer, Radford and Stanko, 1989). The scale of this mistreatment across time and across jurisdictions is immense.

Explaining sex discrimination in policing

Feminist theory

In an article titled 'The Logic of Sexism Among Police', Hunt (1990) identified three main areas of theory that relate to women in policing. 'Socialist feminist theory' focuses on the economic competition between men and women. Male police were initially able to entirely exclude women from the benefits of police work – with its authority, job security, superannuation, paid leave, sickness benefits and career path. In this view, policing was just one more occupation monopolised by men in which salaried men required female support by way of unpaid domestic labour. The establishment of women police sections, staffed by a handful of spinsters, did nothing to directly threaten this regime.

'Role theory' focuses on how males and females are socialised into different expectations about their 'natural' place in the social order. Policing is represented as a male occupation requiring exclusively male traits of aggressiveness, strength, emotional toughness, risk-taking and exercise of authority. In this ideology, stereotypical female traits of emotionality, passivity, nurturing, negotiation, and avoidance of conflict would undermine the police function, especially when combined with women's supposed physical weakness. The presence of women police therefore provokes role conflict. Male police have often reacted by stereotyping women police as misfits, labelling them as 'butch', 'lesbians' or 'sluts' – views that help justify harassment and discrimination. Balkin's (1988) review of studies on male police attitudes to women police emphasised how many policemen depend on the masculine identity of policing for their self-esteem.

The coping strategies that women police adopt also often reinforced their subordinate position and role expectations. Given their extreme minority status, they have tended to keep a low profile, avoiding trouble, adapting as much as possible to the inhospitable environment and lowering career expectations (see Wexler, 1985, on the 'neutral-impersonal style' and Jacobs, 1987, on the 'professional officer' style). This acceptance of a secondary status is reflected in surveys where women police often show a lack of confidence in their own sex to handle the physical side of police work (Hotchkiss, 1992; Niland, 1996). And it occurs despite the extensive research into the performance of women police, which shows they are equally capable with men and are often better at reducing conflict (see Lunneborg 1989). It also occurs despite public opinion supportive of women police (Lunneborg 1989).

The two theoretical viewpoints outlined above help explain why the traditional culture of policing is hostile to women. It should not be surprising that a study in the United States found that 95 per cent of male officers agreed with the statement, 'if it weren't for legal and government pressure, few police departments would hire many female officers' (Weisheit 1987: 147; also Balkin 1988). Hunt, however, adds a third theoretical dimension, which can be termed an 'interpretive/symbolic approach'. She states that:

> The interpretive approach recognises the importance of economic factors and role relations in structuring gender attitudes and behaviours. However, it also draws upon symbolic interactionist views which acknowledge the relevance of symbols and meanings in constructing action (1990: 5).

In particular, Hunt focused on how policing is suffused with binary oppositions about acceptable and unacceptable behaviours, persons and values, framed within a basic male/female opposition. Things which are respected and valued in the traditional police culture – brutality, 'street justice', arresting people, excessive drinking, swearing and lewd jokes, defiance of departmental rules, casual sex, disdain for management, acceptance of corrupt money – are characterised as 'male'. The opposites of these things, which are loathed and despised – due process, showing respect or compassion towards suspects, preventing crime, valuing education, showing emotion, and even homosexuality – are characterised as 'female'.

Hunt's analysis was based on a participant observation study in a corrupt police department. The department had been forced to employ women police under a court order. Hunt found that the increased presence of women, engaged in a range of normal police duties, constituted a profound threat to the whole identity of the majority of male officers and to the way they had been 'doing business' for many decades. Of particular significance was the way in which women police were seen as the 'moral woman' who could not fit in into, and threatened to disclose, the secret world of interconnected male camaraderie, drunkenness, illicit sex, violence and corruption. Women police spoilt the party!

Gender and corruption

As corruption inquiries developed from the 1970s, increasing attention was given to ways in which the police culture supported misconduct (see Chapter 1). However, while most inquiries ignored discrimination as a form of corruption, they also neglected to consider gender as a causal factor in corruption. For example, the relatively recent Mollen Report of 1994 made a detailed analysis of the culture of the NYPD, but it completely ignored gender. Despite its comments on discrimination, the Fitzgerald Report's analysis of police culture and corruption also ignored gender. Only very recently have the connections between gender and corruption begun to receive serious consideration in official reports. For example, the NSW Wood Report made an explicit assessment of the issue in the following terms:

> This royal commission and similar inquiries have found relatively few women police involved in corrupt practices. Where it has emerged it has largely related to process corruption or 'secondary corruption' involving protection of other officers from internal investigations.

Several reasons have been advanced for this, including the suggestions that women are:

- innately less susceptible to corruption;

- excluded from corrupt practices by their male colleagues who refuse to admit them into their tight-knit social groups, or to fully recognise them as operational police; and

- under-represented in those areas of policing, particularly detective work, where the corruption potential is highest.

There is often an assumption that increasing the number of women police will lead to a general raising of the ethical standards in policing because women are less likely than their male colleagues to engage in corruption or tolerate such behaviour (Wood 1997: 42-43).

The Report cited mixed research findings on whether or not women police have more ethical attitudes than male police or are more willing to report misconduct. But, there is a good deal of evidence to show that women are subject to fewer complaints from the public, especially for excessive force and rudeness (Wood 1997: 42-43; Christopher 1991: 84). Hunt's study, described above, is particularly important for showing, from the inside, how women present as an alien culture disruptive of corrupt police networks; and how corruption, brutality, racism and sexism (and homophobia and anti-intellectualism) serve as mutual reinforcers of each other.

The policy implications of this are somewhat problematic. The Wood Commission recommendation on the issue represents something of a balancing act:

> Increasing the number of women ... is not of itself an answer to corruption ... Widening the recruitment base, however, may address some of the problems which result from the homogeneity of the Service which tends to reinforce the negative aspects of its culture and to lock out diversity of ideas (1997: p 258).

This cautious view can be compared with the more positivist view of the National Centre for Women and Policing in the United States. In its report, *Equality Denied: The Status of Women in Policing, 2000*, it took a stronger line on the relationship between male dominance and misconduct:

> The continued under-representation of women in policing is a significant contributing factor to the widespread excessive force and corruption scandals plaguing law enforcement today, scandals that are costing the US taxpayers tens of millions of dollars annually in liability lawsuit payouts for injuries and wrongful deaths of citizens (NCWP 2001: 3).

Preventing discrimination and creating equity

There are three main arguments for increasing the number of women police:

1. To have women police available for members of the public who want 'a woman's touch';

2. To reduce misconduct by recruiting officers predisposed toward ethical conduct, who will also challenge the culture of male solidarity that supports corruption; and

3. For the sake of fairness in making the career benefits of policing available equally across the sexes.

The first two arguments could be criticised as using women as a means to an end. There is also the practical argument that faith in women may be misplaced if they conform to the traditional police culture. However, the third argument has overridden the others in the form of the equity principles embodied in anti-discrimination legislation. Consequently, it is likely that fulfilment of employment equity requirements will contribute by default to the other two goals.

The great benefit of anti-discrimination law is that it assumes that organisations will not voluntarily comply with equity principles. Police departments fall almost universally into this category. Anti-discrimination legislation has been essential to force police to include women. The problem, however, is that most anti-discrimination legislation is essentially passive in simply prohibiting discrimination. Disadvantaged groups such as women cannot be discriminated against because they frequently 'self-select' themselves out of applying for employment, promotion or specialist roles because of career expectations generated in childhood, the potential conflict between work and child rearing responsibilities, and expectations of discrimination (Martin 1990). Aggrieved parties can also be deterred from making complaints of discrimination by cost factors, ignorance of the law, fear of retribution or difficulties proving bias (Thornton 1990).

Consequently, a new generation of EEO and affirmative action legislation was designed to capture the original vision of anti-discrimination legislation, which was not just to *prevent* discrimination but to *promote* equal participation. A number of writers in this area emphasise the distinction between 'formal equality' and 'substantive equality' in organisations (Thornton 1990). When it comes to noncompliance with equity principles, many police departments have 'gotten away with it'; and the case of sex discrimination supports the observations of scholars that police are adept at evading genuine accountability and of maintaining their independence (Palmer 1999).

In response to these problems, affirmative action and equal opportunity legislation has been more demanding of public sector bodies such as police. Equity agencies have been established to which police departments must submit equity plans and performance reports, although these agencies often lack an adequate enforcement capacity (NCWP 2001; Prenzler and Hayes 2000). Strategies currently being used in policing to encourage women's equal participation include the following:

- recruitment campaigns targeted at women,

- pre-application classes,

- the inclusion of women on all selection and promotion panels where there are female applicants,

- career development courses and mentoring programs,

- women's advisory groups to senior management,

- paid maternity leave,

- flexible employment options, including part-time work,

- child care advisory services,

- equity units and sexual harassment officers to receive complaints and provide advice, and

- the inclusion of equity content and anti-harassment information in training courses.

Many of these initiatives also benefit male police who wish to contribute more to family life or who suffered discrimination under the 'old boys' system.

Conclusion

Police commissioners, senior police managers and police union executives have initiated very few improvements in the position of women. In fact, these leaders have, on the whole, resisted gender integration at every turn. Permanent positive change has come almost exclusively from outside policing – initially from lobby groups and politicians, and later from anti-discrimination legislation. Even then police often engaged in forms of active and passive resistance. The lesson from this is that police cannot be trusted to ensure women are treated fairly within the ranks. Individual police managers and the male colleagues of women police may be accepting and supportive at particular times and places, but the winds of patronage can quickly change. In the general area of police ethical conduct, strong independent agencies are needed to prevent corruption (see Chapter 13). The same applies for gender equity. Policing remains a high-risk occupation for sex discrimination. The legacy of misogyny poses an ongoing threat that must be pre-empted with active strategies of support for women.

References

AIC, 2001, *The Composition of Australia's Police Services as at June 2001*, Australian Institute of Criminology.

Balkin, J, 1988, 'Why Policemen Don't Like Policewomen', *Journal of Police Science and Administration* 16(1), 29-38.

Brown, J, 1998, 'Comparing Charges: The Experience of Discrimination and Harassment Among Women Police Officers', *International Journal of Police Science and Management* 1(3), 227-40.

Christopher, W, 1991, *Report of the Independent Commission on the Los Angeles Police Department*.

Faludi, S, 1991, *Backlash: The Undeclared War Against American Women*, Crown.

FCLCV, 1999, *Brute Force II: The Continuing Need for Affirmative Action in the Victorian Police Force*, Federation of Community Legal Centres Victoria.

Fitzgerald, G, 1989, *Report of a Commission of Inquiry Pursuant to Orders in Council*, Goprint.

Heidensohn, F, 1992, *Women in Control? The Role of Women in Law Enforcement*, Clarendon.

Hotchkiss, S, 1992, *Policing Promotional Difference: Policewomen in the Queensland Police Service*, MA thesis, Griffith University.

Hanmer, J, Radford, J and Stanko, E (eds), 1989, *Women, Policing and Male Violence, International Perspectives*, Routledge.

Hunt, J, 1990, 'The Logic of Sexism Among Police', *Women and Criminal Justice* 1(2), 3-30.

Jacobs, P, 1987, 'How Female Police Officers Cope with a Traditionally Male Position', *Sociology and Social Research* 72(1), 4-6.

Knapp, W, 1972, *The Knapp Commission Report on Police Corruption*, George Braziller.

Lunneborg, P, 1989, *Women Police Officers: Current Career Profile*, Charles C Thomas.

Martin, S, 1990, *On the Move: The Status of Women in Policing*, Police Foundation.

Martin, S (1980) *Breaking and Entering: Policewomen on Patrol*, University of California Press.

Mollen, M, 1994, *Commission Report, Commission to Investigate Allegations of Police Corruption and the Anti-Corruption Procedures of the Police Department*, New York City.

NCWP, 2001, *Equality Denied: The Status of Women in Policing*, 2000, National Centre for Women and Policing.

Niland, C, 1996, 'The Impact of Police Culture on Women and Their Performance in Policing', paper presented at the First Australasian Women in Policing Conference, Sydney, 29-31 July.

Owings C, 1969, *Women Police: A Study of the Development and Status of the Women Police Movement*, Patterson Smith.

Palmer, D, 1999, '"Confronting Police Culture" or "The Force is Still With You"? Making Sense of Contemporary Policing in Australia', *International Journal of Police Science and Management* 1(4), 333-46.

Prenzler, T, 1994, 'Women in Australian Policing: An Historical Overview', *Journal of Australian Studies* 42, 78-88.

Prenzler, T, 1996, 'Rebuilding the Walls? The Impact of Police Pre-Entry Physical Ability Tests on Female Applicants', *Current Issues in Criminal Justice* 7(3), 314-324.

Prenzler, T and Hayes, H, 2000, 'Measuring Progress in Gender Equity in Australian Policing', *Current Issues in Criminal Justice* 12(1), 20-38.

Prenzler, T, Jones, L and Ronken, C, 2001, Journey to Equality: An Illustrated History of Women in the Queensland Police, Queensland Police Service.

Sutton, J, 1996, 'Survey of New South Wales Policewomen', paper presented to the First Australasian Women in Policing Conference, Sydney, 29-31 July.

Thornton, M, 1990, *The Liberal Promise*, Oxford University Press.

Tynan, M, 1995, *Eighty Years of Women in Policing, New South Wales, 1915-1995*, NSW Police Service.

Weisheit, R, 1987, 'Women in the State Police: Concerns of Male and Female Officers', *Journal of Police Science and Administration* 15(2), 137-144.

Wexler, J, 1985, 'Role Styles of Women Police Officers', *Sex Roles* 12(7/8), 749-55.

Wood, J, 1997, *Royal Commission into the New South Wales Police Service: Final Report*, Government Printer.

6

The Politics of Police Reform

Jenny Fleming and Colleen Lewis

Police are 'inherently and inescapably political' (Reiner 1985: 2) and police organisations inevitably operate in an environment that is shaped by its political context. In recent years concerns about law and order and police corruption have been prominent on the political agenda of many democracies. These concerns create a number of problems for governments beholden to those who elected them, and for a police service that may or may not have the same goals and aspirations as the government that employs them (Smith 1994: 186). This is true in an ordinary environment but is particularly pertinent when change and reform is the result of a public inquiry into corruption in a police service. When that happens the reform program attracts keen public, media and political interest. This chapter examines two case studies – in the Australian States of Queensland and New South Wales – where politics has had divergent effects on the reform process. In Queensland, the control of reform by an independent commission appears to have made for a more successful process. In New South Wales (NSW), police reform was undermined by an excessive reliance on the police commissioner and the negative politicisation of the reform process.

Background

The political focus on crime and police conduct can have positive or negative consequences. In New York City, for example, Police Commissioner Patrick Murphy was able to capitalise on widespread support for change to ensure the comprehensive implementation of recommendations made by the Knapp Commission in the 1970s (Henry 1994). Conversely 22 years later, the Mollen Inquiry (1994) found that political concerns about negative publicity and crime 'clean up' rates had marginalised corruption prevention in the New York Police Department.

In Ontario, Canada, a lack of political will in the 1970s meant that it took five years and the recommendation of six inquiries before the government acted to create a pioneering external body to oversight complaints against police. In 1995 the newly-elected Conservative government took much less time to dismantle the independent Office of Public Complaints Commissioner (Lewis 1999: 43-44).

In Northern Ireland, changes relating to the accountability of the Royal Ulster Constabulary have often been stymied by the political climate. Recent attempts at meaningful reform focus on the recommendations of the Patten Report, which encouraged implementation of key recommendations of the 1997 Hayes Report. A crucial element in both reports was the link between the success of the reform program and the introduction of an 'open' and 'accessible' process for handling complaints against police that had widespread community support. A review by civil libertarians argued that 'a new beginning for policing in Northern Ireland is possible'. But, 'the political will to change needs to be demonstrated quickly and monitored effectively' (O'Rawe and Moore 2000: 291-292).

As the above examples suggest, it is the nature of the political environment that is fundamental to the progress of reform. In Australia, two major investigations into police corruption have resulted in widespread anti-corruption reforms. In both cases investigations have taken place in a highly charged political environment, which in one instance contributed to a relatively successful outcome and in the other contributed to the breakdown of reform. In examining developments in Queensland and NSW, this chapter demonstrates the political nature of police reform. The lesson to be drawn from these case studies is that an awareness of the centrality of politics in police relations is crucial for those who seek to implement a successful reform process.

Queensland

The Fitzgerald Inquiry

The Queensland Police Force had been the subject of a number of corruption inquiries but none led to serious organisational reform (see for example, Bolen 1997). In early 1987 new corruption allegations led to the *Commission of Inquiry into Possible Police Misconduct and Associated Matters* (the Fitzgerald Inquiry). The Inquiry became a catalyst for significant reform. The Commission's report did not limit itself to detailing what went wrong and recommending the establishment of new institutions, policies and procedures to fix the problem. It also addressed the issue of implementation and foreshadowed the 'many ways in which the reform agenda could be delayed or subverted by political or bureaucratic opponents' (Fitzgerald 1989: 7).

A crucial aspect of the Fitzgerald Report was its focus on the improper relationship that had developed between the Police Commissioner and the National Party government. Fitzgerald showed how the Queensland government's protective attitude toward its police force had led to a situation where corrupt police behaved as if they were immune from official investigation. This situation was able to develop because the unofficial 'quid pro quo' for police compliance with the government's strong law and order policy, which included a ban on street marches, was defending the police against allegations of misconduct.

The influence and autonomy of the police and police union

Prior to the Fitzgerald Inquiry, power in the Queensland Police Service (QPS) was centralised, with most decisions being channelled through the Commissioner's office. The Commissioner himself enjoyed direct access to the Premier. In return for unconditional support for the Police Service, the Commissioner supported the government, especially at election time. For example, during the 1983 Queensland State election Commissioner Lewis made a speech in which he expressed the view that 'the people of Queensland and the police force owe the Premier a very deep gratitude. The free enterprise policy of the Bjelke-Petersen government has been responsible for Queensland's tremendous [economic] growth' (in Whitton 1989: 4). Such a statement from a public servant who is also the head of the coercive arm of the state is improper at any time; during an election campaign it is extraordinary. The fact that Lewis felt comfortable making such partisan political statements demonstrated the depth of the improper relationship that had developed between his office and the government.

Evidence such as this and other examples of the improper use of police power to influence government policy allowed Fitzgerald to legitimately make significant administrative and management decisions about policing issues during the inquiry's two-year duration. In effect, shortly after the Inquiry began, Fitzgerald was acting as '... the defacto commissioner of police' (Lewis 1999: 127).

While the police force is a key stakeholder in any reform process, so too is the powerful police union. The Fitzgerald Inquiry found that the Queensland Police Union (QPU) had opposed previous attempts at reform (Fitzgerald 1989: 212). It also enjoyed an inappropriate relationship with the government in that it frequently met with government ministers and the Premier without police management being present. The Union was, in Fitzgerald's view, improperly involved in police disciplinary matters and management policy, and the QPU had little credibility at the end of the inquiry. When asked why the Union did not oppose the introduction of the far-reaching reform agenda, the President of the QPU admitted that, 'the Union didn't really have anything to horse-trade' (in Lewis 1999: 128).

A change in government consolidated the reform process. After 32 years in opposition the Labor Party formed government in 1989 and honoured its promise to implement all of Fitzgerald's recommendations. The Union's and the Police Service's lack of power, coupled with the election of a government dedicated to cleaning up corruption in Queensland, meant that the immediate post-Fitzgerald police reform phase went ahead without the 'political posturing and bureaucratic obfuscation' that had beset previous inquiries (Fitzgerald 1989: 11). Given Fitzgerald's findings, any suggestion that the government could, or would overtly intervene in the reform process would have been anathema to all concerned. The Commission's 'hands on' approach to implementing the initial stages of reform, the neutralisation of the police union and the government's reluctance to intervene contributed to a much stronger reform outcome than would develop in New South Wales.

The Criminal Justice Commission

During his inquiry, Fitzgerald recognised that a unique independent organisation was needed if Queensland was to achieve meaningful, on-going, reform of the QPS. The Criminal Justice Commission (CJC) was designed so that the structures and processes put into place would guard against the derailment of the reform program once the scandal that surrounded the exposure of police corruption became yesterday's news. The CJC was not only given the power to investigate allegations of police corruption and recommend punishment, but through its research and corruption prevention arms was also given a preventive role. Most importantly, it was charged with 'overseeing the reform of the Police Force' independently from the police and the government. Fitzgerald stated that 'an important consideration underlying the establishment of the CJC' [was] the exclusion or reduction of party political considerations and processes from the decision making process with respect to the administration of criminal justice' (1989: 309).

Fitzgerald also put processes into place to help protect the Office of Commissioner of Police from future abuse by politicians seeking party political advantage. Control over who would be police commissioner, for example, was no longer at the sole discretion of the government. It was now obliged to consult with the CJC. Fitzgerald understood the need to establish an appropriate arms-length relationship between the police and government and to open up the QPS by subjecting it to continued scrutiny and policy input from an expert independent oversight body.

Mundingburra by-election

Reforming the QPS has not been without its problems. Attempts have been made to politicise the process and a change of government in 1996 threatened to undo much of Fitzgerald's reform program. The catalyst for this was the signing of a Memorandum of Understanding (MOU) by the President of the Police Union, the Leader of the Opposition and Shadow Minister for Police before a crucial one-seat by-election, the result of which would determine who formed government. The QPU was openly hostile to the Labor Government and actively and openly campaigned for more police and resources during the by-election. The by-election delivered government to the National-Liberal Party coalition (Lewis 1999: 160-163).

After the by-election it was revealed in the *Courier-Mail* newspaper that the now incoming Premier and Police Minister had agreed in the MOU to reduce the CJC's role in the complaints against police process to 'serious criminal matters only'. They had also agreed to other matters, including union input into the selection or dismissal of a police commissioner.

A public and media outcry followed and Police Minister Cooper was left with little alternative but to forward the document to the CJC that engaged an independent retired judge, Ken Carruthers, to conduct an inquiry. The inquiry was to investigate whether the signing of the MOU represented any misconduct by those involved. The new National-Liberal coalition government then established a commission of inquiry into the future role, structure, powers and operation of the CJC (the 'Connolly-Ryan Inquiry'). This Inquiry had the power to review the ongoing Carruthers Inquiry, *before* Carruthers reported. In response, Carruthers resigned and, with the CJC commenced action in the Queensland Supreme Court alleging bias on the part of the Connolly-Ryan Inquiry. The Court ruled that the Inquiry be terminated on grounds of 'ostensible bias' (Lewis 1999: 166-167). Despite efforts by the government and the QPU to reassert control, the CJC has managed to maintain its role and powers.

Over the past 13 years the QPS has been subject to positive, on going reform. While there have been pockets of corruption revealed, ongoing endemic corruption at the moment at least, is conspicuous by its absence. Much of this reform can be attributed to the CJC's activities (see Preston 1999: 1). The CJC became the buffer between the police and government that helped protect police reform from becoming overly politicised thus contributing significantly to transparent processes. This was not the case in NSW where the reform process, did not include such a buffer. One of the consequences of this was that the reform of the Police Service, to its detriment, was transferred to the political arena in a much more destructive form.

New South Wales

The Wood Inquiry

Like the Fitzgerald Inquiry, the Wood Commission had its genesis in public controversy. It was established in 1994 following allegations of corruption made in the NSW parliament. As noted above, since 1989 the Fitzgerald reforms have essentially remained on track despite some attempts to destabilise the process. In NSW the politicisation of the Wood Commission's program remains a problem. The Commission's reliance on the Police Commissioner to effect reform rather than an independent organisation, and the government's politicisation of the process have combined to undermine reform.

The Wood Commission delivered its first interim report in February 1996. The report identified 'a state of systemic and ... entrenched corruption' and detailed specific measures 'directed towards minimising or reducing the incidence of ... misconduct' (Wood 1996: 1 11). It recommended a fundamental restructuring of the Service (NSWPS), 'establishment of strategies to ensure that the problems identified ... do not re-emerge on a cyclical basis', and established a Police Integrity Commission (PIC) (Wood 1996: 11-117). The PIC was established primarily as an external agency whose function was to investigate serious misconduct and corruption. Unlike the CJC, the agency was not established to oversee the reform process, nor to provide policy input (PIC 1997: 8-9). Instead the Commission called for 'a revolutionary change manager capable of strategic thought, strength and vision ... in whom absolute confidence can be entrusted' to implement reform (Wood 1996: 1).

In 1996, while the Royal Commission was still sitting, former British police officer Peter Ryan was sworn in as Police Commissioner. Wood's acceptance of a man 'who [was] not weighed down by institutional baggage from an old organisation' was explicit in his readiness to allow the new Commissioner to set his own agenda. Two months after his appointment Ryan detailed his proposals, making clear the need for an 'opportunity to actually proceed with ... reform without having to respond to intrusive demands from stakeholders for an account of progress' (Ryan 1996: 4). These included proposals relating to recruitment, transfers and removals from the Service, random drug and alcohol testing of police officers, the dismissal of officers and the disbanding of the Police Board (Ryan 1996: 5). The unexpected hostility exhibited by rank and file police, led by their union, to Ryan's proposals resulted in demonstrations outside parliament. Shocked by the ferocity of the demonstration a meeting of government members voted to reject Ryan's changes and 'give in' to the police. The Labor Premier argued against his colleagues' decision and insisted that they support the Commissioner and the reform process (Williams 2002: 166-168). He succeeded in overturning their decision and Ryan was allowed to continue implementing his reforms, albeit with the approval of the government.

Wood, in conjunction with the government, supported the Commissioner's directives – effectively allowing the NSWPS in some areas to set the agenda for reform and be responsible for implementation. He was concerned however about the level of political control that had exerted itself over the reform process and that Ryan's actions were always subject to government approval (Willams 2002: 199-200). Dixon cites a number of examples where the government successfully intervened in a number of issues that were clearly outside the Commission's understanding of 'operational decisions' (Dixon 1999: 153-156). The Wood Commission understood the importance of separating the formulation and implementation of policy. This is evidenced in its final report where a statutory policy/ operations divide was suggested that would relieve the Commissioner of subjection to ministerial direction and ensure that the 'Police Service not be subject to undue political direction' (Wood 1997: 379 243-245). The government rejected Wood's recommendation; unlikely, as Dixon notes, to allow its Police Commissioner such 'political freedom' (1999: 155). As a result, while the importance of a division between formulation and implementation was acknowledged, it 'remained (inevitably) undefined and ... much reli[ed] upon the ability, trustworthiness, and professionalism of the Police Commissioner' (Dixon 1999: 153). In the absence of an external independent body, the reform process in New South Wales was effectively entrusted to a newly appointed Police Commissioner and a government not averse to involving itself in the process where it was deemed politically expedient. While it could be argued that government support is crucial to effective police reform, as this chapter suggests, the government's support was contingent on public opinion. In its eagerness to score political points with a public increasingly concerned about ostensibly high crime rates, the government's support was limited to rhetoric. It allocated no funding for reform and was not prepared to support any proposals that it deemed would disaffect the public.

The politicisation of the NSW reform process

Ryan enjoyed a significant honeymoon period. In 1998 however, a renewed media focus on the politically sensitive issue of crime rates ensured that the government, the Commissioner's activities and the reform process generally came under close public scrutiny. Publicly, Ryan retained the government's support despite public commentary about the Commissioner's deteriorating relationship with senior officers, accusations that reform was being undermined and that senior officers were disgruntled at the lack of leadership in the Service (Martin 1998).

A State election called in February 1999 gave Ryan the opportunity to showcase his achievements and the government to cash in on its Commissioner's public popularity. Labor pursued a strong law and order rhetoric throughout the election campaign, vying with the opposition to produce the greater law and order policy credentials. It cited the success of the reform process and Ryan's efforts to tackle crime as major achievements (Bernoth 1999: 5). During the election campaign the Commissioner often appeared publicly with the Premier and the Police Minister. As one journalist put it, 'No one can remember a NSW Police Commissioner so openly supportive of a government's attempts to promote its law and order image during the run up to the State election' (Murphy 1999: 35). When Ryan negotiated a lucrative extension of his contract one month before the election, a prominent academic observed that 'the renewed contract announcement reeked of a political fix... It's not the sort of thing that inspires confidence in his independence from the politicians' (in Murphy 1999: 35).

Ryan compounded doubts about his political neutrality when he effectively destroyed the Opposition's attempts to match the government's law and order program. The Police Association had demanded an additional 2,500 police officers and the Opposition promised to deliver if elected. While not making the kind of partisan political speech that Commissioner Lewis had in Queensland, Ryan nevertheless undermined the Opposition's proposition by suggesting 'it was not possible to train such an influx of police without a fall in professional standards' and that he could have told the Coalition so had they consulted him ('Butt Out' 1999: 1). This may have been a valid observation, but in commenting, 'Mr Ryan had allowed unprecedented politicisation of his position and was now dependent on the politicians who employed him' (in Murphy 1999: 35). The Labor Party retained government.

The QSARP Report

In 2001, the PIC-commissioned *Qualitative Strategic Audit of the Reform Process* (QSARP) was released. Its findings served to refocus police reform back on the political agenda. In the absence of an independent body to oversee and implement reform, the Wood Commission had provided a detailed 'checklist', for the external audit to be administered periodically by the PIC (Wood 1997: A246-254). The first Report was caustically critical and found that Justice Wood's prescription for change was being undermined by the Commissioner's determination to bring down crime rates (QSARP 2000: 85).

The Police Commissioner denied that the reform process was 'not in sync with the Royal Commission's vision and that reform achievements have been overstated' (Chulov 2001: 5). The government dismissed the QSARP report as 'management jargon' with the Premier asserting the government's 'full confidence' in its Commissioner ('Police Reform Audit' 2001: 16). Ryan's comments perhaps illustrate contemporary difficulties of implementing police reform in New South Wales. Commissioners Ryan's relationship with the State government, the government's unequivocal support of its highly paid public servant and the focus on crime rates in the media combined to limit the extent to which the government could legitimately intervene and assess the progress of reform objectively. Ryan had always seen crime reduction as his primary task and is on record as saying 'I'm not going to apologise for making our streets safer and for bringing down crime' (in Miranda 2001: 2). This suited a government wedded to crime reduction and law and order imperatives. However, along the way Wood's reform initiatives particularly those relating to changing the culture of the police service, the importance of leadership and people management had become sidelined. These issues became more difficult to achieve, as reform became less of a priority for the government and for its Commissioner. According to the Police Association of New South Wales (PANSW), it was the over emphasis on crime reduction that contributed significantly to the breakdown of the reform process.

The perspective of the Police Association

Despite Wood's negative comments about the 'undesirable conflict' engendered by the Police Association's attitude to reform (Wood 1997: 211-212), the Association insists that it was supportive and saw the Inquiry as a 'window of opportunity' to initiate reform. It made extensive submissions supporting radical change, including integrity testing and greater external oversight. It also provided administrative assistance to support the Inquiry's investigations, was represented on most of the forums that formed the basis of Ryan's reports to the Inquiry, and participated in a range of groups examining specific reform issues (PANSW 2001; Chilvers 2001).

Five years into the reform process, the PANSW concedes that there has been positive structural, technological and legislative change but it has become frustrated by the continued 'obsession with numbers and crime' that, according to the Association has been the hallmark of the NSWPS for many years. The Association's Research Director, Greg Chilvers, sees the focus as misleading:

> NSW is no more dangerous now than it was at the turn of the century ... It's probably less dangerous in terms of crime. Road traffic accidents and deaths are the biggest problem in NSW ... Ryan's arrival coincided with a rise in the State's crime rates. Crime was riding a crest of the wave – not only in NSW but in Australia and throughout the Western world. Now the crest has subsided, Ryan is trying to take credit, pointing to the supposedly successful reform process to explain the numbers (Chilvers 2001).

The Association was also critical of the politics of the reform process. Paul Remfrey, Secretary of the Association, pointed out 'the government appointed Ryan and soon realised that Ryan was electorally advantageous to them. He provides regular advice and therefore they support him. But its support is political, not necessarily about his efforts vis-à-vis the reform process' (Remfrey 2001). Chilvers agreed:

> Whatever Ryan or the government say the reform process is still in its early stages – there is still no real emphasis on changing the culture or successful people management, something the Association has been pushing for years. Its not just about ticking off the Appendix 31 recommendations [and] its not about naively investing extraordinary amounts of power in one person (Chilvers 2001).

It was Ryan's emphasis on rising crime and his perceived relationship with the government that denigrated the reform process in the eyes of many stakeholders. The NSWPS has changed in many ways and is not the same organisation it was before the Wood reforms. The organisation's structure has been radically restructured. Ryan has tightened accountability lines through the Operations and Crime Review process with a focus on crime reduction. New education and training programs have been developed and aligned to the university structure and assessment centres have been introduced into the promotion system. Yet the reform process intended to stifle corruption has not delivered its expected gains. Five years on, and six months after a PIC inquiry into aspects of the reform process began there is evidence of further police corruption said to be 'as bad as anything uncovered during the police royal commission'. Allegations of bribery, illegal 'pay offs' and improper conduct towards drug suspects initiated a new inquiry into corruption in October 2001 (Devine 2001: 16). As the PIC inquiry into corruption continued to make headlines (for example, Mercer 2002: 2), police reform appeared to have lost its resonance with the public and therefore, for the time at least, its political salience. With the loss of its political salience, the Police Commissioner was on his own.

Conclusion

The political environments in Queensland and NSW have in both positive and negative ways determined the shape and direction of reform. Queensland's reform process took place in a highly politicised environment and was greatly assisted by this situation. Positive public and media support forced a commitment by all political parties that, if elected to government, they would implement the Fitzgerald recommendations 'lock, stock and barrel'. Without the politically charged atmosphere of the time such a promise would never have been made and sustained. This conducive milieu for reform contributed significantly to the relative success of the Queensland reform experience.

Fitzgerald's blueprint for reform recognised the dangers inherent in the negative politics of reform and to a significant degree provided mechanisms to limit its impact. Handing the reform process to the CJC was a potent strategy. The reform process also benefited from a sometimes begrudging willingness by the QPS and QPU to support change during the crucial first few years. As a result Queensland was spared from the usual recalcitrant attitude that had been the hallmark of QPS and QPU attitudes during previous attempts at reform.

From the outset the NSW reform process was subject to politicisation. The absence of an independent agency appropriately funded to oversee reform ensured that the process became the responsibility of the Commissioner and a government whose priorities differed from those of the Wood Commission. Both Ryan and the government were politically committed to crime reducing strategies and the pursuit of law and order. Ryan, because he perceived it was his job and the government because it was politically expedient to do so. Both parties pursued their own agendas for survival and, for a time, Ryan's advice, activities and public profile complemented the government's political image of a party committed to law and order. When the reform process came under attack, the government felt obliged to continue its support for Ryan, despite concerns about Ryan's diminishing standing in the community following the PIC inquiries.

Ryan's recent and controversial resignation has freed the government from any obligation to protect its Commissioner (Chulov 2002: 7). The reform of the NSWPS continues, but any success it enjoys in the future will depend largely on whether the process can be removed from power politics. The new Minister's proclivity to intervene and his hands on approach to operational policing issues to date do not inspire confidence in this process (see Williams 2002: 307ff).

In recent years, police reform has been a notable feature of policing studies. Various accounts and case studies add to our overall understanding of reform programs. What we know is that while change occurs in various ways in different jurisdictions, it does not take place in a vacuum. The political environment, whether positive or negative, will largely shape the nature and pace of police reform. If we are to draw a lesson from Queensland and NSW it is that potential reformers must be aware of the centrality of politics in the reform process.

References

Bernoth, A 1999, 'Carr Puts Troops in Law and Order Poll Mode', *Sydney Morning Herald*, 1 February, p 5.

Bolen, J, 1997, *Reform in Policing: Lessons from the Whitrod Era*, Hawkins Press.

Chilvers, G 2001, Interview with Jenny Fleming, 7 February 2001.

Chulov, M 2001, 'Report Savages Ryan Police Reform', *The Australian*, 16 February, p 5.

Chulov, M, 2002, 'Labor Mates Aided Ryan Deal', *The Australian*, 13 April, p 7.

Daily Telegraph, 2001, 'Police Reform Audit', 17 February, p 16.

Devine, M 2001, 'Despite All the Talk, The Force Still Stinks', *Sydney Morning Herald*, 11 October, p 16.

Dixon, D, 1999, 'Reform, Regression and the NSW Royal Commission', in D Dixon (ed), *A Culture of Corruption: Changing an Australian Police Service*, Hawkins.

Fitzgerald, T, 1989, *Report of a Commission of Inquiry Pursuant to Orders in Council*, Queensland Government Printer.

Henry, V, 1994, 'Police Corruption: Tradition and Evolution', in K Bryett and C Lewis (eds), *Un-Peeling Tradition: Contemporary Policing*, MacMillan.

Lewis, C, 1999, *Complaints Against Police, The Politics of Reform*, Hawkins.

Martin, B, 1998, 'Ryan's Blues', *Bulletin*, 14 July, pp 26-38.

Mercer, N, 2002, 'I was Depressed, says a Sobbing Police Star Who Took the Money', *Sydney Morning Herald*, 31 January, p 2.

Miranda, C, 2001, 'Anti-corruption Process "Flawed" – Damning Report Attacks Police', *Daily Telegraph*, 16 February, p 2.

Mollen, M, 1994, *Commission Report, Commission to Investigate Allegations of Police Corruption and the Anti-Corruption Procedures of the Police Department*, New York City.

Murphy, D, 1999, 'Cop This', *Sydney Morning Herald*, 6 March, p 35.

O'Rawe, M and Moore, L 2000, 'Accountability and Police Complaints in Northern Ireland: Leaving the Past Behind', in A Goldsmith and C Lewis (eds), *Civilian Oversight of Policing: Governance, Democracy and Human Rights*, Hart.

PANSW, 2001, *Discussion Paper Regarding Some Issues of Reform in the NSW Police Service*, August, Police Association of NSW.

PIC, 1997, *Annual Report 1996-97*, NSW Police Integrity Commission.

Preston, N, 1999, 'Public Sector Ethics in Queensland since Fitzgerald', paper presented at the *Australian Society of Archivists Conference*, Brisbane, July.

QSARP, 2000, *The Qualitative Strategic Audit of the Reform Process Report*, The Hay Company, Sydney.

Reiner, R, 1985, *The Politics of the Police*, St Martin's Press.

Remfrey, P, 2001, Interview with Jenny Fleming, 7 February.

Ryan, P, 1996, *'Reform of the NSW Police Service – Phase 1'*, Royal Commission exhibit 2820/1, 19 November.

Smith, D, 1994, 'The Political and Social Constraints to Reform', in K Bryett and C Lewis (eds), *Un-Peeling Tradition: Contemporary Policing*, MacMillan.

Sydney Morning Herald, 1999 'Butt Out – Politics is My Beat, Chikarovski Warns Ryan', 9 September, p 1.

Whitton, E, 1989, *The Hillbilly Dictator: Australia's Police State*, ABC Enterprises.

Williams, S, 2002, *Peter Ryan The Inside Story*, Viking.

Wood, J, 1996, *Royal Commission into the New South Wales Police Service, Interim Report (1)*, NSW Government Printer.

Wood, J, 1997 *Royal Commission into the New South Wales Police Service, Final Report, Volumes I-III*, NSW Government Printer.

INNOVATIONS IN CREATING ETHICAL POLICE DEPARTMENTS

7

Monitoring Integrity

David Brereton

Substantial resources are devoted to the prevention, detection and investigation of police misconduct in Australia. Every police service now has its own Ethical Standards Department, or equivalent, and each State has some form of external complaints investigation mechanism in place (Lewis and Prenzler 1999). In three States, standing Royal Commissions of Inquiry have been given jurisdiction to investigate serious misconduct by police: the Criminal Justice Commission (CJC) in Queensland, the Police Integrity Commission in New South Wales and, the Anti-Corruption Commission in Western Australia. In addition, over the last decade several major public inquiries have been initiated into aspects of police corruption; most notably, the Fitzgerald Inquiry in Queensland (Fitzgerald 1989), the Wood Royal Commission into the New South Wales Police Service (Wood 1997) the Carter Inquiry into Police and Drugs in Queensland (CJC 1997a) and the recently established Royal Commission in Western Australia.

Notwithstanding the effort that has been put into addressing the problem of police misconduct, instances of serious wrongdoing continue to come to public attention. Doubts have also been raised about the commitment of some police services to carrying through reform agendas (Dixon 1999) and the effectiveness of some of the recently established investigative bodies (Prenzler 2000). These on-going concerns highlight the need for oversight agencies and police services to improve how they monitor and report on police integrity within their jurisdictions. Enhancing this capability will assist these bodies to improve their own performance and, hopefully, improve the quality of public discussion about police reform issues.

This chapter describes how one oversight agency – the Queensland CJC – has approached this challenge. The CJC is an independent statutory body, established in 1990, in the aftermath of the

Fitzgerald Commission of Inquiry. (In January 2002, the CJC was merged with the Queensland Crime Commission to form the Queensland Crime and Misconduct Commission. As this chapter is focused entirely on the period prior to the merger, it uses the pre-2002 name.) Its functions include investigating alleged misconduct by Queensland Police Service (QPS) members and monitoring and reporting on the progress of reform within the Service. The CJC has put considerable resources into monitoring the incidence of, and trends in, police misconduct in the QPS, including by conducting periodic surveys of police clients and members of the public, and organizational 'ethical climate' surveys. In addition, it regularly reviews the procedures and processes which the QPS has put in place to reduce corruption risks.

Apart from producing a large number of reports and papers on specific aspects of this monitoring program, the CJC has published two summary reports on the overall progress which has been made in improving standards of conduct in the QPS (CJC 2001; CJC 1997b). This chapter presents the key findings of these reports and makes some more general observations about the utility of the different monitoring strategies that have been employed.

Complaints data

Uses and limitations of complaints data

The most readily available source of data on police misconduct is complaints statistics. These data have the advantage of being continuously collected, comprehensive in coverage and readily accessible. Used properly, they can be a valuable source of information about police practices and organisational processes, and the quality of 'customer service' being provided. In addition, careful analysis of complaints data can assist in identifying officers who have shown a propensity to act inappropriately, and in flagging at-risk areas and work units (see Chapter 9).

While complaints data are undoubtedly very useful, they need to be treated with caution (Brereton 2000). The fact that a person has made a complaint is not, of itself, proof that the alleged behaviour actually occurred. As police are quick to point out, some complaints are deliberate fabrications or are made by people whose judgment and recall have been clouded by anger, alcohol or other drugs. Many other allegations cannot be investigated productively, because of weak or conflicting evidence Conversely, the absence of complaints should not necessarily be taken as evidence that police are acting appropriately. People who have suffered at the hands of the police may not know where or how to complain, or may be fearful of reprisals. Some serious forms of misconduct, such as the giving and receiving of bribes, are consensual and therefore not likely to be the subject of a complaint. In some instances, people may not even be aware that they have been the victims of police misconduct (such as when confidential information about them has been released).

Finally, complaint numbers can rise or fall for reasons that are unrelated to the level of police misconduct. For example, the public's knowledge of and/or confidence in the complaints system may change over time; high-profile inquiries may prompt an upsurge in some types of complaints; or organisational procedures for recording and classifying complaints may alter. The amount and type of contact between police and members of the public can also affect complaint levels. If there are more police, or if individual police are more active in enforcing the law, this will result in more contact with members of the public. Assuming that the propensity of individual officers to act rudely or aggressively is constant, more contact will mean more complaints, even though the probability of a complaint arising from any one contact has not altered. For these reasons, it is important always to be aware of possible alternative explanations for changes in the level and type of complaints.

What the data show

Figure 7.1 shows the number of complaints of police misconduct received annually by the CJC in the years 1991-92 through to 1999-2000, plus the number of complaints per 1000 sworn officers. (Less serious 'breach of discipline' complaints are not included, because these fall outside of the CJC's jurisdiction.)

It can be seen that the number of misconduct complaints per 1000 sworn officers was quite stable from 1992-93 onwards, with the exception of a 'spike' in 1996-97. This upturn corresponded with the Carruthers Inquiry into the Queensland Police Union Memorandum of Understanding with the National Party, the aborted Connolly-Ryan Inquiry into the CJC and the Carter Inquiry into Police and Drugs. These high profile events generated considerable publicity about the CJC and police corruption issues, which in turn appears to have led to a temporary increase in complaints from the public.

Figure 7.1: Number of Misconduct Complaints Received and Rate per 1,000 QPS Sworn Officers, 1991-92 to 1999-2000

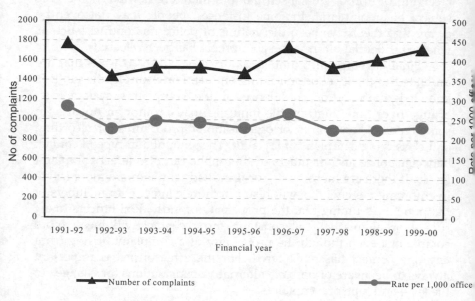

Sources: 1. Complaints: CJC Complaints Database; 2. QPS sworn officers: QPS *Statistical Reviews* 1991-92 to 1999-2000.

When analysing complaints data, it is important to look not only at overall trends, but also at the trends for specific types of complaints, as aggregate stability can sometimes conceal some significant changes in the complaints 'mix'. The CJC explored this issue in detail in its 1997 report, *Integrity in the Queensland Police Service*. As documented in that report, between 1991-92 and 1995-96 there was a substantial drop in complaints about 'behaviour' and 'duty failure' (in part due to fewer of these matters being classified by the CJC as misconduct matters). On the other hand, there were marked increases recorded in allegations of assault, misuse of powers and improper searches. Taken at face value, this would seem to indicate that police conduct got worse over this period. However, on further examination the most likely explanation for the rise in these complaints was an increase in police enforcement activity. The increase in complaints relating to searches was matched by a corresponding increase in the number of reported drug offences. Similarly, the rise in assault complaints tracked the growth in the amount of street-level law enforcement, as measured by the number of recorded drug and good order offences (CJC 1997b: 81-5; 1997c).

In the latter half of the 1990s the complaint mix was more stable, in part because complaints classification procedures were more settled than in the early years of the CJC and also because police enforcement activity leveled off. The main changes of note were a temporary increase in allegations relating to police involvement with illicit drugs, most probably as a result of the publicity generated by the Carter Inquiry (see above), and an increase in complaints about improper release of information in 1999-2000, which was also associated with another well-publicised Inquiry (CJC 2000a).

Overall, the complaints data suggest that there has been relatively little change in the underlying level of police misconduct in Queensland since the early 1990s. While there have been increases in certain types of serious complaints, such as those relating to assault and involvement with illicit drugs, these can plausibly be accounted for in terms of extraneous factors such as the publicity generated by public inquiries and changes in the level of police enforcement activity. Given, however, that complaint trends are sensitive to changes in recording or reporting practices, it is important also to examine alternative data sources, such as surveys, to see if they provide independent confirmation of this conclusion. This will be the focus of the next section.

Survey findings

Uses and limitations of survey data

Well-designed surveys can provide valuable information about the nature and extent of contact between police and members of the public. When conducted at regular intervals, with comparable questions and sampling strategies, surveys can also be employed to track changes over time in the willingness of people who are aggrieved by police conduct to formally complain. However, large samples are required to obtain statistically reliable indicators of change, especially for general population surveys, as most members of the public have had little or no contact with police, except in highly structured traffic enforcement situations.

Surveys, by their nature, measure perceived rather than actual misconduct. In some instances, this may lead to the frequency of certain types of misconduct being over-stated: for example, what a person regarded as excessive force by a police officer may have been appropriate in the eyes of an objective observer. Another limitation of surveys is that they are not very useful for identifying, and monitoring changes in, the more covert forms of police misconduct.

The CJC has used two types of surveys to collect information about public perceptions and experience of police misconduct: general population surveys conducted in 1995 and 1999 (CJC 2000b) and surveys in 1996 and 1999 of defendants in criminal prosecutions (CJC 2000c). The latter surveys were considerably more costly and logistically difficult to administer than the public attitudes surveys, because of the reliance on face-to-face interviews. However, an obvious benefit of surveying defendants is that all have had recent substantial contact with the police, whereas this is not the case for most members of the general public. Police critics of these surveys have raised concerns about the accuracy of the information provided by defendants, but assuming a constant 'error rate' this factor should not affect the reliability of the surveys for measuring *changes* over time.

Public attitudes surveys

The two general population surveys undertaken by the CJC were carried out by telephone, with the samples being drawn from Queensland residents aged 18 years or over. Around 900 people were surveyed in 1995, with this being increased to 1500 in 1999. In both surveys, respondents were asked whether they had been dissatisfied with the behaviour of a member of the QPS in the last 12 months towards themselves or someone else, what this behaviour involved, and whether they had complained formally about it. Earlier surveys in this series, conducted in 1991 and 1993, asked only about general public confidence in the police, rather than respondents' experiences of specific incidents.

In the 1999 survey around 11 per cent of respondents claimed to have been dissatisfied with police behaviour towards themselves or someone else in the previous 12 months (see Table 7.1). This was a similar result to the 1995 survey, when 12 per cent of respondents expressed dissatisfaction. In both the 1995 and 1999 surveys, the most commonly stated grounds for dissatisfaction were that police had been unfriendly, rude or arrogant, or had acted unreasonably or unfairly. Less than one per cent of the sample in each survey claimed to have been the victim of, or a witness to, a police assault or some other illegal act.

The main change identified by the 1999 survey was a statistically significant drop in the proportion of dissatisfied respondents who said that they had felt like making an official complaint – from 56 per cent in 1995 to 44 per cent in 1999. The proportion of dissatisfied respondents who reported actually making a complaint declined from 21 per cent to 16 per cent over the same period, although this was not a statistically significant change (see Table 7.1). The drop in the complaint rate was most likely attributable to a decline in the perceived seriousness of the behaviour engaged in by police (CJC 2000b: 5).

Table 7.1: Level of public dissatisfaction with police behaviour and action taken in response to that dissatisfaction, CJC Public Attitudes Surveys 1995 and 1999

	1995 (n=900) No.	% of all respondents	1999 (n=1502) No.	% of all respondents	p
Dissatisfied with police behaviour in the last 12 months	109	12.1	161	10.7	ns
Respondents dissatisfied with police behaviour in the last 12 months who:	61	6.8	71	4.7	*
felt like making an official complaint against the officer	23	2.6	26	1.7	ns
made or tried to make an official complaint					

Source: CJC 2000b. Notes: differences between the two years were examined using the chi-square test; ns: not significant; *: p<0.05.

The 1999 survey also highlighted some substantial differences in the way in which different sections of the population view police. As shown by Figure 7.2, respondents in the 18-24 years age bracket were much more likely than the rest of the sample to express dissatisfaction with police behaviour. This age group also had generally more negative attitudes towards police. Data from other sources, such as police statistics on 'cleared' crimes, indicate that younger people are much more likely than the rest of the population to be subject to enforcement action by police, which may help to explain this finding.

Figure 7.2: Proportion of respondents reporting dissatisfaction with police behaviour in the last 12 months: by age group, CJC Public Attitudes Survey 1999

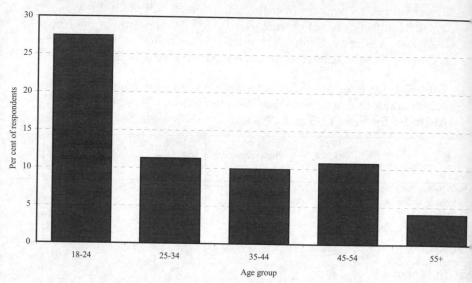

Source: CJC, 2000b.

Defendants surveys

In 1996 and 1999 the CJC surveyed defendants appearing at several large Magistrates' Courts throughout Queensland about their experiences of police treatment and the arrest process. Respondents were approached by independent interviewers prior to their first court appearance and asked if they would be willing to participate in a short, anonymous, survey about their experiences. Around 500 defendants were surveyed in 1996, with this number being doubled in 1999 to facilitate more intensive analysis of the findings. These surveys were undertaken primarily to monitor the impact of new police powers legislation in Queensland, but they also provided the opportunity to collect valuable data about police behaviour towards arrestees. (See CJC 2000d: 6-15, for a full description of the survey structure, rationale and methodology.)

In both surveys, respondents were asked whether they were unhappy with any aspect of their treatment by police, what they were unhappy about, and whether they had made a formal complaint about the alleged incident. Not surprisingly, defendants had a considerably more negative view of their contact with police than did the general public. In both the 1996 and 1999 surveys, just under 50 per cent of the respondents said that they were dissatisfied with some aspect of their treatment by police, with the most commonly expressed concerns relating to the use of force by police and the ways in which police spoke to the defendant. However, while the overall proportion of dissatisfied respondents was the same in both years, there was nonetheless evidence that police behaviour towards defendants had improved between 1996 and 1999. Specifically, a smaller proportion of respondents to the 1999 survey said that: they had been assaulted; the police had been impolite, rude or verbally abusive; or the police had not informed them about their rights.

The proportion of dissatisfied defendants who reported having complained to someone about their treatment fell from 25 per cent in 1996 to 18 per cent in 1999 – a statistically significant drop. This may be partly attributable to fewer serious allegations being made against police in 1999 than in 1996.

Table 7.2: Main concerns expressed by defendants about police treatment, Defendants Surveys 1996 and 1999

Type of concern	1996 (n=489) % of total sample	1999 (n=1005) % of total sample	p
No concern expressed	53	55	ns
Excessive force			
Assault	8	4	**
Rough treatment	11	11	ns
Impolite, rude or verbally abusive	13	7	**
Didn't tell me my rights/provide information	7	4	*
Manner of treatment	9	11	ns
Conduct of Search	5	6	ns

Source: CJC 2000c. Notes: 1. Multiple responses were permitted, so percentages may add up to more than 100%. 2. 'Assault' includes striking or hitting. 'Rough treatment' includes pushed, shoved, rough handling, use of force, grabbed, thrown, heavy-handed, twisted fingers around, dragged from car, tight holds, tight handcuffs, drove car roughly, coercion generally. 3. 'Manner of treatment' includes 'intimidated, harassed, victimised or humiliated me', or 'tried to provoke, upset or frighten me'. 4. ns: not significant; *: p<0.05; **: p<0.01. Not all responses are shown. For a full break down see CJC 2000c.

In general, the picture provided by the defendant surveys is somewhat more positive than the general population surveys, which showed little change between 1995 and 1999. The most likely explanation for this apparent discrepancy is that more fine-grained comparisons could be made with the defendants surveys, because the number of dissatisfied respondents was much larger and the survey allowed for open-ended responses.

Measures of police attitudes

Another area monitored by the CJC has been the ethical climate of the QPS itself. Since 1995, regular surveys have been administered to intakes of First Year Constables (FYCs) after they have been 'in the field' as operational police officers for about six months. The primary purpose of these surveys has been to ascertain FYCs' level of awareness of ethical issues and obligations as police officers, but the surveys are also a useful guide to the state of police 'rank and file culture' generally. The surveys are administered during Academy training courses, which ensures a near 100 per cent response rate (see CJC 1999a for a description of the survey methodology).

The surveys have proved to be an easy and cost-effective way of tracking cultural change amongst junior police officers. The main limitations of the surveys are, firstly, that they measure attitudes rather than behaviour, and secondly, that coverage is restricted to new entrants to the QPS. Logistic difficulties have to date prevented similar surveys being administered on a regular basis to other groups within the QPS, such as detectives and middle-level managers and supervisors.

One of the questions asked of FYCs is how well equipped they feel to deal with ethical problems. Figure 7.3 shows a steady increase from 1995 onwards in the proportion of respondents considering themselves to be 'fairly' or 'very' informed about how to deal with ethical problems. This corresponded with a greater emphasis being placed on ethical decision-making in the QPS Initial Service Program.

The surveys also included a series of scenarios describing various forms of unethical conduct by police officers, with respondents being asked to rank, on a scale of 1 to 10, how seriously both they themselves and a typical officer would regard the behaviour described in each scenario. This type of question is used quite widely in surveys of police about ethical issues (see for example,

Figure 7.3: Proportion of First Year Constables considering themselves to be "fairly" or "very" informed about how to deal with ethical problems (1995 to 1999)

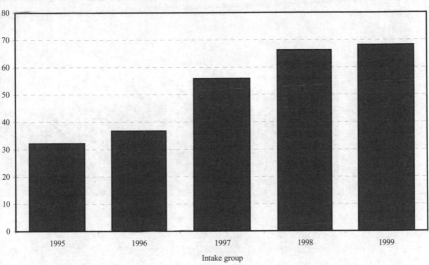

Intake group

Source: CJC 1999a.

McConkey, Huon and Frank 1996; and Klockars, Ivkovich, Harver and Haberfield 2000). In summary form, the scenarios are:

1. off-duty officer tries to avoid Random Breath Test (RBT)

2. officer at bottle shop break-in pockets cigarettes

3. officer retaliates against youth who assaulted female officer

4. accident by police misrepresented in report

5. words added to suspected rapist's statement

6. pick-up outside of patrol area

7. registration check to get details of attractive woman

8. officers accept cartons of beer for Christmas party

9. officer forcefully moves youth on

10. skimming from drug exhibits

Figure 7.4 shows, for each scenario, the average 'seriousness' ratings that respondents said a 'typical officer' would assign to that behaviour. It can be seen that since 1995 the seriousness ratings have increased for

Figure 7.4: The average seriousness rating of scenarios of unethical conduct (typical officer) QPS First Year Constables (1995 to 1999)

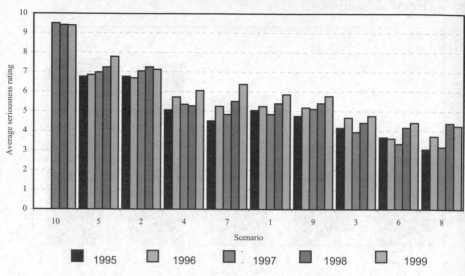

Note: Scenario 10 was not included in the first two surveys. Source: CJC 1999a.

most of the scenarios, albeit only marginally in some cases. The responses relating to respondents' personal views exhibit a similar trend.

For each scenario, FYCs are also asked whether they would be prepared either to formally report an officer who engaged in the behaviour described, or to informally bring the incident to the attention of a senior officer. Figure 7.5 shows that since 1997 there has been some increase for most of the scenarios in the proportion of FYCs indicating a willingness to report, formally or informally, another officer. However, the proportions are still quite low for some of the scenarios, given that the *Police Service Administration Act* 1990 (Qld) imposes a statutory obligation on police to report suspected misconduct by other police.

Overall, the ethics surveys indicate that *some* positive cultural change has occurred amongst junior officers in the QPS since 1995. FYCs declare themselves to be better equipped to deal with ethical issues, seriousness ratings have increased for most scenarios (albeit only marginally in some cases) and stated willingness to report fellow officers for misconduct has also risen. As indicated, the surveys measure only stated views, not actual behaviour. The also cover only junior officers: it cannot necessarily be assumed that similar changes

Figure 7.5: Proportion of First Year Constables willing to take action that would result in official attention for each scenario of unethical conduct (1995 to 1999)

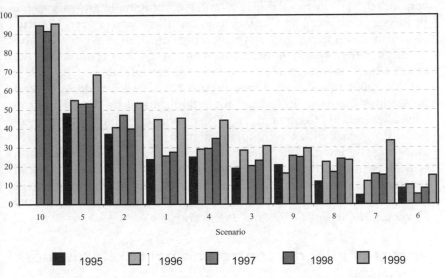

Source CJC 1999a.

have occurred at other levels of the organisation. However, viewed in conjunction with other data sources such as the defendants surveys, these findings add weight to the conclusion that there has been some improvement in integrity levels within the QPS in recent years.

Analysis of organisational controls

Another key component of the CJC's oversight strategy has been to monitor and report on what the QPS as an organisation is doing to reduce misconduct and corruption risks and promote higher standards of conduct. On several occasions the adequacy of the controls in particular areas of activity have been scrutinised in detail, as part of a larger CJC inquiry. For example, the 1997 Carter Inquiry into Police and Drugs focused on the systems that the QPS had in place to prevent drug-related corruption by police (CJC 1997a; 1999b). Similar exercises were undertaken in 2000, as part of an investigation into the unauthorised release of confidential information by police (CJC 2000a) and in the context of a review of police strip-searching practices (CJC 2000e). In addition, the CJC routinely monitors progress in a range of areas by obtaining periodic updates from the QPS and participating in QPS working groups and internal reviews.

The 1997 report *Integrity in the Queensland Police Service* concluded that 'in most respects' current complaints and discipline processes were working satisfactorily, but there was 'a need to focus more on developing and implementing preventive strategies and modifying the organisational climate of the QPS to ensure that the gains which have been made to date are consolidated' (CJC 1997b: 11). The 2001 update noted that progress had been made in several areas since that time, including: the establishment by the QPS of the Ethical Standards Command in 1997; provision of improved protection for internal witnesses; implementation of stricter procedures for assessing the integrity of potential recruits and greater emphasis on ethical issues in training programs (CJC 2001). However, several outstanding issues were identified, including the need to implement the outstanding recommendations of the CJC's reports on *Police and Drugs* and *Protecting Confidential Information*.

Impact of integrity controls on police effectiveness

In addition to monitoring integrity standards, the CJC has addressed the issue of whether increased controls have had an adverse effect on police operational effectiveness. This has been done in response to assertions by some Queensland police officers, and others in the community, that police in the post-Fitzgerald Inquiry era have become more fearful of being the subject of a complaint investigation and therefore less willing to 'do their job'.

A simple way of testing this claim is to examine trends in the level of discretionary police activity, as measured by such indicators as the number of good order and drug offences detected and recorded by police. There is much more scope for police to cut back on proactive as opposed to reactive enforcement activity (such as responding to crime reports and other calls for service). Therefore, if police were being constrained by a fear of complaints, this should be reflected over time in a reduction in the number of 'discretionary' offences that are being enforced. Figure 7.6 shows, on an annual basis, the trend in the number of drug and good order offences per officer for the period 1991-92 through to 1999-2000. For both offence categories there was a strong upward trend over the course of the decade. This is persuasive evidence that the increased focus on integrity and accountability issues has not had an adverse impact on police operational effectiveness.

Figure 7.6: Number of "drug" and "good order" offences detected per sworn officer (1991-92 to 1999-2000)

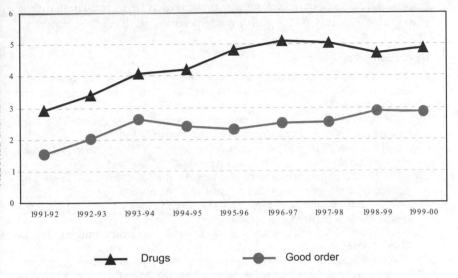

Source: *QPS Statistical Reviews*, 1991-92 to 1999-2000.

Conclusion

While each of the information sources used by the CJC has some limitations, collectively they present a consistent picture of gradual improvement in standards of conduct within the QPS. Specifically, the data show that, since the mid-1990s: the rate of complaints has remained fairly stable, the treatment of defendants has improved, some positive cultural change has occurred amongst junior police, and some additional integrity controls have been implemented by QPS management. Further, these gains have been achieved without any apparent diminution in police operational effectiveness.

There is undoubtedly scope for the CJC to extend and refine its monitoring strategies further, particularly in regards to the more covert forms of misconduct. However, the work undertaken to date has highlighted the potential benefits of using multiple strategies to monitor integrity levels within policing organisations. The challenge now is to persuade policing and oversight bodies in other jurisdictions, and the policy-makers who fund these bodies, of the benefits of this multi-pronged approach.

Acknowledgement

This chapter draws heavily on the 2001 CJC report, *Integrity in the Queensland Police Service: Reform Update*, of which I was principal author. I am grateful to the CJC for granting me permission to use this material.

References

Brereton, D, 2000, 'Evaluating External Oversight', in A Goldsmith and C Lewis (eds), *Civilian Oversight of Policing: Governance, Democracy and Human Rights*, Hart.

CJC, 1997a, *Police and Drugs: A Report of an Investigation of Cases Involving Queensland Police Officers*, Criminal Justice Commission.

CJC, 1997b, *Integrity in the Queensland Police Service: Implementation and Impact of the Fitzgerald Inquiry Reforms*, Criminal Justice Commission.

CJC, 1997c, *Reducing Police-Civilian Conflict: An Analysis of Assault Complaints Against Queensland Police*, Criminal Justice Commission.

CJC, 1999a, *Ethics Surveys of First Year Constables: Summary of Findings 1995-1998*, Criminal Justice Commission.

CJC, 1999b, *Police and Drugs: A Follow-Up Report*, Criminal Justice Commission.

CJC, 2000a, *Protecting Confidential Information: A Report on the Improper Access to, and Release of, Confidential Information from the Police Computer Systems by Members of the Queensland Police Service*, Criminal Justice Commission.

CJC, 2000b, *Public Attitudes Towards the QPS*, Criminal Justice Commission.

CJC, 2000c, *Defendants' Perceptions of Police Treatment: Findings from the 1999 Queensland Defendants Survey*, Research Paper Series, Vol 6, No 1, Criminal Justice Commission.

CJC, 2000d, *Police Powers in Queensland: Findings from the 1999 Defendants Survey Report*, Criminal Justice Commission.

CJC, 2000e, *Police Strip Searches in Queensland: An Inquiry Into the Law and Practice*, Criminal Justice Commission.

CJC, 2001, *Integrity in the Queensland Police Service: QPS Reform Update*, Criminal Justice Commission.

Dixon, D (ed) 1999, *A Culture of Corruption: Changing an Australian Police Service*, Hawkins Press.

Fitzgerald, G, 1989, *Report of a Commission of Inquiry Pursuant to Orders in Council*, Goprint.

Klockars, C, Ivkovich, S, Harver, W, and Haberfield, M, 2000, *The Measurement of Police Integrity*, National Institute of Justice.

Lewis, C and Prenzler, T, 1999, *Civilian Oversight of Police in Australia*, Australian Institute of Criminology.

McConkey, K, Huon, G and Frank, M, 1996, *Practical Ethics in the Police Service: Ethics and Policing – Study 3*, National Police Research Unit.

Prenzler, T, 2000, 'Civilian Oversight of Police: A Test of Capture Theory', *British Journal of Criminology* 40(4): 659–674.

Wood, J, 1997, *Royal Commission into the New South Wales Police Service: Final Report*, Government Printer.

8

Alternative Strategies for Resolving Complaints

Andrew Ede and Michael Barnes

Police organisations are increasingly looking for better ways of dealing with complaints against police. They are turning away from relying exclusively on a traditional investigative approach towards such methods as informal resolution, mediation and managerial resolution. This chapter describes the main features of these different methods, explains their rationales, and discusses their advantages and disadvantages using surveys of police and complainants. The chapter argues that it is crucial to adopt the most appropriate approach when dealing with a particular complaint, and it proposes a set of criteria for deciding which approach is best in which circumstances.

Background

This study is based on developments in police complaints management in Queensland, Australia. In 1989 the report of the Fitzgerald Inquiry was highly critical of the two per cent substantiation rate from investigations conducted by the police Internal Investigation Branch. The report recommended the establishment of an independent body to deal with complaints against police (Fitzgerald 1989). Consequently, the Criminal Justice Commission (CJC) was created in 1990 (now the Crime and Misconduct Commission). On average, about 1,700 'misconduct' complaints and 1,200 'breach of discipline' complaints are recorded against members of the Queensland Police Service (QPS) every year. Breach of discipline matters typically involve incivility, rudeness, intimidation, inappropriate behaviour, inaction or failing to comply with procedures. Misconduct, which is more serious, is defined by s 1.4 of the *Police Service Administration Act* 1990 (Qld) as conduct that:

(a)   is disgraceful, improper or unbecoming an officer; or
(b)   shows unfitness to be or continue as an officer; or
(c)   does not meet the standard of conduct reasonably expected by the community of a police officer.

While these 'misconduct' matters are the more serious allegations, most do not involve serious criminal activity or corruption. Primarily, the matters pertain to officers performing their duties inadequately or inappropriately. For example, while the most frequently made complaint alleges a police officer has assaulted or used excessive force while carrying out his/her duties, in most cases there is no allegation that bodily harm resulted. Over the ten years from 1991-92 to 2000-01, approximately 26 per cent of matters related to allegations of assault, excessive force or other arrest issues. Custody or search related matters accounted for nine per cent; while eight per cent related to an officer's demeanour or attitude; 12 per cent to inadequacies in investigations, evidence handling or prosecutions; seven per cent to harassment or victimisation, six per cent to information breaches; and ten per cent to duty failures or non-compliance with procedures. Only about 14 per cent of matters involved serious criminal conduct or corruption. (The remaining few percent were spread across a variety of 'other' categories.) Thus, it can be seen that there is a large volume of complaints passing through the system with only a small proportion of these complaints involving serious criminal conduct or corruption.

The rate at which complaints against Queensland police are now substantiated has increased dramatically since the pre-Fitzgerald Inquiry days. Depending on how complaints are counted, and what is included in the category of 'substantiated', the rate is around the ten per cent mark (CJC 1997). This rate is common in many jurisdictions (IPCC 1996; Home Office 1997; NSW Ombudsman 1999) and could be said to help deter potential police misconduct. However, a substantiation rate of 10 per cent might translate, in a police officer's mind, into a low perceived probability of suffering a penalty for engaging in misconduct. In fact, a CJC (1995) study found that a sample of 65 experienced officers gave consistently low ratings to the chances of being caught for a variety of disciplinary offences. For example, on a scale of one, indicating 'not at all likely' to seven, indicating 'very likely', in response to the hypothetical scenario of an officer assaulting an arrestee in a jail cell, the average perceived likelihood of detection was 3.7.

What of the 90 per cent of complaints against police that are not substantiated? It seems unlikely that they would all be false complaints, which suggests that a significant number of people who have contact with police are justifiably dissatisfied with aspects of police conduct (Maguire and Corbett 1991). But engaging in thorough investigations of these complaints may not be the best response. Homel (1997: 43) has summarised the criticisms of the investigative model, stating it is,

> predominantly reactive, relying on third parties to lodge a complaint; it has an individualistic, 'bad apple' focus that makes it difficult to attend to systemic issues; it seeks culpability rather than explanation and must negotiate formidable legal, evidentiary, and procedural hurdles; it invokes the notion of deterrence while delivering rates of detection and punishment that are generally below the threshold of effectiveness.

The scope for increasing the 'deterrent power' of complaints investigations systems also appears limited. Putting more resources into complaints investigations is unlikely to lead to a significant increase in the probability of a complaint being substantiated and a sanction imposed because of the difficulty of obtaining sufficient evidence. So, while the quality of formal investigations has undoubtedly improved in jurisdictions such as Queensland, this type of response may not always be the best one and, for at least some complaints, might not be appropriate at all.

Options for responding to complaints

Recognition of the limitations of the investigative response has prompted some police services to look for alternatives. However, when considering options, it is essential that the limitations of the various methods are also identified. One can begin this process of evaluation by going back to a basic question: What should a police complaints system do? The short answer is: detect and prevent misconduct. But, of course, a police complaints system can do much more. It can also:

- enable individual members of the public to express their concerns about police actions (or inaction) and to have these concerns taken seriously and contribute to improved policing practice,

- dispense 'justice' by ensuring that allegations against officers are properly investigated, that innocence or guilt is established, and appropriate sanctions imposed,

- deter future inappropriate behaviour by the officer concerned,

- deter future inappropriate behaviour by other officers,

- inform the Service about the performance of individual officers, their supervisors and the organisation in general, so that remedial action can be taken, and

- maintain public confidence in the integrity of police.

In considering the advantages and disadvantages of different police complaints-handling systems, it is important to be aware of these various functions and to be conscious of the fact that it is unlikely that all functions can be adequately addressed by a single response. For example, if responding to a complainant's concerns about an officer's conduct is to be given priority, then mediation or conciliation processes – in which the complainant plays a major role in determining how a matter is handled and helps decide the outcome – may be more satisfactory. If, however, the allegations raise concerns that the subject officer may be unfit to serve, then the response must focus on establishing the truth of the allegations in a manner that will enable the dismissal of the officer if the complaint is substantiated. In these circumstances, the satisfaction of the complainant cannot be a priority. Their prime role will be as a witness whose testimony will be relied upon when deciding the matter.

The four systems of complaint resolution currently used in Queensland are:

1. formal investigation,

2. mediation,

3. informal resolution, and

4. managerial resolution.

Investigation involves the systematic gathering of evidence to verify an accusation made against someone or to identify the person responsible for an offence. This usually involves a finding of guilt or innocence and the application of a penalty to those found guilty. Evidence gathering can be very complex and scientifically sophisticated, and can involve controversy about the evidentiary value of material. Evidence can include such things as witness statements, or incriminating documents or videotape footage.

Mediation (sometimes called 'conferencing') is an alternative method of dispute resolution that involves trained neutral mediators. (In Queensland these are provided by the Dispute Resolution Centre in the Department of Justice and Attorney-General, and thus are independent of the QPS). Mediation aims to assist the parties to discuss the events and resolve the matter in a way that is mutually satisfactory. Mediators do not take sides, decide who is right or wrong, or tell people what to do. Mediation may be used whether complaints come from police or members of the public. Mediation theory originally required voluntary participation. However, in recent years compulsory mediation has become more common, and studies show that many of the benefits of voluntary mediation are not lost when the parties are required to participate (Spencer 2001).

Informal resolution (sometimes called 'conciliation') is a process where an 'Authorised Member' of the Service, with the verbal or written agreement of the complainant, attempts to informally resolve a complaint made against a police officer. Generally speaking, complaints are considered to be informally resolved when the complainant acknowledges satisfaction with the outcome of the process. The process also aims to address the inappropriate conduct of erring members without the risk of formal punishment or threat to promotional prospects. The process is not designed to establish fault. The member dealing with a complaint by informal resolution undertakes the role of a conciliator rather than an investigator. The Authorised Member speaks to the complainant on behalf of the Service to determine the basis of the complaint. The complaint is then discussed with the subject member in an attempt to obtain one or more of the following outcomes:

1. an explanation of the incident, where the conduct of the member appears to have been both lawful and reasonable,

2. an apology from the member to the complainant if the member admits the conduct and such apology is warranted (the apology may be given either by the Authorised Member on the member's behalf with their knowledge or personally by the member),

3. an apology from the Authorised Member to the complainant on behalf of the Service if inquiries establish that the complaint has substance and no apology is forthcoming or is warranted by the subject member, and

4. where there is no substantiation of either version of the incident, to explain that fact to the complainant and invite acceptance that nothing further shall be done by the Service.

Managerial resolution is a relatively new process being trialled in two of the eight Queensland police regions. It is a flexible process for the efficient and expeditious resolution of complaints against police involving breaches of discipline and less serious misconduct. It is designed to encourage and empower managers and supervisors to effectively address and respond to complainants' concerns relating to a member's competence or conduct through remedial strategies such as guidance, coaching or specialised training. It can include an apology by the officer or by a police service representative. It asks managers and supervisors to take responsibility for staff performance, rather than assuming that responsibility for complaint resolution lies solely with an internal investigation unit or an external agency. The priority goal of the Managerial Resolution process is to improve the conduct of police and prevent re-occurrences of similar complaints. To this extent, managers are not required to formally apportion blame or record detailed information about what happened.

Research findings

Surveys of complainants have consistently shown high levels of dissatisfaction with traditional complaints investigation processes, regardless of whether the complaint was dealt with through internal police systems or by an external oversight agency. For example, Perez (1994) studied three United States jurisdictions with different oversight arrangements (by police internally, by total civilian oversight, and by civilian review after the internal police investigation is completed). In all three cases complainants held negative perceptions of the thoroughness, fairness and objectivity of the complaints systems. In Britain, Maguire and Corbett (1991) found that respondents whose complaints investigations were supervised by the Police Complaints Authority held slightly better views of the process than complainants of unsupervised investigations. However, the majority of both groups were critical of the system. In Queensland, in 1993, the Police Service introduced informal resolution as an option for dealing with minor complaints. As part of a CJC evaluation of the effectiveness of the new system after its first year, complainants who had been involved in a formal investigation and complainants who had participated in informal resolution were surveyed (CJC 1994). Table 8.1 compares complainants' satisfaction with the outcome, and Table 8.2 compares their satisfaction with the way the investigation or resolution was handled. It is evident that the informal resolution sample was far more satisfied than the formal investigation sample on both measures. For both samples, there was greater satisfaction with the process than with the outcome. Surveys conducted in Britain also confirm that citizens whose complaints were informally resolved are more likely to be satisfied with both the outcome and the way in which the matter was handled (Maguire and Corbett 1991).

Table 8.1: Complainant satisfaction with outcomes

	Formal investigation % (n = 144)	Informal resolution % (n = 241)
Very satisfied	9.0	17.4
Fairly satisfied	18.8	42.7
Fairly dissatisfied	18.8	19.5
Very dissatisfied	53.5	20.3
Total	100.0	100.0

Notes: Eight complainants in the formal investigation sample and four in the informal resolution sample declined to answer this question. Chi-square = 26.91, df 3, p <.01.

Table 8.2: Complainant satisfaction with how the investigation or resolution was handled

	Formal investigation % (n = 148)	Informal resolution % (n = 243)
Very satisfied	16.2	34.6
Fairly satisfied	23.6	41.6
Fairly dissatisfied	18.2	13.2
Very dissatisfied	41.9	10.7
Total	100.0	100.0

Notes: Four complainants in the formal investigation sample and two in the informal resolution sample declined to answer this question. Chi-square = 30.94, df 3, p <.01.

Similar results were found in a telephone survey conducted as part of the evaluation of the trial of managerial resolution (Table 8.3). This survey revealed that a majority of complainants experiencing managerial resolution were very or fairly satisfied with the outcome and the process, whereas a minority of those whose complaint was formally investigated was very or fairly satisfied with the outcome and the process.

Table 8.3: Complainant satisfaction with managerial resolution compared to investigation

	Managerial resolution % (n = 39)	Formal investigation % (n = 20)
Very or fairly satisfied with outcome	57	30
Very or fairly satisfied with process	58	40

Note: Caution should be used with these results as the sample sizes are very small. Because of these small sample sizes Chi-square tests were not conducted.

Table 8.4: Complainant achievement of aims

Aims	Formal investigation % (n = 151)	Informal resolution % (n = 242)
Achieved	21.2	32.6
Perhaps	26.5	34.7
Not	52.3	32.6
Total	100.0	100.0

Notes: One complainant in the formal investigation sample and three in the informal resolution sample declined to answer this question. Chi-square = 11.33, df 2, p <.01.

Another part of the informal resolution evaluation involved surveying Authorised Members (the senior police officers who conducted the informal resolutions). Ninety-three of the 188 Authorised Members (49%) who responded to the questionnaire had conducted both formal investigations and informal resolutions. The large majority of these officers thought that informal resolution was a better system for dealing with minor complaints than formal investigation (Table 8.5).

Table 8.5: Comparison of authorised member views of formal investigation and informal resolution in dealing with minor complaints

Response	% (n = 92)
A lot better	89.1
A little better	8.7
A little worse	1.1
A lot worse	1.1
Total	100.0

Notes: Table shows responses only for Authorised Members who had conducted both an informal resolution and a formal investigation. One respondent declined to answer this question.

The informal resolution evaluation also involved the examination of file data to examine the length of time taken to resolve an issue (Table 8.6). This information revealed that for cases received between 1 July 1993 and 30 June 1994 that were classified as suitable for informal resolution, the average (mean) time to process the complaint was 55 days. A comparison was conducted with completed minor allegations not resolved via informal resolution. These allegations were of a similar type and seriousness as those matters that had undergone the informal resolution process. For these allegations, the average time taken to deal with an allegation was 142 days. It can be seen that for minor allegations informal resolution took only about half as long as the formal investigation procedure.

Table 8.6: Time taken to process allegations

	Mean (days)	Median (days)	90th Percentile (days)
Informal Resolution (n = 452)	55	47	111
Formal Investigation of Minor Allegations (n = 3,416)	142	99	293

Note: The comparison group of minor allegations comprised of allegations from the following categories: Behaviour – Incivility/Rudeness/Language (n = 912), Behaviour – Inappropriate (n = 650), Duty Failure – Inaction (n = 1,050), Harassment – Victimisation/Intimidation (n = 506), Traffic – Manner of Vehicle Use (n = 298).

There is also little doubt that informal resolution is considerably cheaper than the formal investigation process. In 1995 the QPS Professional Standards Unit (PSU) conducted a costing survey of investigator time involved in the resolution of complaints. The figures produced do not include time frames and costings for Regional office staff or personnel at the PSU and the CJC involved in processing these matters, only costs based upon the time invested by QPS investigators. All officers conducting complaint investigations were requested to complete one survey form for each complaint investigation or informal resolution worked on for the period 1 July to 30 September. Information was sought on the time spent and distance travelled for each task, and the investigators were asked to make a costing of their time based on hourly salary costs. A total of 212 survey returns were received. Of these 106 matters were identified as investigations, 77 as informal resolutions 14 as resulting in no further action, and five as discipline hearings (ten of the surveys gave no indication as to action taken). The figures show that informal resolution was much less time consuming and much less expensive than formal investigations (Table 8.7).

Table 8.7: Comparative costs in processing allegations

	Average time (hours)	Average cost ($)
Formal Investigation (n = 107)	18.3	500
Informal Resolution (n = 77)	4.9	138

The above findings indicate the value of alternatives to formal investigations according to a number of criteria such as complainant satisfaction, timeliness and cost. However, it is necessary to remain aware of other potential drawbacks to the different complaint responses.

Other limitations of the different methods

A **prosecution-focused investigation**, in which all witnesses are closely questioned and independent corroborating evidence is sought, can leave complainants feeling that they were not believed and subject officers believing that they were presumed guilty. If the allegation is not substantiated, as is often the case, it is difficult to see what benefit flows from the process. If the allegation was true, does the fact that the subject officers were able to avoid being held accountable embolden them to act with less restraint in future? If the allegation is baseless, does the investigation leave the subject officers feeling unsupported? This could undermine their loyalty to the Service and commitment to the job. Investigations, especially lengthy ones, can also be extremely stressful for the subject officer.

Mediation may help complainants convey their personal perspective of the incident to the subject officers and may even result in the officers becoming more self-aware and consequently improving their behaviour. But it will provide little or no information that the police service can use to determine whether any monitoring of subject officers or their superiors is warranted, nor whether any changes to work practices are necessary to avoid complaint-generating behaviour in the future.

Informal resolution may provide speedy and simple relief to complainants in minor matters, but there must be doubt about its positive impact on the behaviour of subject officers, let alone its ability to deal with systemic issues.

A danger with **managerial resolution** is that supervisors will try to minimise the seriousness of allegations or cover up evidence they discover in order to avoid negative implications for their management evaluations. They may also try to dissuade complainants from persisting with a complaint or appealing against an unsatisfactory outcome.

The potential benefits and drawbacks of the four response options for complaints against police are summarised in Table 8.8.

Developing guidelines for matching responses to complaints

From the data and discussion presented above, the following guidelines have been developed which can be applied when considering the appropriateness of each complaint-response mechanism.

Investigations

An investigation may be called for if the allegation is so serious that, if substantiated, it would indicate that the subject officer is unfit to serve. In the most serious cases the nature of the allegation alone may dictate that an investigation should proceed, even if only to allay public concern. In all other cases, an investigation (with all its attendant negative effects) can only be justified if there are good prospects of the allegation being substantiated, and none of the other mechanisms can satisfy the needs of the police service.

Table 8.8: Comparison of formal investigation, mediation, informal resolution and managerial resolution

	Formal Investigation	Mediation	Informal Resolution	Managerial Resolution
Primary purpose	Determine if disciplinary or criminal offence committed	Resolve conflict to parties' mutual satisfaction	Ensure complainant is satisfied that complaint has been dealt with appropriately	Address behaviour of subject officers that gives rise to complaints
Current use in QPS	More serious allegations	Mainly minor allegations	Minor allegations only	Mainly minor allegations. Can be part of resolution for more serious matters

	Formal Investigation	Mediation	Informal Resolution	Managerial Resolution
Conducted by	Commissioned officers or senior sergeants	Neutral qualified mediators	Authorised Members	Subject officer's supervisor
Outcome	Complaint substantiated or not substantiated Criminal or disciplinary sanction	Written or oral agreement (if successful) No sanction	Flexibility allowed Mainly an apology, 'explanation accepted' or 'agree to differ' No sanction	Wide range of strategies available, eg, remedial training, apology, change to supervision No sanction
Benefits	Justice by way of criminal or disciplinary sanction Clearance for the accused Possible specific and general deterrence	High complainant satisfaction Possible specific deterrence	High complainant satisfaction Quick and cheap Benefits complainant and Service when subject officer is uncooperative No negative impact on subject officer	Customised response Addresses systemic issues Moderately quick and cheap
Limitations	Costly and time consuming Low substantiation rates Low complainant satisfaction No systemic improvement (when outcomes are not linked to research) Negative impact on subject officer	No finding No sanctions No general deterrence	No sanction No general or specific deterrence Minimal remedial effect	Possibly low complainant satisfaction Limited general and specific deterrence No sanction

This involves considering such matters as:

- the subject officer's complaints history,
- an assessment of the likely available evidence to support the allegation,
- the complainant's views as to what is warranted,
- the prevalence of allegations similar to the matter under consideration,
- the subject officer's initial response to the allegation, and
- the likely duration and cost of an investigation.

As the seriousness of the allegation decreases, the weight to be given to these considerations varies.

Mediation

Mediated agreements can include agreements to pay compensation and so can be used where a complainant is seeking this remedy. As no formal sanction can be imposed, mediation would not be suitable if the conduct concerned indicated the subject officers were unfit to remain in the Service or unfit to remain at their current rank. One of the problems of the mediation approach is the difficulty in maintaining confidentiality while at the same time satisfying the police service's need to record the outcome of complaints. However, this can be overcome if both parties agree to waive confidentiality. There is no reason for the proceedings to involve only the officer complained against. If the officer maintains that work practices or policies contributed to the complaint-generating behaviour, more senior officers could participate – including those whose lack of supervision or training contributed to the behaviour that led to the complaint. Therefore, the process may be suitable for use in more serious complaints than informal resolution and is particularly useful in circumstances in which the parties might be expected to have continuing contact.

Informal resolution

This method is primarily suitable for minor complaints that raise no concern about the subject officer's ongoing behaviour. Many complainants just want to be heard and acknowledged. When no other interests of the police service need to be considered, informal resolution may be an entirely suitable response. In addition, if more information can be provided about the circumstances of the complaint, this can feed into data used to develop prevention initiatives. At a minimum, the complaint would be entered into the officer's complaint history, which would be considered when future complaints are assessed.

Managerial resolution

The array of responses available under 'managerial resolution' (including guidance and remedial training) offers considerable flexibility in tailoring responses to fit offending behaviour or the circumstances in which a complaint arose. It will be particularly suitable for responding to complainants who have no strong wish to meet with the officer concerned. As managerial resolution does not usually involve the gathering of evidence suitable for a disciplinary or criminal proceeding, it is unlikely to be the right choice for serious matters – that is, those matters that indicate the subject officer should be dismissed or demoted if the complaint is true. To date, there is little information about how satisfied complainants are with this method of resolution. However, provided sufficient care is taken to explain what is being done and why, there seems to be no reason why managerial resolution would be any less effective in satisfying complainants than informal resolution.

Applying these guidelines requires information. The best way to obtain as much useful information as possible is for a complaints officer to work systematically through a set of questions. In many jurisdictions the decision about how to proceed with a case might be made internally by the police service, externally by an oversight agency or by a combination of both (depending upon the seriousness of the alleged offence). Irrespective of who is making the decision, in order to determine the most appropriate complaint resolution method, expertly trained officers should ask the following questions.

1. **How serious is the complaint?** As the seriousness of the allegation is an important determinant, this must be ascertained as soon as possible. Initial inquiries probably need to be made by a complaints officer who is a lawyer or trained detective well versed in precedents and prevailing standards.

2. **What is the complainant's objective?** As complainant satisfaction is an important outcome, it is necessary to find out what complainants want to see happen as a result of making the complaint.

Usually complainants will have little knowledge of the various responses available, and so these need to be explained in a manner that enables them to understand that there are other options apart from a formal investigation that can satisfy their concerns. This can be done face-to-face or via telephone. Care must be taken not to influence complainants to accept a 'soft option'.

3. **What is the subject officer's complaints history?** To avoid repeated use of ineffective responses it is essential to review the subject officer's complaints history to see if there is a pattern of complaints and remedial responses that have already been tried. It may also be useful to consider the complaints history of the unit in which the subject officer works and that of other officers who have been supervised by the subject officer's supervisor. These data need to be comprehensive and should not be limited to the outcome of previous matters.

4. **What is the subject officer's version of events?** Traditionally, the subject officer is not officially spoken to about a complaint until all of the evidence available from other sources has been gathered. It may well be that if spoken to immediately the incident comes to notice the officer will make concessions that will help decide how the matter should be dealt with. Concerns about induced confessions have no application in circumstances where officers can be directed to answer questions. Officers can be re-interviewed if the matter proceeds to investigation.

Conclusion

Each complaint made against police can be looked at as an opportunity to pursue one of the various objectives of the complaints-resolution system to a greater or lesser extent. When deciding which particular objectives will be pursued, it is necessary to consider the advantages and disadvantages of the available response options and seek a balance that best meets the interests of the police service, the complainant and the subject officer. Before deciding which process will be embarked upon, it is essential to gather sufficient information to enable the likely consequences of each of the various processes to be accurately gauged. The aim of this paper has been to facilitate improved 'selection decisions' as to what might be the most effective resolution process in any given circumstance.

References

CJC, 1994, *Informal Complaint Resolution in the Queensland Police Service: An Evaluation*, Criminal Justice Commission.

CJC, 1995, *Ethical Conduct and Discipline in the Queensland Police Service: The Views of Recruits, First Year Constables and Experienced Officers*, Criminal Justice Commission.

CJC, 1997, *Integrity in the Queensland Police Service: Implementation and Impact of the Fitzgerald Inquiry Reforms*, Criminal Justice Commission.

Fitzgerald, G, 1989, *Report of a Commission of Inquiry into Possible Illegal Activities and Associated Police Misconduct*, Government Printer.

Home Office, 1997, *Statistical Bulletin: Police Complaints and Discipline* 21, Research and Statistics Directorate.

Homel, R, 1997, 'Integrating Investigation and Prevention: Managing the Transformation of the Criminal Justice Commission', *Queensland Review* 4(2), 37-49.

IPCC, 1996, *Report of the Independent Police Complaints Council*, Hong Kong.

Maguire, M and Corbett, C, 1991, *A Study of the Police Complaints System*, Her Majesty's Stationery Office.

NSW Ombudsman, 1999, *Annual Report 1998/99*, New South Wales Ombudsman.

Perez, D, 1994, *Common Sense About Police Review*, Temple University Press.

Spencer, D, 2001, 'Mandatory Mediation in New South Wales: Further Observations', *Australasian Dispute Resolution Journal* 12(3) 141-145.

9

Complaint Profiling and Early Warning Systems

Meredith Bassett and Tim Prenzler

Complaint profiling is a new strategy being developed to proactively manage complaints against police and to assist in the prevention of misconduct. Profiling, and associated early warning systems, systematically examine past activities in order to identify future risk areas for complaints and for misconduct. Profiles (or risk assessments) may be made of an individual police officer or other employee, an organisational unit (such as a police station) or a procedure (such as the execution of search warrants or prosecution of offences in the courts). This chapter offers a number of examples and highlights the general principles underlying early warning systems to identify and help prevent misconduct.

Background

Policing in many countries has been faced with recurrent crises of corruption, as well as continuing high volumes of complaints about police conduct. One response to this problem has been to create external agencies with powers to investigate and discipline police (see Chapter 13). At the same time, many police departments are responding to the challenge of external oversight with more creative strategies to minimise misconduct. The need for these strategies was identified by a speaker at a 1999 Australian Internal Investigations Conference:

> A new paradigm for internal investigations is currently emerging as a consequence of the revelations generated from police scandals in the last half century. At the core of this new model is the imperative that the police must take the initiative to vigorously and pro-actively attack and reduce serious misconduct and corruption within the ranks of law enforcement (Knoll 1999: 4).

One component of this 'new paradigm' is the development of early warning systems, and a core component of early warning systems is complaint profiling. Early warning systems attempt to systematically and comprehensively identify, catalogue and assess all factors that may be predictive of future misconduct, and develop interventions to prevent the misconduct occurring (Walker, Alpert and Kenney 2001).

A key predictive factor in an early warning system is complaints against police. Standard mechanisms for dealing with complaints limit investigations to the immediate circumstances of the complaint or related allegations. This ensures that the investigation is not tainted by assumptions based on previous conduct, especially unsubstantiated complaints. While this process is procedurally fair in determining the outcome of particular complaints, it does not contribute to the identification of complaint patterns and profiles of risk. For example, police officers may have substantiated complaints against them with penalties that have not led to dismissal. Over the years the number of substantiated complaints my build up without supervisors being aware of the situation. In these terms, the New South Wales Ombudsman recently reported that:

> Preliminary research by my office suggests in excess of 200 police officers have complaint histories which indicate they may present a significant risk to the police service and community. Some of these officers have very serious substantiated complaints against them, including criminal matters. Others have between 20 and 40 complaints of varying degrees of seriousness (2002: 8).

Processing of complaints therefore has the potential to go beyond investigations, to 'attempt to determine whether there are any organisation-wide implications for the way in which the police service manages its staff or prevents and detects serious misconduct' (Urquhart 1999: 4).

This potential is significant even when complaints are not substantiated. While many complaints are deemed 'unsubstantiated', this is often due to difficulties in obtaining independent witnesses rather than the absence of any problematic behaviour by police (CJC 1997; Maguire and Corbett 1991). However, problematic behaviour may become apparent when an individual police officer, or a particular police unit, is subject to very similar complaints over a period of several years. This is illustrated in a study of excessive force complaints by the Christopher Commission (which followed the Rodney King beating in Los Angeles):

Of approximately 1,800 officers against whom an allegation of excessive force or improper tactics was made from 1986 through 1990, over 1,400 officers had only one or two allegations. But 183 officers had four or more allegations, 44 had six or more 16 had eight or more, and one had 16 allegations (Christopher 1991: 36).

Consequently, the examination and monitoring of complaints can provide police managers with the capacity to identify possible or probable behaviour problems; predict their continuation or escalation; and devise, implement and test preventive interventions (Walker, et al 2001).

The strategies of profiling and early warning systems fit within the four basic rules identified by O'Dowd (1999: 26-28) as essential for effective corruption prevention:

- **'Cast the net wide'** – Profiling casts the net across the whole organisation.

- **'Never stop'** – Profiling is an ongoing long-term strategy.

- **'Be proactive'** – Profiling assesses areas at risk, allowing interventions before the problem compounds.

- **'Make it a leadership problem'** – Profiling is a management tool that allows for expanded supervision capability and information sharing with staff in the pursuit of the organisational goal of integrity.

The challenge for law enforcement is to provide a method for profiling and early warning systems that offers objectivity, fairness and flexibility. At present there is very little information officially available on the extent and outcomes of complaint profiling. Nonetheless, Australian law enforcement agencies are currently collaborating under the sponsorship of the Australasian Police Professional Standards Forum to develop these methods. The New South Wales Ombudsman has also emphasised the urgent need for internal affairs departments to use complaints in a 'comprehensive strategy to identify and assess high risk police officers' (2002: 8). The following sections elaborate on some of the core principles behind this emerging strategy to enhance police conduct.

Principles of early warning systems

An organisation-wide early warning system collects and integrates data concerning a variety of subjects with the aim of identifying circumstances in which misconduct is likely to occur. Because early warning systems are relatively new in terms of their systematic application there has been very little research on them to-date. In 1981 a recommendation was made by the United States Commission on Civil Rights that all police departments have early warning systems to identify and manage 'problem officers'. However, a national survey of a large sample of departments found that only 27 per cent had a system in place in 1999 (Walker, et al 2001).

The study by Walker et al. included three in-depth case studies focused on the impact of early warning systems. The departments selected were Miami-Dade County, Minneapolis and New Orleans. The study concluded that introducing the systems had a 'dramatic effect' on reducing poor performance records and complaints. In summary, the following results were reported:

* In Minneapolis, the average number of citizen complaints received by officers subject to early intervention dropped by 67 per cent one year after the intervention.

* In New Orleans, that number dropped by 62 per cent one year after intervention.

* In Miami-Dade, only four per cent of the early warning cohort had zero use-of-force reports prior to intervention; following intervention, 50 percent had zero use-of force reports (Walker et al 2001: 3).

Discussions by the first author of this chapter with Australian Law Enforcement agencies in 2001 showed that the majority had a simple system in place based on a multiple complaint file approach. Typically, a warning flag is raised when thee to five complaints are received in a given timeframe – typically 12 months. This can be very useful for quick results through interventions with individuals who may have a rapidly escalating behaviour problem. However, 'the key to a successful system is to include as much data as possible. The blending of a wide range of indicators may well bring an officer to the top of the list where a review of a single aspect would not' (Berkow 1996: 24). Little empirical work has been done to identify a full range of valid indicators; nonetheless, the following types of indicators would be useful in a comprehensive warning system (Berkow 1996; Walker, et al 2001):

1. citizen complaints,

2. internal complaints/disclosures,

3. discharge of firearm,

4. unusual absenteeism/sick leave,

5. high speed pursuits,

6. resisting arrest cases,

7. injury to arrestee,

8. failure to attend court,

9. use of force incidents,

10. adverse work performance reports,

11. suspensions, fines or other disciplinary outcomes,

12. litigation,

13. failed prosecution briefs.

These indicators need to be considered in context – for example, the type of duty a police officer performs can influence the number of complaints received. Duty types that have a high number of public interactions, such as traffic duties, tend to receive more complaints (Ede, Homel and Prenzler 2002). Comparing complaint profiles of an officer in traffic with an officer in a criminal investigation branch would be inappropriate. Consequently, an understanding of the different task environments needs to be built into the early warning system. This, in turn, requires the identification of normative behaviours for the organisation and reasonable expectations about what is appropriate conduct in different situations. These conduct benchmarks must be quantified, on a provisional basis, in order to develop a computer-based early warning system that automatically analyses risk data. The benchmarks would incorporate means and variances of demographic groups and organisational units within an organisation. Violations of the appropriate benchmark would automatically signal a warning. Hence, the early warning system essentially identifies individuals or units who most go outside the norm (or benchmark) for other officers engaging in the same types of duties (Berkow 1996).

Early warning systems can vary from the simple to the very complex depending on the variables and indicators used. There are two major types: a simple flag or point system and a multifaceted model. Most Australian law enforcement agencies use a flag system. This consists of a multiple complaint file and makes for a very simple and quick early warning system. Various indicators flag an officer for detailed profiling or intervention – for example when three external complaints are received in a 12 months period or when use of force reports or internal reprimands for poor work performance are recorded. The disadvantage of this system is that it only uses one type of indicator and may overlook other questionable behaviours. This problem may be overcome by including other indicators through the use of a point or index system. Thus several variable scores are added together to come up with an index. Higher scores should show greater risks and identify targets.

A simple example of a point system is $P = A+B+C$, where P is an index or score and A, B and C are variable (or indicator) ratings:

P could be called the Profiling Index
Variable A = number of external complaints
Variable B = number of internal complaints
Variable C = number of use of force incidents.

However, this does not consider the seriousness of each indicator. For example, Officer A receives four complaints within a year, three relating to rudeness and one for intimidation. All of these are conciliated through work place resolution or conciliations, with no apportionment of blame. Officer B may receive two unsustained complaints both relating to sexual harassment. Officer A would score more highly on the profiling index than Officer B, as he has twice as many complaints. However, complaints of sexual harassment are generally considered more serious than complaints of rudeness and intimidation, particularly when Officer B's complaint history shows him receiving at least one unsubstantiated complaint of sexual harassment per year. This pattern shows the need for a more complete profile of Officer B to assess his behaviour. A second example develops this issue of weighting. Officer A is subject to four external complaints and two use of force reports, but no internal complaints. Officer B receives two external complaints, one internal complaint and one use of force report. The result is as follows.

Officer A   4+0+2 = 6
Officer B   2+1+1 = 4

Again, Officer A has a higher score and would more likely be subject to a profile than Officer B. However, the seriousness of the complaint was not considered. The fact that internal complaints are generally considered more serious than external complaints has not been taken into account.

As can be seen from these examples, outcomes from investigations are not necessarily considered when identifying issues of concern, but they should be taken into account within the detailed examination of the profiling process. If a thorough investigation identified the officer as exonerated of the complaint, this should be recognised. By contrast, withdrawn complaints should be considered in the initial review because they may suggest threat or intimidation by the subject of the complaint; or they may be withdrawn for other reasons unrelated to the original conduct, such as a lack of resources by the complainant to continue with the matter.

A major problem with an early warning system based solely on complaints is that complaints alone do not necessarily reveal all potential misconduct. The New South Wales Royal Commission report (Wood 1997) showed that some corrupt detectives had no previous complaint problems. This is because corruption is often a consensual activity and participants are often unlikely to complain. Therefore, there is a need to look for other signs or indicators of corruption, apart from just complaints. These might include intelligence from informants, or adverse comments from judges or prosecutors. Combining the indicators into an early warning system may help identify issues of concern where using only one indicator would not.

In contrast to a simple flag and point system, a multifaceted computer model allows for a more detailed technical approach. It produces more specific results, more suitable for prediction, and provides enormous memory with rapid retrieval of information (van Lanen, Hack-ten Broeke, Bouma and de Groot 1992). The basic strength of modelling is its ability to divide a highly complex reality into interrelated sub-processes that are mathematically defined. Models allow for sensitivity analysis and scenario planning by changing one attribute and demonstrating the potential outcome. Consequences can be estimated by modelling the outcomes of an event or set of events, or by extrapolation from experimental studies or past data. Table 9.1 summarises the main advantages and disadvantages of the two main types of early warning systems.

The following factors should be taken into account when developing an early warning system (adapted from Amendola 1999; Berkow 1996; Walker et al 2001).

1. It should be a component of a broader corruption prevention program.

2. The responsibility for use of the early warning system should rest with Internal Affairs (or Professionals Standards Unit) to ensure uniformity and department-wide coverage.

Table 9.1: Advantages and disadvantages of early warning system types

Type	Advantages	Disadvantages
Simple Flag and Point Systems	Provide quick results. Suitable with minimal data Easy to present Useful for reactive work Can include any variable type Easy to apply consistently Takes into account the combined effect of variables.	Ignores person or situation traits and interactions Difficult to incorporate seriousness ratings. Fails to indicate the real impact of a singular event. Based mainly on complaint or work performance measures and ignores the environment interactions Errors are compounded Only a limited number of variables can be used.
Multifaceted Model	Quantifiable Rapid and cheap after establishment Time compression Continuous updating and modification Sensitivity analysis possible Incorporates all variables Provides a single, accessible, organised body of reference Reproducible	Large data requirements Initial development expensive and labour intensive Validation required Often very complex Inaccuracies may compound results May tend to over-emphasise one aspect of the system. Predicted behaviour may be open to legal challenge

3. It must be based upon risk analysis and understanding of the organisational and task environments.

4. It must be continually monitored and updated.

5. It must provide for early interventions tailor-made to the suspected problem; such as counselling, therapy, training, a warning or an integrity test to confirm suspicions.

6. It must integrate as many sources of data as possible.

7. It must openly practice procedural fairness and the presumption of innocence (see below under 'Individual Profiles').

8. It must promote positive performance.

9. It should always consider factors beyond the individualised 'problem officer', such as gaps in training or better supervision requirements.

10. It should include a communication strategy for conveying plans and summaries of outcomes to employees.

The last point is vital in that staff need to be brought on side by emphasising the value of an early warning system in safeguarding the organisation's reputation and in explaining safeguards to officers' reputations and employment position (Fridell, Lunney, Diamond and Kubu 2001: 43).

Principles of profiles

This section examines profiling of individual officers and of organisational units as core components of an early warning system. It also looks at the issue of profiling vexatious complainants. Although the term 'complaint profiling' has currency, concerns have been expressed that it implies an adverse profile. Some agencies have adopted the terms 'complaint history' or 'risk assessment' instead. We have retained usage of 'complaint profile', but 'risk assessment' appears potentially a more appropriate broad term as it encompasses both an outline and examination and assessment of the issues without any presumption of guilt.

Individual profiles

A profile incorporates an assessment of a member's overall performance and provides appropriate management intervention options and recommendations. The task is probably best carried out by a specialist risk assessment unit within an internal affairs department and separate to an investigations unit. A good relationship with oversight agencies and professional associations will assist with external accountability through the sharing of intelligence and through external scrutiny and assessment of reports. The options outlined in a profile are not meant to be exhaustive or prescriptive. The profile should provide the decision-maker with the best available information to assist with their deliberations. Intervention strategies for profiles should initially be focussed on assistance rather than punitive action. Types of intervention strategies may include psychological counselling, reassignment, remedial training, warnings, performance related undertakings or, in extreme cases, the employment suitability of the officer may be questioned.

It is extremely important that staff understand profiling is an objective process conducted 'without prejudice and with a presumption of innocence' (Ede et al 2002: 9). Officers will feel threatened by the prospect of disciplinary action. They will also be concerned that 'having a record', even if they have been cleared of wrong doing, will prejudice their career prospects or affect people's view of their character. It is therefore vital from the point of view of both organisational morale and ethical practice that subject officers are given the opportunity to explain. The New South Wales Ombudsman has also cautioned that officers should, in most cases, know what their complaint history is, and how it is being used in performance and promotion assessments. Officers should also 'have the right to have noted on their complaint history matters which are disputed' (2002: 15; also Wood 1997). In preparing the profile, analysts may choose to speak with the subject. Speaking with the subject of the profile gives them a chance to explain personal issues that may be affecting their performance and helps decide on remedial strategies. A meeting will often highlight broader issues unknowable from the examination of hard data alone. However, feedback to the subject should be strictly limited to work related explanations (Girodo 2000).

It has been suggested that police departments may resist introducing early warning systems or profiling for fear the files may be subpoenaed and used in litigation. However, having a risk assessment system in place is more likely to protect a department from liability because it shows that proactive measures are being taken to maximise integrity (Walker, et al 2001). Coble (1997) examined the legal aspects of early warning systems and profiles in relation to United States legislation. He concluded that 'fear of liability exposure from having such a system should never be allowed to keep an agency from doing something which it believes is in furtherance of the law enforcement mission and its obligation of accountability to the public' (26). A similar legal examination will be undertaken in Australia as part of the early warning system and profiling development process occurring under the auspices of the Police Professional Standards Forum.

The failure to consider previous complaints when investigating current complaints or when responding to behavioural issues is graphically illustrated in the following two cases reported by the New South Wales Ombudsman (2002: 8).

(1) The Ombudsman recommended that the police service review the management of a detective suspected of perjury. The detective's complaint history included allegations of theft, corruption and bribery. The services *Threat Assessment* did not consider details of his complaint history nor were investigators of those complaints consulted. The assessment determined the officer posed a low risk of corruption. Three years later, the officer's longstanding corruption has been exposed in public hearings before the Police Integrity Commission.

(2) An instructor with a history of sexual misconduct was moved from the Police Academy to reduce his unsupervised contact with student officers. Despite high-level advice barring him from training positions, he was promoted to acting education officer at his new local command. Subsequently he returned to the academy a few weeks later, where he allegedly sexually assaulted a student officer and was criminally charged.

Officers with significant complaints may continue in a pattern of unethical conduct because they feel they can get away with it or because other factors – such as psychological problems – are not being addressed. Figure one, below, illustrates what should happen theoretically if an intervention is made when there is problematic behaviour underlying a history of complaints. The example shows the need for continued monitoring and follow up interventions.

Figure 1: Theoretical model of complaint profiling effect on an individual police officer

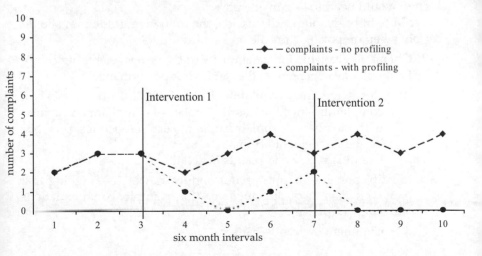

The following case study from the New South Wales Ombudsman's report is a partial demonstration of this model in action. It illustrates how a quick response and a tailor-made intervention can have a positive effect on an officer's future behaviour (2002: 12).

> A supervisor was unaware that an officer who had recently been transferred from a nearby command was still being investigated for her involvement in the unlawful arrest and serious assault of an Aboriginal woman. The investigation was prompted by concerns raised by a colleague and included an inquiry into the officer's alleged attempts to influence her colleague's version of events.
>
> We alerted the officer's new supervisor to the officer's complaint history, which included other allegations of assaults and customer service issues. The supervisor initially placed her under closer supervision and ensured ongoing support before allowing her to resume full duties.
>
> Once alerted to the officer's complaint history, the supervisor immediately recognised the risk of further damaging confrontations with the community. Another incident would also have significantly undermined any attempts by the officer to get her career back on track. There have been no reports of significant concerns about this officer since the supervisor acted.

Readers might be concerned that an officer suspected of a serious assault is allowed to continue working with the public. However, the Ombudsman also cautioned that 'patterns of unusual or uncharacteristic behaviour [may] indicate an officer is suffering from stress or otherwise having difficulties which affect the officer's ability to cope' (2002: 9). Were the ongoing investigation to result in substantiation of the complaint, then a range of penalties or major remedial action would need to be considered.

In light of the above discussion, the following guidelines should apply when preparing a profile on an individual:

- Obtain all available information about the issues, including complaint outcomes, personnel files and work performance;
  - o Detail the full complaint history including the number of complaints since file raised, number of complaints compared with members of similar length of service/postings, previous local management action.
  - o Examine recent complaints in detail.
- Identify possible inappropriate conduct as well as anything that may be in favour of the employee (for example, commendations and letters of praise);
  - o Comment on trends/patterns.

o   Include any local management comment on member, include positive and negative aspects and refer to any contradictions.

o   Analyse information for descriptive statistics (for example, gender ratio of complainants).

o   Make assessment of member's overall work performance.

o   Comment on member's response to any previous non-disciplinary initiatives and any disciplinary action.

o   Provide assessment of likelihood of member rectifying complaint history, especially in current work environment.

• Maintain an objective view of all information.

• Refer to source information in preference to inferences/opinions by other parties.

• Raise any discrepancies concerning source information that may render it an unsound basis for a decision.

• Where practicable, interview the member near the end of the profile process.

• Always provide options and recommendations for intervention;

o   Include a rider that local management's knowledge of the member and local environment may result in more appropriate options being identified.

Profiling work units

While the focus of profiling is generally on individual officers, it can also be used to examine work units or locations as part of a comprehensive risk management and early warning system. Crime mapping and associated hot spot analysis are used in policing to show areas with a high concentration of crime, such as burglary or armed robbery, as a way of targeting preventive efforts. In a similar fashion, in a recent study, Ede et al (2002) showed that complaints are not necessarily spread evenly across a police department but can cluster in certain units, including more intense 'hot spots'. Controlling for type of work done by police (task environment) and the size of organisational units, they found that some police stations and specialist units in their study received many more complaints than others. At a deeper level of analysis, some units had large numbers of complaints because a small number of officers attracted a disproportionate number of complaints (a high concentration). In other cases, the high volume of complaints was spread relatively evenly across a unit (a high prevalence). Where a high concentration of complaints is identified, remedial interventions are most likely to be effective when targeted at the individuals concerned. A high prevalence is more likely to require changes to management style, supervision and police procedures.

Responding to vexatious complaints

Just as some officers get many complaints, some citizens complain on a frequent basis. Some of these may be justifiable but others may be harassing or malicious (NSW Ombudsman 2002). Profiling can also be used to examine this type of complaint. Like an officer, a complainant is identified by the number of times they complain within a given time frame or within a particular frequency. Examining these complaints may highlight a pattern. This could show whether there is a genuine basis for the complaints or if they truly are malicious. There is a trend for oversight agencies to prosecute malicious complainants as a way of deterring this abuse of the complaints system and as a way of reassuring police that their interests are being protected (NSW Ombudsman 2002).

Conclusion

Profiling is an evolving technique and there are a number of limitations and problems that need to be acknowledged. These include the difficulty of identifying genuine misconduct from unsubstantiated complaints, the fact that complaints may be vexatious, and that some police misconduct (such as consensual corruption) may not lead to complaints. In addition, legal considerations associated with profiling and early warning systems have not been fully explored. There certainly need to be safeguards in place to prevent complaints being used unfairly to label police or jeopardise their careers. Initial first responses to adverse assessments should also focus on learning and assistance, rather than punitive disciplinary responses. But, as part of a larger early warning system, complaint profiling – or risk assessment – is emerging as a potentially valuable tool for managing police behaviour and reducing misconduct.

References

Amendola, K, 1999, *Early Warning Systems For Law Enforcement*; Institute for Integrity, Leadership and Professionalism; Police Foundation.

Berkow, M, 1996, 'Weeding out problem officers' *Police Chief* 63(4) 22-29.

Christopher, W, 1991, *Report of the Independent Commission on the Los Angeles Police Department*.

CJC, 1997, *Integrity in the Queensland Police Service: Implementation and Impact of the Fitzgerald Inquiry Reforms*, Criminal Justice Commission.

Coble, P, 1997, 'Early warning Systems: Identification and Correction of Problem Behaviour', *The Journal of California Law Enforcement* 31(1) 23-27.

Ede, A, Homel, R and Prenzler, T, 2002, 'Reducing Complaints Against Police and Preventing Misconduct. A Diagnostic Study Using Hotspot Analysis', *Australian and New Zealand Journal of Criminology* 35/1 27-42.

Fridell, L, Lunney, R, Diamond, D, and Kubu, B, 2001, *Racially Biased Policing: A Principled Response* Police Executive Research Forum.

Girodo, M, 2000, 'Ethical Standards for Profile Assessment, Analysis and Feedback Sessions', in *Behaviour Risk Assessment and Strategic Systems (BRASS), Selected Documents Related to Testing and Profile Feedback in the BRASS Program*, School of Psychology, University of Ottawa.

Knoll, P, 1999, 'Re-Engineering Internal Affairs', paper presented at the *Corruption Investigations Beyond 2000* conference, Sydney, September.

Maguire, M and Corbett, C, 1991, *A Study of the Police Complaints System*, Her Majesty's Stationery Office.

NSW Ombudsman, 2002, *Improving the Management of Complaints: Identifying and Managing Officers with Complaint Histories of Significance*, New South Wales Ombudsman.

O'Dowd, D, 1999, 'Perdition to Probity: Four Steps Towards Ethical Policing', paper presented to the *Corruption Investigations Beyond 2000* conference, Sydney, September.

van Lanen, H, Hack-ten Broeke, M, Bouma, J and de Groot, W, 1992, A Mixed Qualitative/Quantitative Physical Land Evaluation Methodology, *Geoderma* 55, 37-54.

Walker, S, Alpert, G and Kennedy, D, 2001, *Early Warning Systems: Responding to the Problem Police Officer*, National Institute of Justice.

Wood, J, 1997, *Royal Commission into the New South Wales Police Service: Final Report*, Government Printer.

Urquhart, P, 1999, Opening Address, *Corruption Investigations Beyond 2000* conference, Sydney, September.

10

Changing Police Procedures

Tess Newton Cain

This chapter examines examples of changes made to policing processes and procedures in recent years that have had an impact on police integrity. The changes are considered in terms of how they have contributed to the introduction or maintenance of ethical practices and the prevention of corrupt activities by police officers. While the furtherance of 'ethical policing' was the primary rationale for some changes, in other cases some other primary focus for change has had additional effects on ethical standards of policing. A central theme is that indirect changes often have the most significant impacts on what police do, how they do it and their attitudes to both.

In this chapter 'corruption' almost exclusively means what is often termed 'process corruption' in American literature or 'noble cause corruption' in the United Kingdom and, to a lesser extent, Australia (see Chapter 1). This can be defined fairly simplistically as 'illegal actions that violate the rights of citizens for moral considerations' (Harrison 1999: 2). Malpractice of these types has contributed to numerous miscarriages of justice and undermines the rule of law in democratic countries (see Chapter 2). This chapter draws primarily on the United Kingdom experience and in this discussion 'police work' is used to mean criminal investigations by uniformed or plain-clothes officers.

The chapter begins by considering how changing the law can bring about ethical development in policing organisations, given that the law forms a significant part of the context or 'field' of policing (Chan 1997). The second part of the chapter discusses changing police training as a means of affecting procedural and attitudinal change. Reference is made to a case study that examined the impact of the introduction of the national training package for investigative interviewing in the United Kingdom (Newton 2000). More generally, training that aims to foster an ethical approach to policing is discussed. The third part of this chapter examines how alterations to relationships within policing organisations can change the nature of policing and the means by which it is carried out, with particular attention to management and supervisory relationships. Fourthly the chapter considers the impact of changes on the context of policing including consideration of public perceptions about policing and the impact of royal commissions on policing. The chapter ends with some brief conclusions and recommendations for the future.

Changing the law

Some legislative changes are enacted with the primary purpose of changing the way that policing is carried out. A good example is the *Police and Criminal Evidence Act* 1984 (UK) (PACE). Although PACE was concerned with a number of aspects of police investigations, some of its most significant effects were observed in the related areas of interviewing of suspects and the significance attached to confession evidence by the courts. PACE introduced procedural changes such as the creation of the position of 'custody officer' in police stations and the establishment of several codes of practice. One of the most significant changes made by PACE was the introduction of audio tape-recording of suspect interviews conducted in police stations. This is now commonplace in the United Kingdom and, in some areas, interviews are also videotaped. In Australia, there is much more enthusiasm for the videotaping of interviews (Dixon 1997; Karstaedt 1997). Although audiotaping is used in some parts of Australia, it has not been established in the same routine way that is evident in the United Kingdom. This procedural change dramatically reduced the occurrence and the risk of police officers 'verballing' suspects; that is, misrepresenting or fabricating what was said by a suspect in police custody. This has been achieved largely through the simple practical impact of taping of interviews, in that it is possible for them to be scrutinised after the fact (Brown 1997) even if this does not happen very often.

It is important to remember that simply introducing a new law, even one so radical as PACE was when it came into effect in 1986, is not the whole story. The way in which the law is accepted by police officers and the gradual effect that it has on practices and procedures is a relationship that is 'interactive' (Dixon 1997). The effect of legislative change on the way police officers carry out their duties, and on police culture and attitudes, are matters of debate. This is particularly significant within the area of reforming policing practices and policing organisations. McConville, Sanders and Leng (1991), drawing on an extensive empirical study, argue that the introduction of PACE and its associated Codes of Practice had little real effect on the 'working rules' (Smith and Gray 1985) that govern police tasks such as investigative interviewing. They maintained that both before and after the introduction of PACE the process of interviewing suspects was one based around bargaining (whether the bargaining was about bail, charge, other offences or other suspects).

However, this position of 'New Left Pessimism' has been criticised elsewhere (Dixon 1992). Dixon's primary complaint about the thesis of the 'Warwick School' (Dixon 1997) is that their portrayal of police officers as seeking to evade and avoid legal regulation is a misleading oversimplification and that often the approach of police officers to new forms of regulation is 'one of grudging but resigned acceptance' (1992: 523). Dixon, with reference to his own empirical evidence, does not argue that PACE has been an unqualified success in bringing about police reform and indeed would maintain that no legal reform could achieve such a goal. However, he does maintain that legal regulation does have a significant role to play in changing police procedures and that to deny that it has any effect on how police officers work is fallacious (Dixon 1997). McConville and Sanders (1995) subsequently sought to justify their position in terms of a concern with the capacity for police officers to subvert attempts at legal regulation in the furtherance of a crime control agenda and this is certainly an issue that merits consideration. However, it continues to be apparent that any attempt to construct police (in)activity as homogenous, non-reflexive and impervious to a changing context and framework is untenable.

The impact of changes in the law continues to be significant in changing policing, both directly and indirectly. The changes to the privilege against self incrimination brought about by the *Criminal Justice and Public Order Act* 1994 (UK) have had a marked effect on the attitudes of police officers towards the presence of legal advisers during interviews with suspects as evidenced in responses to an attitudinal survey (Newton 2000) indicating that police officers see the presence of legal advisers in interview situations to be as much for their benefit (to prevent complaints) as for the benefit of interviewees. It is not fully clear as to how the *Human Rights Act* 1998 will affect policing in the United Kingdom but it is undeniable that some changes will be seen (Newton 1998; Palmer 2000; Wadham 1999). For example, the issue of disclosure of evidence to defence lawyers by the police is a significant issue within the context of Article 6 of the European Convention on Human Rights which guarantees the right to a fair trial. The move towards more intelligence-led policing with its emphasis on surveillance poses challenges for police operations in the context of Art 8 which enshrines the right to privacy. At a more conceptual level, the culture of policing continues to require reform in order to change the attitude of officers towards legal regulation from one which considers the law to be a hindrance to police work to one which recognises and upholds the essential integrity of due process and the rule of law (Dixon 1999).

Changing the training

Training in all areas of work is a major priority of policing organisations, but to what extent can training be expected to have an impact on developing an ethical approach to policing and establishing integrity in individual officers and police services as a whole? To focus more closely on the particular task of interviewing suspects, it is probably the case that education is the most desirable means of promoting an ethical approach – if only because it is likely to promote a greater sense of 'ownership' and although it is not always easy to evaluate its effectiveness. Training in this area could be expected to be well received by trainees as this task is rated very highly by police officers in terms of importance to their job and training needs (McGurk, Carr and McGurk 1994). However, elsewhere it has been noted that police officers can maintain a high degree of resistance to training that is expressly aimed at ethical issues (Bryett 1992).

This tension is not one that is easy to reconcile either for individual trainers, those responsible for developing training courses or policing organisations more generally. In the early 1990s the Central Planning and Training Unit (CPTU) in the United Kingdom developed a new national training package aimed specifically at interviewing skills in police officers. Until then each police force had devised and delivered its own training courses. Some commentators viewed this as an ethical framework for interviewing (Williamson 1994; Mortimer 1994). However, the training package introduced in 1992 made no explicit reference to the significance of ethics in this area in either of its key components (CPTU 1992a 1992b). While the training package stressed the importance of 'effective' interviewing, no reference was made in either the package or its accompanying statement of principles to the concept of 'ethical intèrviewing'. In *A Guide to Interviewing* there is a short paragraph that deals with 'Investigating with Integrity'. It points out that evidence obtained from an interview with a suspect may be ruled inadmissible by a court, even where PACE and its associated Codes of Practice have been followed strictly. The paragraph refers to the 1988 case of *R v Mason* [1988] 1 WLR 139 CA. In that case the Court of Appeal held that evidence obtained in an interview should have been excluded at trial even though there had been no breach of PACE or the relevant Codes of Practice because the interviewing officers had lied about having found fingerprints at the scene of the crime. In the judgement Watkins LJ made no reference to the breaking of any Code of Practice. The deception of the appellant and his solicitor during the questioning process was considered to be a material consideration that the trial judge should have considered under either s 76 or s 78 of PACE (dealing with courts' discretion to exclude confession evidence) as it was as a result of these deceptions that the confession had been obtained.

Ashworth (1998) notes that the deception of Mason was in fact an act of coercion and that this coercion was then compounded through the deception of his solicitor. What is most striking about the inclusion of this case in the training materials is that its emphasis is on explaining how to ensure that evidence will not be ruled inadmissible by a court. The primary focus of this part of the training materials is one of evidence and protection of evidence rather than ethics. This approach is reflected in *The Interviewer's Rule Book* as well. The effect of this type of approach, which fails to deal with ethical issues and dilemmas in a robust fashion, is that this aspect of the training becomes increasingly marginalised first in the minds of trainers, then in the tone and content of the training that they deliver, next in the minds of trainees and eventually in the attitudes and practices of those trainees in their working environments. Therefore, it continues to be difficult to make ethics real for police officers (Newton 1998).

For many years, police recruits and officers further along in their careers were very critical of training that had nothing to do with 'real' police work or that was theoretical and abstract in nature. To a certain extent, this remains the case (Frank, McConkey, Houn and Hesketh 1995). However, juxtaposed against this is a growing trend towards the 'academicisation' of police training. This is particularly noticeable in Australia where there have been several partnerships established between policing organisations and academic institutions to develop and deliver courses in policing and police studies as part of the overall training programme. A recent example is the launch of the Diploma of Policing Practice developed jointly by New South Wales Police and Charles Sturt University. This is a product of a growing concern within policing organisations that they perceive themselves and are perceived by others to be professionals. However, the tension between an increasingly academic approach to policing and the entrenched belief that it is 'getting the job done' that counts remains and will no doubt continue to do so for a long time to come.

Changing the relationships

The relationships that are significant to policing procedures and processes are numerous and operate at several different levels. Whilst the micro-level of individual relationships cannot be discounted, it is necessary to focus on systemic or organisational issues as a means of identifying corruption risks and managing those risks most effectively. Thus, it is probably more instructive to look at the macro-level relationships that are at play both within policing organisations and also between policing organisations and other key actors and agencies. This section focuses on issues that are particularly significant within the context of management models, especially as exhibited in detective units. Some of the issues and concerns that arise when considering relationships between policing organisations and other actors and agencies in the criminal justice system are addressed in the next section of this chapter.

Within policing organisations, relationships are structured in a fairly rigid organisational hierarchy. However, it remains the case that relationships can be fluid and flexible. The questions of leadership and management are entwined in a consideration such as this although the two terms are not necessarily interchangeable. Alongside this, it is important to keep in mind that within policing organisations, it is those officers who are at the bottom of the hierarchy who exercise the greatest amount of discretion. In many cases these exercises of discretion take place in an environment in which there is little supervision and accountability; that is, on the street. Therefore, it is not so much the direct effect of supervision, management and leadership on working practices that is significant. Rather, it is the indirect effects on the ethos and attitudes of police units and teams that will be the most crucial in determining whether malpractice is encouraged, condoned, ignored or condemned.

A review of the literature in this area reveals a number of strands. The idea of supervision is not one that many police offices are comfortable with, preferring to describe their working relationships as one of teamwork or a partnership. One of the reasons for this unease is that even in the investigation of serious offences, the officer in charge may often be of a relatively junior rank. In a study into the supervision of serious criminal cases conducted for the British Royal Commission on Criminal Justice, officers of the rank of constable were in charge of investigations in 49 per cent of the cases concerned (Baldwin and Moloney 1992). Whilst junior officers appreciate the importance of leadership, this is not necessarily associated with senior management levels within the organisation. Junior officers are likely to perceive chief and senior officers as remote figures who are out of touch with the harsh realities of everyday policing. This can lead to a degree of resistance towards policies, initiatives and procedures that are presented and implemented on a 'top down' basis.

The greatest influence on the working ethos of junior police officers is the example shown to them by their (immediately) senior colleagues, but senior officers can hope to influence rank and file behaviour only if they maintain their credibility with junior staff. Maguire and Norris (1992) used the term 'charismatic' to describe the model of management and supervision that prevailed in Criminal Investigation Departments (CID) in the United Kingdom. A feature of this type of management is that supervision is based on trust, which means that operational officers view monitoring with suspicion. In addition, a great deal of activity within the CID is difficult to monitor. Supervising officers may often adopt the attitude that so long as the results continue to be achieved there is no need to examine too closely the methods by which they have been delivered or the quality of the work that is involved. This, in turn, can lead to a lack of adequate emphasis on the importance of formal and procedural rules in the investigation context (Maguire and Norris 1994).

The dangers of the 'charismatic' model are exacerbated if particular units are allowed to become almost autonomous with certain officers spending prolonged periods of time in the same team and senior officers having a significant input into selection of new personnel. In the past the culture and operation of the CID have tended to foster conditions such as these sometimes with disastrous results as in the case of the West Midlands Police Serious Crime Squad where there were witnessed numerous instances of misconduct by officers including the fabrication of evidence and the covering up of procedural infractions by others (Kaye 1991).

This 'charismatic' model is highly if not wholly dependent on the integrity of the individuals involved. This integrity is fundamentally influenced by environmental factors within operational detective work. If the occupational culture creates undue pressures to obtain results, then this model of management is unlikely to provide sufficient safeguards against either malpractice or, perhaps more significantly, the potential for malpractice to occur if the pressure becomes too much. One means of alleviating such problems is to affect a cultural shift in the supervision and management structures within CID units towards a more 'bureaucratic' model (Maguire and Norris 1992). Such a shift may be affected by defining roles within investigation units more clearly. For example, this would mean that Detective Sergeants would have to see the supervision of junior officers as a distinct and primary function of their rank. The blurring of the roles of supervision and investigation appears to be less of a problem in major enquiries but remains an issue of concern within the context of more routine investigations (Baldwin and Moloney 1992).

A further aspect of 'bureaucratic' management is the move towards monitoring investigative processes by reference to issues of 'quality control' (Maguire and Norris 1992: 113ff). Such a shift is essential if the culture of criminal investigation is to be weaned off the belief that obtaining the 'right' result is the single most important criterion for evaluating the work of individual officers, teams or the police service as a whole. If such an ethos is to be achieved, it is necessary for policing organisations to create a working environment in which the integrity of the process (that is, compliance with legal and procedural rules and precepts essential to ethical investigations) must be demonstrated rather than merely assumed with no institutionalised method of monitoring or assurance. Such a 'quality control' system is based on the twin ideas of independence and randomness (Maguire and Norris 1992: 115). The independence requirement is largely satisfied by the separation of supervisory and monitoring activities from operational duties.

This is exemplified in the use of the Home Office (Large) Major Enquiries System (HOLMES) (Maguire and Norris 1992). To satisfy the requirement of randomness, it is necessary that supervisors undertake the random checking of various detective activities. An example of this, suggested by research commissioned by the Royal Commission on Criminal Justice, is the monitoring of audiotapes of interviews with suspects as a means of ensuring that the 'quality' of the interviewing practice is maintained and/or enhanced (Maguire and Norris 1992). The model that police officers are taught in training sessions would provide an appropriate benchmark for this type of monitoring. From July 1995, it has been a requirement in the United Kingdom that all police officers with a supervisory function (from Tutor Constable upward) undertake this form of monitoring of tape-recording of interviews with suspects (CPTU 1994).

Changing the context

The socio-political context of policing is one that is constantly changing and constantly presenting new challenges to police officers as individuals, to policing organisations and to those who seek to reform policing practice and procedure whether from within or without. As in many other areas of the public sector, the police are increasingly subject to managerialist concerns of accountability (whether fiscal or otherwise), quality of service delivery and 'client' satisfaction. In amongst all this is a continuing concern that the police become 'professionalised' and as part of this professionalisation process a concern as to issues of integrity and ethics continues to prevail.

It is the impact of changing contexts that shows that indirect changes and impacts often have the most significant effects in terms of changing the way police officers conduct themselves. An example from the United Kingdom illustrates this. In 1985, the government enacted the *Prosecution of Offences Act 1985* (UK). Its main effect was to create the Crown Prosecution Service (CPS) and to transfer to it responsibility for prosecuting all offences, including those previously handled by police officers in the magistrates' courts. It was not the primary intention of this piece of legislation that the CPS should act as supervisors of the police. The two agencies were to maintain their independence but obviously were required to establish an effective working relationship. The interplay and its associated tensions are too numerous and complex to explore here but a very simple example can be given to illustrate the sort of effect this type of change can have. Although the United Kingdom law relating to the admissibility of confession evidence (or a damaging admission) does not preclude either a conviction based solely on a confession or the admission of a confession or damaging admission that has not been recorded, the nature of the relationship between policing organisations and the CPS is such that detectives are unlikely to refer a case to the CPS in the absence of any additional evidence knowing that it is doubtful that such a case would proceed to court. It is evident that this relationship is one that is essentially pragmatic in nature. It is also evident that an indirect result or effect of this relationship is that police officers take more trouble to pursue other lines of investigation and evidence collection where previously they might have focussed solely on obtaining a confession from a suspect, with the problems attendant on such an approach (Ainsworth 1995; Gudjonsson 1992; Leo 1996).

Other aspects of the changing context of policing are significant in terms of addressing issues of malpractice and how it is best reformed. Fleming and Lafferty (2000) have argued that recent changes to organisational structures and management models within the policing organisations of New South Wales and Queensland were direct responses to revelations of systemic corruption and misconduct by the Fitzgerald Inquiry in Queensland and the Wood Inquiry in New South Wales. Similarly, the number of agencies and organisations involved in oversight, review and monitoring of the (in)actions of those who work in the criminal justice system has increased markedly in recent years. Examples include the United Kingdom Criminal Cases Review Commission (see Chapter 2), the Independent Commission Against Corruption (ICAC) in New South Wales and the Criminal Justice Commission in Queensland. These form part of a broader movement aimed at increasing and improving the effectiveness of civilian oversight of policing (Lewis and Prenzler 1999).

Conclusions and recommendations

The perception of corruption has the potential to be nearly as damaging as its actual occurrence. Therefore, it is not surprising to find that some changes in police practices and procedures are aimed at preventing such perceptions arising or being maintained. However, it is necessary to ensure that proposed changes or reforms are aimed at substance and not just form. Changing the terminology or the rhetoric may have a significant symbolic impact but this is insufficient in the absence of actual changes to the way things are done. It is also important to beware of rhetoric that deflects attention from areas that continue to be problematic and which are not being addressed either adequately or at all (Newton 1995).

The issue of supervision and monitoring of police activities is central to this consideration of how changing the way police officers do investigative work. This in turn leads to recognition of the increasing bureaucratisation of policing. Again, this is underpinned by a movement away from a 'charismatic' and individualistic style of policing to a more systematic approach (Maguire and Norris 1992). Aspects of this systematic approach are increases in supervision and record keeping as a way of potentially improving accountability. A recognisable example of this sort of development is demonstrated in the changes in the way that detectives run informers in New South Wales. Prior to 1987, there was little or no supervision. However, during the last 15 years, a systematic system of supervision, monitoring and record keeping has been developed with a view to minimising the risks associated with this aspect of police investigations, including the risk of corruption.

This bureaucratisation is linked to an increasingly managerialist philosophy in policing which has been evident in recent times. In addition, there has been a growing professionalisation of policing and a developing concern on the part of policing organisations to portray themselves as professionals. This type of development is not restricted to the policing services; a similar trend has been observed elsewhere in the public sector (Liverani 1997). However, the development of effective systems of monitoring and supervision must go further than increasing the amount of record keeping that police officers are involved in. There is also a need for 'active monitoring' of police activities. This can be resource intensive and costly so is best focussed in areas where there is greatest risk of corruption or malpractice.

References

Ainsworth, P, 1995, *Psychology and Policing in a Changing World*, Wiley and Sons.

Ashworth, A, 1998, 'Should the Police be Allowed to Use Deceptive Practices?', *Law Quarterly Review* 114(January): 108-140.

Baldwin, J and Moloney, T 1992, *Supervision of Police Investigations in Serious Criminal Cases, Royal Commission on Criminal Justice Research Study No 4*, Her Majesty's Stationery Office (HMSO).

Brown, D, 1997, *PACE Ten Years On: A Review of the Research*, Home Office.

Bryett, K, 1992, 'The Preparation of Police Recruits Queensland Style', *Police Journal* 65(1): 49-55.

Chan, J, 1997, *Changing Police Culture: Policing in a Multicultural Society*, Cambridge University Press.

CPTU, 1992a, *A Guide to Interviewing*, HMSO.

CPTU, 1992b, *The Interviewer's Rule Book*, HMSO.

CPTU, 1994, *Investigative Interviewing: Developing Interview Skills*, HMSO.

Dixon, D, 1992, 'Legal Regulation and Policing Practice', *Social and Legal Studies* 1(4): 515-541.

Dixon, D, 1997, *Law in Policing: Legal Regulation and Policing Practice*, Oxford University Press.

Dixon, D, 1999 'Issues in the Legal Regulation of Policing', in D Dixon (ed), *A Culture of Corruption: Changing an Australian Police Service*, Hawkins Press.

Fleming, J and Lafferty, G, 2000, 'New Management Techniques and Restructuring for Accountability in Australian Police Organisations', *Policing: An International Journal of Police Strategies and Management* 23(2): 154-168.

Frank, M, McConkey, K, Houn, G and Hesketh, B, 1995, *Individual Perspectives on Police Ethics: Ethics and Policing Study 2*, Australian National Police Research Unit.

Gudjonsson, G, 1992, *The Psychology of Interrogations, Confessions and Testimony*, Wiley and Sons.

Harrison, B, 1999, 'Noble Cause Corruption and the Police Ethic', *FBI Law Enforcement Bulletin* 68(8): 1-7.

Karstaedt, A, 1997, 'Videotaping Police Interviews with Suspects', *E Law – Murdoch University Electronic Journal of Law*, 4(1): <http://www.murdoch.edu.au/ elaw/issues/v4n1/karst.htm>.

Kaye, T, 1991, *'Unsafe and Unsatisfactory?' Report of the Independent Inquiry into the Working Practices of the West Midlands Police Serious Crime Squad*, Civil Liberties Trust.

Leo, R, 1996, 'Inside the Interrogation Room', *The Journal of Criminal Law and Criminology* 86(2): 266-303.

Lewis, C and Prenzler, T, 1999, *Civilian Oversight of Police in Australia*, Australian Institute of Criminology.

Liverani, M, 1997, 'Police Get in Step with Teachers and Nurses', *The Law Society Journal* (NSW), 35(6): 54-71.

McConville, M, Sanders, A and Leng, R, 1991, *The Case for the Prosecution*, Routledge.

McConville, M and Sanders, R, 1995, 'The Case for the Prosecution and Administrative Criminology' in L Noaks, M Levi and M Maguire (eds), *Contemporary Issues in Criminology*, University of Wales Press

McGurk, B, Carr, M and McGurk, D, 1994, *Investigative Interviewing Courses for Police Officers: An Evaluation, Police Research Series Paper 4*, HMSO.

Maguire, M and Norris, C, 1992, *The Conduct and Supervision of Criminal Investigations, Royal Commission on Criminal Justice Study No 5*, HMSO.

Maguire, M and Norris, C, 1994, 'Police Investigation: Practice and Malpractice', *Journal of Law and Society* 21(1): 72-84.

Mortimer, A, 1994, 'Asking the Right Questions', *Policing* 10(2): 111-124.

Newton, T, 1995, 'Cop Talk: the Changing Rhetoric of the Police Service', *New Law Journal* 145(6712): 1362-1363.

Newton, T, (1998) 'The Place of Ethics in Investigative Interviewing by Police Officers', *The Howard Journal of Criminal Justice* 37(1): 52 -69.

Newton, T, 2000, *Reducing Miscarriages of Justice: Police Training and the Development of 'Ethical' Interviewing*, PhD thesis, University of Wales.

Palmer, P, 2000, 'Human Rights and British Policing', *The Police Journal*, 73(1): 54-60.

Smith, D and Gray, J, 1985, *Police and People in London*, Gower.

Wadham, J, 1999, *Crime, the Human Rights Act and Public Law*, <http://www.liberty-human-rights.org.uk/mhrp6c.htm>.

Williamson, T, 1994, 'Reflections on Current Police Practice', in D Morgan and G Stephenson (eds), *Suspicion and Silence*, Blackstone.

11

Integrity Testing

Ross Homel

Integrity testing involves placing elected officials or employees of public or private organisations in situations that have been constructed in such a way that a clear opportunity to behave in a dishonest, negligent, or otherwise improper manner is available. Such situations occur routinely on a daily basis as part of the normal work environment of tested individuals, but their behaviour in those situations is not normally observed by management or by other responsible authorities.

The essential purpose of integrity testing is to add the element of *surveillance*, without inducing or enticing a person to act improperly. Should a situation be constructed in such a manner that inducements to act improperly were present that are not a normal feature of the work environment, a court would most likely find that the test constituted entrapment and was therefore not legal (Prenzler and Ronken 2001). Ideally, the situations and opportunities utilised in integrity testing are indistinguishable from those occurring 'naturally.'

In the United States and some other countries, integrity testing is widely used as a tool by large organisations to check the behaviour of employees. Testing of public officials in the United States is by no means restricted to police, although the high visibility of police corruption in New York and other cities has ensured that testing of police has received a great deal of publicity (Anechiarico and Jacobs 1996; Marx 1992). An example of a random test used by the NYPD is to have a factory or shop set up with an open door, or to have it exhibit other signs that it has been burgled. The premises will be fitted with covert videos to monitor the actions of officers (Shawyer 1997: 4).

In this chapter I argue two propositions:

1. That *random integrity testing* is the only way to create a general deterrent impact in police agencies that will be substantial and

permanent; targeted testing will fail to achieve this effect, but should nevertheless be used in tandem with random testing as part of a proactive enforcement strategy.

2. That in a social context where there is strong community pressure to make policing more professional and accountable, random integrity testing can make a major contribution to *improvements in police culture and ethical standards* precisely because it coerces behaviour change rather than attempting (in the first instance) attitude change.

I take it for granted that integrity testing is *only a tool* and must be embedded in a broad management strategy for the prevention of misconduct (Homel 1997; Goldsmith 2001). The tool is however often poorly constructed or misapplied because the theory of deterrence that underpins its use is not well understood.

Integrity testing is usually thought of as either *targeted* or *random*, but in reality there is a more complex continuum. Strictly speaking, random testing involves the use of rigorous statistical procedures to draw a probability sample of individuals or situations, but in practice it usually simply means that individuals who are not under suspicion for any specific kind of misconduct or corruption are selected in a more or less haphazard fashion and tested. In addition, most forms of random testing are based on intelligence about problem areas or organisational sub-units and are therefore not random across the whole organisation, although they may be effectively random in how they are implemented *within* the area or section. Similarly, targeted testing need not involve a specific individual since it may not be known exactly who is engaging in corrupt practices, but it may be clear that one or more individuals in a small group are involved. The group in that situation becomes the target.

Integrity testing can be applied both to serious corruption (such as taking bribes or protecting drug dealers) and to less serious forms of misconduct (like being drunk on duty or accepting gratuities), but generally where implemented it is directed at more serious matters (Prenzler and Ronken 2001). This is partly because these offences warrant the kind of strong response that integrity testing embodies, and partly because other remedies, such as improved supervision and video surveillance, are more appropriate for many acts of misconduct. Nevertheless what is genuinely serious, or what is minor but could be a stepping stone to what is serious, requires careful thought.

The current policy of police services in Australia is to support targeted testing, although only New South Wales and Victoria police have moved from policy to practice (Prenzler and Ronken 2001). The Criminal Justice Commission in Queensland has also conducted targeted testing in consultation with police (Carter 1997). Random testing is currently 'off the agenda' in all States and Territories. Since police unions generally support targeted testing but all vehemently oppose random testing, and since police services in this country are not yet under sufficient political pressure to introduce such radical measures, random testing has little chance of being implemented in Australia in the near future. A reasonable long-term goal would be the implementation of targeted testing in all jurisdictions, followed some years later by random testing regimes when practical and procedural problems have been resolved and the need for random testing is perceived politically to be inescapable. Targeted testing could continue as a parallel program.

In many respects the current situation is analogous to the time when breath testing technology was being introduced in Australia in the late 1960s. It took time for the police and the community to get used to the idea of the targeted enforcement of drink-driving laws using the new technology, and it was not until 1976 in Victoria and 1982 in NSW that random breath testing (RBT) was introduced (Homel 1988). Moreover, random testing was not introduced without considerable argument and debate, which really centred around civil liberties concerns as well as the concept of *general deterrence*. Of course there are essential differences between RBT and random integrity testing, especially the fact that when an RBT is conducted the offence has already been committed, but these differences are not in my view sufficient to nullify the useful parallels between the problems and the techniques, and I draw repeatedly on the parallels between the two kinds of tests in this chapter.

The chapter is divided into four sections. The first argues the need for integrity testing. This is followed by a discussion of deterrence, including a defence of random integrity testing as the only form of integrity testing that has the potential to really reduce corruption. The third section addresses criticisms of random testing, and finally some implementation issues are discussed.

The need for random integrity testing

The literature on police corruption is replete with references to the police code of silence, and more generally to the malign influences of police culture on professional standards and public accountability.

Goldstein (1975: 30) for example refers to 'the blue curtain – the conspiracy of silence among police.' Police see the worst side of humanity, and discover that dishonesty and corruption are by no means restricted to those the community sees as criminal. The average police officer sees in her career many individuals of high reputation engaging in practices such as defrauding insurance agencies by false claims or hiding earnings to avoid tax, so she often develops a cynical attitude which views corruption as a game in which every person – including police – is out to get his share.

Bayley observes that the people who join the police '… have a tremendous need to fit in, to belong, to demonstrate that they are a reliable part of the group' (1995: 100). Thus it is not surprising that loyalty to fellow officers is an important part of the police culture, and that this is sometimes a factor in becoming involved in corrupt practices. As the New York Knapp Commission noted: 'Accepting payoff money is one way for an officer to prove that he is one of the boys and that he can be trusted' (in Goldstein 1975: 15).

Many Australian police officers still express a reluctance to report misconduct by their peers, partly because of fear of ostracism. A Queensland study of ethical decision making by recruits, first year constables, and experienced police indicated that a large majority would not formally report six kinds of behaviours that clearly constitute misconduct under the *Police Service Administration Act 1990*, and (except for the recruits in some scenarios) most would not even report the incident informally (CJC 1997).

Recent revelations of the Mollen Commission in New York City, the Wood Royal Commission in NSW, and the Carter Inquiry in Queensland strongly support the research findings of the CJC, that police corruption and the attitudes and practices that foster it are extremely difficult to eradicate. Carter (1997) is particularly scathing in his comments on the effects of police culture on the ability of the complaints investigation system to deter misconduct. He notes that there was not a single 'rank and file' police officer who provided useful original information that was worthy of investigation. Misconduct must be understood not as the actions of a few 'bad apples' but as a systemic problem that is an inevitable by-product of an organisation's activities that routinely bring a likely offender and an opportunity for misconduct into alignment, in the absence of a capable guardian (Homel 1997).

If therefore a deterrence model is to be relied on as a mechanism for behaviour change, a more effective means of delivering a deterrent threat than reactive complaints investigations must be found. The essential aim of such a program should be to increase the perceived risk of detection and punishment, especially for serious forms of misconduct such as drug-related offences.

General deterrence and random integrity testing

Deterrence can be thought of as the omission of an act as a response to the perceived risk and fear of punishment for contrary behaviour. In general, we can be deterred from certain actions by their inconvenience or cost (which includes but is not limited to legal penalties), we can be deterred by the fear of being publicly embarrassed in certain situations, and frequently we are deterred by our own consciences. Non-legal or informal aspects of deterrence are as important in police organisations as they are anywhere else. For example, the great majority of police are honest most of the time. This is not usually because they are constantly looking over their shoulders wondering whether they'll be detected, but because they have been brought up to believe that 'honesty is the best policy.'

However, it is a mistake to assume that more than a small minority of people in any walk of life, including police, are honest in *all* possible situations. Most people occasionally commit small acts of dishonesty when faced with certain temptations and opportunities, and a few people are consistently dishonest when they think they can get away with it (Gabor 1994). Thus it is a mistake to divide police into the 'corrupt' and the 'non-corrupt,' as if these were attributes of individuals that are fixed for all time. People can learn dishonest practices, and they can unlearn them through training, through example, or through effective enforcement. And dishonest or corrupt practices that the rank and file might be tempted to commit can be prevented by tightening up management systems or by powerful deterrent methods like random integrity testing.

Like the force of conscience, fear of embarrassment or looking silly is as potent for police as for anyone else. Sometimes this works to encourage law abiding behaviour, since the thought of being publicly disgraced after being found out for some serious act of misconduct is probably a particularly important consideration for many police. On the other hand, fear of embarrassment can work to the advantage of a corrupt pocket of police, as in the example quoted earlier from the Knapp report, and is undoubtedly one factor contributing to the code of silence. This illustrates that informal deterrence can sometimes operate to *discourage* compliance with the law. On the other hand legal deterrence can in some circumstances *reinforce informal sanctions* that encourage compliance with the law, or undermine informal sanctions that discourage compliance. Random integrity testing could have similar effects to RBT in this respect (Homel 1988). Because a genuine program of random testing would be *unavoidable*, there would be no loss of face for a young officer to refuse an invitation from a more experienced officer to become involved in a corrupt act. Indeed, he could argue that the officer making the offer might be an undercover operative engaged in integrity testing! This could be a very important dimension of random integrity testing.

Another way that RBT has influenced the behaviour of motorists over time is by making it *less morally acceptable* to drive after drinking (Homel 1988). If behaviour change is coerced (people are forced to do the right thing), eventually they may change their beliefs to fit in with their new behaviour. In the context of police misconduct, this suggests that major long-term changes in police attitudes and police culture could be affected by a vigorous, well-publicised regime of random integrity testing.

To summarise these points, an effective deterrent like random testing can help undermine the negative effects of police culture by providing a face-saving excuse to refuse invitations to become involved in corrupt activities. It can also have a long-term educative effect on the whole organisation by causing beliefs to fall into place with behaviours altered through fear of detection and punishment.

Deterrence is hard to achieve and is unstable

Criminological research has repeatedly found that the certainty of punishment is far more important than severity (Nagin 1998). In fact *perceived* certainty is the key. Deterrence must be understood primarily as a communication process that depends for its success on extensive publicity. For a rational offender to be influenced by the threat of punishment, he must believe that there is a reasonable chance that the punishment will actually be imposed. If he considers that he is too smart to get caught – quite a common attitude – it doesn't matter how tough the penalties are.

It is the central importance of the perceived chances of detection and punishment that makes randomised enforcement programs so much more effective than targeted approaches. For years police in Australia used targeted enforcement methods to detect drinking drivers, but even with the huge boost provided by the introduction of breathalyser technology alcohol-related road deaths continued to rise until random breath testing became widely used. RBT did what targeted testing failed to do: it increased the perceived chances of detection to the point where the driving population radically changed their lifestyles. The essence of RBT is its *unpredictability* – people are left guessing as to whether the chances of detection are actually high or low on any given occasion, so they over-compensate by assuming for safety that the chances are higher than they really are. This phenomenon of 'ambiguity aversion' underlies the success of all randomised enforcement regimes (Nagin 1988: 10; Sherman 1990).

Random enforcement programs like RBT only work when they are conducted in a highly visible manner and are well publicised. The publicity reinforces the impression of ubiquity or omnipresence, and means that a deterrent effect is achieved even when the actual number of random testing operations is fairly low. However, unless potential offenders actually see random testing in operation at least occasionally, or hear about it from others, they are not likely to be deterred by the publicity for very long. Publicity is necessary but not sufficient – it must be reinforced by regular, highly visible, unpredictable random enforcement.

One particularly important property of random testing already noted is that it takes away one of the key defences of the offender who considers that he is too smart to get caught, since there is nothing he can do through his own cleverness to avoid being tested. It follows that undetected offenders can only be deterred by testing that is known to be random, since they do not believe that they will ever be targeted. Even if they *are* targeted and caught, it is only after a long period of offending that should have been prevented before it became entrenched.

However, any deterrence-based program is inherently unstable in its effects, and must be kept up and even intensified over time until genuine attitude change takes place in the target population. Officers who do the right thing because they fear getting caught could become discouraged if they never see or hear of random integrity testing, and decide eventually to take the risk involved in committing a corrupt act. Once a person has offended and not been caught (the most likely outcome), he will be further encouraged in his criminal career. On the other hand, if an officer refrains from corruption through fear and is constantly observing or hearing of random testing, his decision to comply with the law will be reinforced and might eventually become a habit. It is also quite possible that once an officer ceases to cultivate his old associates and engages in alternative (lawful) activities, it becomes more difficult for him in the future to engage in corrupt practices because the old opportunities are not so readily available.

These scenarios clarify the dynamic nature of the deterrence process, with potential offenders constantly reassessing the official threat and modifying their behaviours accordingly. Because the enforcement pressure must be kept up in order to maintain a compliant population, it is essential that random enforcement be supported by other measures, including publicity, management system reforms to reduce opportunities, and ethics training.

Criticisms of random integrity testing

The theory may be fine, but what happens when one tries to put these ideas into practice? Anti-random testing arguments may be found in the New South Wales Royal Commission Report (Wood 1997), in a KPMG (1996) report to the New York City Commission to Combat Police Corruption, in Marx (1992), Anechiarico and Jacobs (1996) and in some other sources. The chief criticisms (apart from those to do mainly with ethics and entrapment) are that random testing:

1. could not be tailored to the same degree nor be as sophisticated as targeted tests;

2. mostly involved officers in groups rather than individually;

3. sometimes did not work as a test since the opportunity for corrupt conduct was not recognised or officers realised they were involved in a 'set up;'

4. does not produce an accurate measure of corruption since (in New York) no criminal prosecutions ensued in the first three years;

5. has a negative effect on morale since police feel they are not trusted, and generally fails to promote a professional and ethical workplace;

6. impedes efficiency since police are constantly 'looking over their shoulders' wondering if they are being checked;

7. drains resources from targeted testing or from other covert methods that have a better chance of apprehending offenders.

8. elides the question whether an officer is 'corruptible' into the question whether he or she is 'corrupt'.

Some of these criticisms are difficult to address at the empirical level, since there is little research to guide discussion. The argument that random integrity testing could cause serious morale problems is clearly important, but would depend critically on how it is implemented and managed. If it is marketed in a positive way, many police could in fact be very supportive, arguing that the honest officer can only benefit.

A specific aspect of the morale argument, raised by Dorothy Bracey (in Cornish 1997), is that integrity testing focuses too much on the decision-making and actions of lower ranking police, and is not directed at people higher in the organisation who can make corrupt decisions. As a result, most police will eventually become cynical about integrity testing and become more distrustful of their superiors. This suggests that there should be developed a specific integrity testing program for senior officers, or that at the very least transparent measures to improve accountability should be introduced.

I have already argued that random testing can over time contribute to an improved ethical climate in the police, and so am not persuaded by arguments that it simply creates a climate of fear that inhibits the growth of proper professional attitudes. Nor am I much persuaded by arguments based on the distinction between 'corrupt' and 'corruptible' police, since as I have already suggested the distinction is theoretically and empirically incoherent.

The potentially most damaging criticisms of random integrity testing are that it is operationally too difficult and too expensive to implement in a way that delivers a meaningful deterrent. From the KPMG report the criticism that officers cannot be randomly tested in isolation appears to have substance, since the average number of officers involved was slightly more than two. However, this is not necessarily a fatal objection to random testing. The real question is whether the situations used mimic the real life situations faced by officers. In practice police frequently work at least in pairs, particularly in responding to calls for service, and so would not necessarily be faced with temptations and opportunities for misconduct on their own.

More generally, the problem of police misconduct is so serious that determined development and evaluation of random integrity testing is required, beginning in a small way and drawing on the experience of New York and other relevant agencies. The main requirement in the process of development is that the general deterrent aims of random testing be kept clearly in focus. *It is not a device for catching offenders.* For this, targeted testing and other covert methods are necessary.

The KPMG report makes much of the fact that the 'hit rate' with random testing in New York City is very low. In 1995 and the first six months of 1996, 826 random tests were conducted involving 1,811 officers. These resulted in one criminal failure that was not prosecuted. When procedural failures were also counted in 1996, there were seven failures out of 762 officers tested. To put this in perspective, the failure rate for criminal offences was only 0.06 per cent or zero, depending on whether the single non-prosecution is counted. However, the failure rate in other forms of random testing is also low. For example, RBT typically has a hit rate of about 0.35 per cent in NSW, which if applied to 1,811 tested officers would result in about six criminal failures. Moreover, most positive blood alcohols detected in RBT are at the low end of the spectrum – very few are higher than 0.15, or the most serious or criminal range of the distribution. In fact, the blood alcohol concentrations (BACs) detected are more like the procedural failures counted in the KPMG report. If these are included with the single criminal violation, the hit rate becomes 0.4 per cent, very similar to RBT.

The point is that it is of course not valid to evaluate the success of RBT on the basis of detected drinking drivers, although this was in fact a frequent criticism in the early days. The impact of RBT is only validly assessed by determining its deterrent effects on accidents, and we know from extensive research (eg, Henstridge, Homel and Mackay 1997) that this impact is very considerable, *despite the very low hit rate.* So the real question to ask about random integrity testing is not 'what is the hit rate?' but 'what is the general deterrent effect?' At this point the KPMG report is actually quite supportive of random testing, concluding that a 'sense of omnipresence' might well have been achieved, or if it wasn't, it had the potential to be achieved.

As the report concludes, random testing has face validity as a deterrent, and needs to be refined and focused rather than abandoned. The amount of skill and the degree of resources required to mount sophisticated random tests that are not easy to see through and which offer meaningful opportunities for misconduct are clearly quite considerable, and will undoubtedly limit the number of random tests conducted in any year. More time is required to properly evaluate the technique using valid measures. Indicators of organisational change could be developed through regular use of ethical scenarios in surveys, while direct measures of the deterrent effect of random testing could also be developed in surveys of police repeated over time, supplemented by focus group discussions and time series analyses of the complaints statistics. Statistical methods for the analysis of rare events should also be applied to data collected over a long period on the numbers of police who fail random tests.

Implementation of random integrity testing

A regime of testing designed both to be an effective deterrent and to be practical would have certain distinct features. Drawing on deterrence theory and on the experience of the NYPD some of these are discussed briefly in this concluding section.

1. The regime must be accepted, supported, and implemented by the police, ideally in partnership with an external oversight body. The NYPD program is incorporated into a *departmental philosophy* endorsed by the Commissioner and supported by managers who are held accountable for implementing corruption prevention and detection strategies. Managers can assist through a policy of inclusion whereby they are called upon by Internal Affairs to procure whatever is necessary to implement a test. Internal Affairs is no longer a secret and isolated unit, and commanders are involved in its operations on a revolving basis.

2. The unions represent a particular set of interests that predispose them to be very suspicious of measures perceived as attacks on the integrity and working conditions of police, but in New York support is secured so that *responsibility for corruption prevention permeates the organisation at all levels, including the union.*

3. Random integrity testing must be widely and continuously publicised, and should be carried out all the time; it is not sufficient to advertise something that is rarely conducted. Any potential offender must believe *that there is nothing they can do through their own cleverness to avoid being tested.* Moreover, publicity protects the Service from the criticism that it is acting in an underhand way, or persecuting particular individuals.

4. Testing must not have a punitive emphasis with the aim of trapping and punishing as many officers as possible. Penalties for misconduct detected as a result of random testing should be no more severe than the penalties that are applied when misconduct

comes to notice in other ways. Wherever possible in minor matters the offender should be offered assistance, education and mentoring.

5. There is a need for constant monitoring and evaluation in terms of behaviour, morale and attitude change using measurement techniques not dependent on the results of tests. The possibility of unanticipated results should be anticipated (for example, in New York some officers are engaging more in off-duty corruption). *The results of random integrity tests and other integrity programs should be reported publicly every year.*

6. Operational details are best worked out by local police. In New York there are no permanent scenario writers, with test scenarios being brainstormed by team members on an ongoing basis. 'Being creative in the development of suitable scenarios is the most difficult job they have at the unit' (Shawyer 1997: 3). Many practical problems must also be overcome, such as the need to avoid the use of the 911 (000) phone call due to growing police awareness that they may involve a test.

Acknowledgements

I am indebted to Inspectors Christopher Reeves and Ron Vincent of the CJC and to members of the *Small Group to Develop Proposals Regarding Enhanced Professional Responsibility Within the Queensland Police Service* who commented on an earlier draft of this paper.

References

Anechiarico, F and Jacobs, J, 1996, *The Pursuit of Absolute Integrity: How Corruption Control Makes Government Ineffective*, University of Chicago Press.

Bayley, D, 1995, 'Getting Serious About Police Brutality', in P Stenning (ed), *Accountability for Criminal Justice: Selected Essays*, University of Toronto Press.

Carter, W, 1997, *Police And Drugs: A Report of an Investigation of Cases Involving Queensland Police Officers*, Criminal Justice Commission.

Cornish, P, 1997, *United States Models of Corruption Prevention Including Integrity Testing*, South Australia Police Service.

CJC, 1997, *Integrity in the Queensland Police Service: Implementation and Impact of the Fitzgerald Inquiry Reforms*, Criminal Justice Commission.

Gabor, T, 1994, *'Everybody Does It!': Crime by the Public*, University of Toronto Press.

Goldsmith, A ,2001, 'The Pursuit of Police Integrity: Leadership and Governance Dimensions', *Current Issues in Criminal Justice* 13(2): 185-202.

Goldstein, H, 1975, *Police Corruption: A Perspective on its Nature and Control,* Police Foundation.

Henstridge, J, Homel, R and Mackay, P, 1997, *The Long-Term Effects of Random Breath Testing in Four Australian States: A Time Series Analysis,* Federal Office of Road Safety.

Homel, R, 1988, *Policing and Punishing the Drinking Driver: A Study of General and Specific Deterrence,* Springer-Verlag.

Homel, R, 1997, 'Integrating Investigation and Prevention: Managing the Transformation of the Queensland Criminal Justice Commission', *Queensland Review,* 4(2): 37-50.

KPMG, 1996, *Report to the New York City Commission to Combat Police Corruption: The New York City Police Department Random Integrity Testing Program,* KPMG.

Marx, G, 1992, 'When the Guards Guard Themselves: Undercover Tactics Turned Inward', *Policing and Society* 2(3) 151-172.

Nagin, D, 1998, 'Criminal Deterrence Research at the Outset of the Twenty-First Century', in M Tonry (ed), *Crime and Justice: A Review of Research,* vol 23, University of Chicago Press.

Prenzler, T and Ronken, C, 2001, 'Police Integrity Testing in Australia', *Criminal Justice: The International Journal of Policy and Practice* 1(3), 319-342.

Shawyer, J, 1997, *Integrity Testing Research Documents,* Victoria Police.

Sherman, L, 1990, 'Police Crackdowns: Initial and Residual Deterrence', in M Tonry and N Morris (eds), *Crime and Justice: An Annual Review of Research,* University of Chicago Press.

Wood, J, 1997, *Royal Commission into the New South Wales Police Service,* Final Report, Government Printer.

12

Civil Litigation

Jude McCulloch

Civil litigation against police is an emerging issue internationally and in Australia. The trend towards more civil litigation has been combined with substantially larger judgments and settlements for plaintiffs. All indications are that the upward trend in civil litigation will continue unless timely and proactive action is taken.

Focusing on policing in the Australian State of Victoria, this chapter examines the extent and nature of civil litigation, including factors – internal and external to policing – that are contributing to the increased frequency and cost of these actions. It also looks at risk and risk management factors and the potential for civil litigation to provide a remedy for police misconduct. Although the primary function of civil litigation is to resolve disputes between litigants and award compensation for injury, it nevertheless comprises a potentially significant aspect of a police force's legal accountability. Whether this potential is realised depends on a number of factors including the financial impact of such litigation and the readiness of police organisations to systematically analyse successful litigation with a view to avoiding or minimising the risk of future litigation. Until recently it appears that Australian police organisations had made little attempt to measure and examine the extent and nature of civil litigation.

Nature of the problem

Civil litigation allows people injured by the wrongful acts of police, including assault, false imprisonment, trespass and negligence, to be compensated or paid civil damages. Incidents resulting in civil litigation comprise a very select subset of encounters between police and citizens. These incidents can be conceptualised as atypical aberrations or the tip of the iceberg, depending on the circumstances and one's perspective. However, regardless of whether cases litigated fairly represent police behaviour, it is likely that they present a legitimacy problem. Litigation often publicly highlights problematic or contentious aspects of policing, particularly use of force (see, for example, *Herald-Sun*, 24 May 2000: 3, 'Police to pay bashed burglar'; *The Age*, 24 February 2001: 3, '$315,000 in damages for 'spiteful' raid'). Additionally, the drain on public funds from settlements and awards in favour of plaintiffs attracts critical public comment (see, for example, *Herald-Sun* 5 June 2001: 1). The potential for criticism over the cost of civil litigation is heightened as policing, rightly or wrongly, is increasingly viewed as a business where value for money is measured in terms of key performance indicators (Edwards 1999).

Accurate and comprehensive information about the number and type of civil litigation actions taken by citizens against police is difficult to obtain (Kappeler 1993). Despite the large volume of civil suits against police in the United States, information about these suits is distributed across a number of government agencies with little coordination or feedback (Adams, Alpert, Dunham, Garner, Green-fild, Henriquez, Langan, Maxwell and Smith 1999). In Australia the systematic collection of information on civil litigation against police even within one jurisdiction is the exception rather than the rule. Additionally, there is no comparable data between jurisdictions and there are certainly no national data publicly available (*Aust Torts Rep* 2000 35-070: 43,072).

Despite the lack of data it is possible to discern an upward trend in civil litigation against police: 'police are now, as never before, becoming targets of civil actions against them by aggrieved citizens' (*Aust Torts Reporter* 2000: ¶35-070 at 43,072). In the 1950s and 1960s courts tended to be unsympathetic to actions against police, because to impose civil liability would discourage police from doing their duty. However, this judicial benevolence has diminished, and successful civil actions against the police are on the increase (Dixon 1997). The London Metropolitan police was ordered to pay out £200 in damages in 1973 compared to £745,324 in 1990 (*Aust Torts Reporter* 2000: ¶35-070 at 43,072). United States commentators point to a sharp increase in civil suits against police since the 1960s (Kappeler, Kappeler and del Carmen 1993; Skolnick and Fyfe 1993). In 1992 it was predicted that 'Civil liability stemming from the use of force may well become the top legal topic in municipal circles in the 1990s replacing road design as the primary liability drain on taxpayers' funds (Roberts 1992: 16). Events in Los Angeles prove this prediction prescient. In 2000 the Police Chief in that city estimated that a new raft of lawsuits alleging excessive use of force could cost the city $125 million (*The Age* 16 February 2000: 13). Subsequently the estimate was revised to more than $200 million (*New York Times* 30 August 2000).

The problem in Victoria

This chapter was motivated by the perception that civil litigation against police has emerged as a major issue in Victoria, which with New South Wales, has been the main Australian hot spot for such litigation throughout the 1990s (Freckelton 2000). An indication of the significance of this litigation in Victoria was the passing of the *Police Regulation (Amendment) Act* (Vic) in 1999. One purpose of the amendment was to protect police from civil litigation arising from the performance of their duties (*Victorian Hansard* 2001). (Police in South Australia and New South Wales have similar indemnity.) Additionally, in April 2000 Victoria Police set up a new civil litigation division to cope with the escalating number of actions (*Herald-Sun*, 5 June 2001: 1).

Between 1994/1995 and the end of March 2001, Victoria Police paid $9,338,899.23 in damages and costs from civil litigation. This figure includes settlements as well as court awards but excludes payments made to serving or former police (Victoria Police 2001). It is difficult to put this figure in context given that there are no comparable figures from other States and no Victorian figures from previous years. At the very least, however, the total suggests that civil suits against police need to be carefully examined to avoid this continuing and escalating drain on public funds.

Policing events leading to litigation

Ascertaining and analysing the nature of the cases and types of issues involved presents some difficulties as most of this litigation is initiated in County Courts where judgments are unreported. Nevertheless, media reports cross-checked with the small number of lawyers litigating in this area has produced seven judgments and one jury verdict between 1996 and January 2002. Six further settled cases, some involving multiple plaintiffs, were identified through media reports, making a total sample of fourteen. The allegations involved in these settled cases were verified through formal statements of claim or another credible version of events (such as an Ombudsman's report or Coroner's finding). The settlement of litigation does not usually involve an admission of liability. Nevertheless, compensating plaintiffs in these circumstances means, at the very least, an assessment that the risks in continuing to judgment outweigh the costs of settling. It is quite likely that there are other settled cases from the relevant time not included in this study. While court processes are public events that, in litigation against police, almost certainly attract publicity, settlements are usually made confidentially, and some plaintiffs prefer to avoid publicity.

The types of policing events leading to successful civil litigation include forced entry raids, fatal shootings, assaults – punching, kicking, stomping and strikes using batons and a hockey stick – strip searches, pressure point holds, fabrication of evidence, and the policing of demonstrations. Many of these categories overlap. For example a forced entry raid may lead to an assault or fatal shooting, and the policing of a demonstration to assault by batons or the use of pressure point holds, as shown in the case descriptions in the table below.

With one exception, policing events associated with successful litigation in this study did not arise in the heat of the moment. In the exceptional case, two police officers responded to a call to a mentally disturbed man stabbing himself. Shortly after arriving the two officers fatally shot the man, having failed to convince him to drop the knife and believing they were in danger (Victoria State Coroner 1994). In some of the other cases where officers seem to have acted in a hot-headed fashion they were not responding to a policing crisis, but instead to a perceived personal affront (see for example *Frazer v Obeid* 2000; *Witney v Victoria* 1998). Overwhelmingly, the events were planned, routine or, particularly in the case of assaults at police stations and private homes, largely within the control of the officers involved. The picture that emerges is at odds with the view that litigation arises when police are caught in crisis situations and are forced to make on the spot decisions.

The conclusion that civil litigation only rarely occurs in the context of heat of the moment or split-second decisions is good news for risk management. While it might be difficult to plan to reduce exposure to unpredictable, sudden risks, it should be easier to reduce and manage risks from poor planning, training, supervision or systemic and routine problems. In each case in the study I looked for indicators that might have alerted a diligent risk manager to potential problems. By identifying the risk prediction factors in these cases, risk management techniques to assist in reducing or containing future civil litigation can be formulated and implemented.

Table 12.1 Cases settled and judgments for plaintiffs in civil actions against Victoria Police

Date of incident	Case details	Circumstances
26 Nov 1990	Witney v Victoria 1998	Assault at police station. Police 'motivated by animosity and vengeance'. Settling an old score.
13 Dec 1991	Montoya v Victoria 1998	Forced entry drug raid by Major Crime Squad (now disbanded). Assault on occupant at house and at police station. Assault apparently designed to extract location of drugs (no drugs located).
16 Dec 1991	Settlement regarding Anthony Drennan deceased	Fatal shooting during forced entry raid (Victoria State Coroner 1994). Settlement in favour of mother and girlfriend of deceased.
31 Dec 1991	Plater v Habel 1998	Assault at police station. Apparently gratuitous. Cannabis planted on accused. Malicious prosecution and unlawful imprisonment.
28 Nov 1992	Shaw v Kyte 1997	Wrongful arrest. Strip search at police station.
13 Dec 1993	Settlement regarding Richmond Secondary College protesters	Police batons used against passive protesters. Settlement in favour of 30 protesters.
3 Jan 1994	Settlement regarding Edward Hulsman deceased	Psychiatrically disturbed man stabbing himself with knife at his parent's home. Police shot man after failing to persuade him to drop the knife and fearing for their lives (Victoria State Coroner 1995)
10 Feb 1994	Settlement regarding anti-logging protesters.	Seven plaintiffs. Use of pressure point holds, including neck holds at demonstration.
20 May 1994	Gray v Hatch 2001	Jury decision. Strip search at police station. Woman taken into custody over unpaid parking fines.
7 Aug 1994	Gordon v Graham 1996	Strip search of 423 Tasty Night Club patrons.
7 Aug 1994	Tasty Night Club settlement	Settlement in favour of other Tasty Night Club patrons.
8 Mar 1996	Horvarth v Christensen 2001	Forced entry raid on private home. Assault on plaintiffs.
19 Mar 1997	Settlement regarding Devine (writ no.9902520)	Alleged assault at police station. Plaintiff claims hit around body and leg with hockey stick. Leg broken. Also kicked and stomped on. Motive unclear.
7 Mar 1998	Frazer v Obeid 2000	Assault in police station. Police officer avenging affront to his ego.

Litigation risk factors

Four of the cases in the sample had no apparent risk factors prior to the policing event that led to the litigation. All involved assaults or alleged assaults at police stations (*Witney v Victoria* 1998; *Frazer v Obeid* 2000; *Plater v Habel* 1998). While these cases provide no obvious warning signs for litigation risk, the judgments in the two of the three cases that went to trial (one was settled out of court) indicate ways to lessen the exposure to damages once the risk has materialised, a topic returned to below.

Two cases from the early 1990s involved fatal shootings by police. Both settled out of court (Victoria State Coroner 1994 1995). As early as the mid-1970s a study had singled Victoria Police out for criticisms over their use of firearms and related management practices (Harding 1975). By the late 1980s there was growing criticism by professional, church and community organisations about the nature and number of fatal shootings by Victorian police (McCulloch 1996). A 1985 incident where a police officer shot and seriously wounded a psychiatrically disturbed man resulted in a successful civil suit against the officer and the State of Victoria (*Zalewski v Turcarolo* 1994). In 1989 a public meeting called on the government to set up a judicial inquiry into fatal police shootings (Flemington/Kensington Legal Service 1992). Between 1984 and 1995 Victoria Police shot and killed just over twice as many people as did all other police forces in Australia (McCulloch 2001). These factors – critical academic comment, widespread public criticism, a disproportionate number of shootings, and the previous court judgment in favour of a shot plaintiff – can be viewed as litigation risk indicators. Had they been viewed in this light by police management it is possible that the settled litigation from the two fatal shootings in the 1990s could have been avoided. This is not to argue that shootings can necessarily be avoided, only that the risk can be minimised. By the mid 1990s, unable to ignore the escalating shooting toll, Victoria Police changed their firearms training and successfully reduced the number of fatal shootings and consequent exposure to civil litigation (McCulloch 2001).

In two cases, police actions at public protests resulted in settlements in favour of multiple plaintiffs. The first took place on December 1993 when police used batons against protesters on a picket line outside Richmond Secondary College. The Ombudsman concluded that the police tactics were a 'radical departure' from those previously used, and that 'the standard of reasonable force was exceeded' (Deputy Ombudsman 1994a: 74, 78). The baton drill used at

Richmond was part of a training package specifically designed for a (then) new crowd control group. Despite the baton training being 'radically' different – in that it sanctioned the use of batons against passive protesters – Victoria Police did not seek any legal advice prior to its development (Deputy Ombudsman 1994a: 67). The second incident involved the use of pressure point holds, including neck holds, against passive demonstrators in early 1994. The Ombudsman found in this case that the 'tactics used by police had the potential of causing serious injury or even death... The evidence clearly indicates that the action was grossly excessive and without justification'. Victoria Police did not seek medical or legal advice prior to the use of the holds (Deputy Ombudsman 1994a: 90, 95 101). In addition, the holds were used by Victoria Police five months *after* the Commonwealth Ombudsman criticised their use against passive demonstrators and pointed out their potentially lethal consequences (Commonwealth Ombudsman 1993).

Three of the cases involved strip searches by police. The first involved an incident in 1992 where a woman was mistakenly arrested on suspicion of being involved in a drug deal and strip-searched at a police station (*Shaw v Kyte* 1997). It is not obvious that there were risk factors present prior to this incident. However, the power to strip search is an extremely invasive one, and police in 1992 were not keeping any records relating to the number and nature of such searches, a situation which surely added to the potential for abuse (FCLC 1994). The second case arose out of an incident in 1994 where a woman was strip searched at a police station after being arrested for non-payment of two parking fines (*Gray v Hatch* 2001). Prior to this a diligent risk manager may have picked up litigation risk factors. First, the claim over the 1992 incident could have triggered a review of the strip search policy. Secondly, there had been a settlement in favour of another strip-searched woman in 1993 (*Herald Sun,* 22 May 1994; personal communication Jan Gray 1994). Moreover, by 1993 there had been trenchant public criticism over strip searches by Victorian Police (George 1993), and in May 1994, several months prior to the third incident, several community organisations wrote to the Attorney-General expressing concern about strip searches by police. The letter included case studies and examples and argued that civil actions against police in relation to strip searches were likely to increase (FCLC 1994). This letter and the 1993 settlement were the subject of a full page article headed 'Police 'abusing strip searches'' in the *Herald-Sun* newspaper several months prior to the third incident, the Tasty

Night Club raid in August 1994, when 423 people were strip-searched. Clearly, the mounting risk factors had been ignored.

Three cases involved forced entry raids (Victoria, State Coroner 1995; *Monloyu v Victoria* 1998; *Horvath v Christensen* 2001). The first, in 1991, resulted in a fatal shooting by the police Special Operations Group. The coroner subsequently concluded there 'was no pressing need to conduct a forced entry raid, something which is by its very nature confrontational and which should only be used as a last resort' (Victoria State Coroner 1995). By 1991, after two controversial shootings, New South Wales police had dramatically decreased their forced entry raids and changed their approach in high risk situations to one of containment and negotiation, with raids only as a last resort (York 1996; see also Wootten 1991). As early as 1989 the *Sun* newspaper, commenting on a bungled forced entry raid by Victoria Police, argued that, 'Given public reaction to the recent death of a 'suspect' in a similar raid in Sydney, one would think the police might have considered some other method of flushing out their quarry. Why not surround the house and wait for them to emerge as they eventually would have?' (*Sun*, 3 June 1989: 25). In 1991, despite the risks, the Special Operations Group were still conducting forced entry raids as a first option. They did not move away from forced entry raids as a primary tactic until the mid-1990s (McCulloch 2001). In the late-1980s, the Deputy Ombudsman (Police Complaints) conducted a public interest inquiry into police raids after receiving 'several hundred' complaints from members of the public. Despite changes to raid guidelines subsequent to the Ombudsman's report, newspapers continued to report heavy handed and bungled raids during the early-1990s (McCulloch 2001; Deputy Ombudsman 1994b). The change in policy in New South Wales, the Ombudsman's report and public complaints can all be viewed as litigation risk indicators signalling a need for policy review or greater accountability in the area of forced entry raids.

Damage control

In a recent Victorian case a jury awarded a woman a total of $337,000 damages for an illegal strip search by police (*Gray v Hatch* 2001). If the evidence points to an increase in the number of civil actions brought against police, the amount of damages awarded in individual cases has also increased significantly. Freckelton's 1996 article 'Suing the Police: The Moral of the Disappointing Morsel', lamented the relatively small amount of damages typically awarded to plaintiffs in these actions. Today the sums awarded in compensatory damages are increasing and exemplary damages designed to punish defendants, once relatively rare, are also regularly awarded (Freckelton 1996).

In a leading New South Wales case, $100,000 in exemplary damages was awarded to the victim of police trespass to property, assault, false arrest and false imprisonment. Priestley JA held that: 'The amount should also be such as to bring home to those officials of the State who are responsible for the overseeing of the police that police officers must be trained and disciplined so that abuses of the kind that occurred in the present case do not happen' (*Adams v Kennedy* 2000 at 87). In Victoria all five cases involving court awards after 1997 included exemplary damages. The trend towards higher compensatory and exemplary damages is likely to increase the nexus between civil actions and police accountability and reform. Given the extent of the monetary penalties courts are now prepared to impose for police misconduct, police managers will increasingly need to focus on litigation risk as a core component of procedures, training, and supervision.

The Victorian judgments suggest that the conduct of police *after* the event in question compounded the damage to the plaintiff, resulting in awards of aggravated damages. The courts have found aggravating factors to include gratuitous attacks on the credibility and character of the plaintiff, lack of apology for wrongdoing, and police interfering with and lying to investigators in cases of formal complaint. In light of this, police need to give serious attention to how investigations of complaints and legal defences are conducted, and whether consideration should be given to more freely apologising to plaintiffs for any mishandling or mistakes that occur.

The rise and rise of civil litigation against Victoria Police

Several factors contribute to the increase in litigation. Lawyers are now more frequently willing to engage in civil litigation against police (Freckelton 2000). Victorian Chief Commissioner, Christine Nixon, in an 'unprecedented attack', urged the legal community 'to put civil responsibility before profit' and argued, 'It is now commonplace for some legal firms to actually tout for business on a no-win, no-fee basis... The practice has exposed police members to the risk of speculative litigation' (*The Age* 13 September 2001: 16). Under 'no win no fee' arrangements lawyers agree to take a case on the basis that they will not charge professional costs unless the plaintiff is successful (see Lawson 1998). These arrangements remove the financial barrier for plaintiffs, but lawyers will only take cases on this basis if there is a strong chance of success rather than risking financial loss in terms of billable time. No-win no-fee arrangements facilitate the pursuit of strong civil cases by people who otherwise would not be able to afford to litigate, but do not give rise to the circumstances that make the litigation viable and worth the risk for plaintiff lawyers. On the other hand, advertising gives victims of police abuses the chance to consider the option of litigation when this may not have occurred to them previously.

United States academics speculate that community-oriented policing has the potential to increase police exposure to civil liability (Worrall and Marenin 1998). I have argued elsewhere that in many jurisdictions, and particularly Victoria, while community policing rhetoric has been strong the dominant trend in policing is para-military (McCulloch 2001). Paramilitary policing, briefly stated, involves the use of high levels of force often against groups of people conceived as enemies The adoption of paramilitary tactics, reflected in Victoria in the high number of fatal shootings, aggressive forced entry raids and the use of high levels of force against protesters, increases police exposure to civil litigation. Because paramilitary tactics have a tendency to be used against groups they can give rise to multiple plaintiffs, as in the cases of the Tasty Night Club raid, Richmond Secondary College, and the use of pressure point holds against protesters. These cases involve certain economies of scale for lawyers and spread risk for plaintiffs making civil actions more viable and thus more likely.

Additionally, the perceived failure of police complaints procedures to produce satisfactory outcomes for complainants may fuel litigation. This would certainly appear to be the case in Victoria, given that it seems courts are more likely to find in favour of plaintiff/complainants than the Victorian Ombudsman or the Victoria Police Ethical Standards Department (see, for example *Horvath v Christensen* 2001; *Frazer v Obeid* 2000; *Gray v Hatch* 2001). In these circumstances, a review of the formal complaints system specifically with a view to its relationship with civil litigation seems warranted. Possible reforms include a changed lowered standard of proof, the more liberal use of apologies, and a system of ex gratia compensation designed to reduced costly litigation.

Ultimately civil litigation against police has grown and is likely to continue to do so because it appears to be delivering results to plaintiffs. Successful cases create a snowball effect: publicity surrounding awards and settlements flushes out new plaintiffs and inspires lawyers to take on cases. There is no doubt that the litigation genie is out of the bottle as far as police are concerned. Getting it back in will not be easy, but it is a task that needs urgent attention.

Conclusion

Litigation is a drain on public funds and police resources. It can undermine the reputation of a police service by placing the spotlight on the worst or most problematic aspects of police behaviour. It is also a source of stress for individual police officers named as defendants and those who regard it as a hazard of the job (Jellett, Pope and Voges 1994; see also Nixon comments, *The Age*, 13 September 2001: 16). On a more positive note it can provide a valuable feedback mechanism and impetus for reforms. It has been argued that liability claims in America have pushed police forces 'towards the development of a professional stance and standards far more quickly than appeals to do so made by academics and politicians' (McKenzie 1994: 103). Before the good as well as the bad of civil litigation can be realised in Australia there are a number of prerequisites that must be met. First is a commitment to collecting data within jurisdictions and nationally. Ideally this data should be comparable between jurisdictions. Second, serious attention needs to be paid to analysing this data so that the type of situations that are leading to litigation can be documented and ultimately minimised. The review of successful litigation against Victoria Police contained in this chapter suggests that training and procedures can be analysed in terms of civil litigation risk in order to manage and minimise that risk.

References

Adams, K, Alpert, G, Dunham, R, Garner, J, Greenfild, L, Henriquez, M, Langan, P, Maxwell, C and Smith, S, 1999, *Use of Force by Police: Overview of National and Local Data*, National Institute of Justice.

Commonwealth Ombudsman, 1993, *Ombudsman's Report of Investigations into Complaints Arising from Demonstrations held at AIDEX, November 1991, Australia.*

Deputy Ombudsman (Police Complaints), 1994a, *Investigation into alleged excessive force by the Victoria Police Against Demonstrators at the Richmond Secondary College on Monday 13 December 1993 and Investigation into Crowd Control Methods used by the Victoria Police against Demonstrators outside the Department of Conservation and Natural Resources Headquarters Victoria*

Parade East Melbourne on Thursday 10 February 1994, Government Printer, Victoria.

Deputy Ombudsman (Police Complaints), 1994b, *Commerce Club: Investigation of Police Raid on the Commerce Club (Tasty Night Club) on Sunday 7 August 1994*, Government Printer, Victoria.

Dixon, D, 1997, *Law in Policing: Legal Regulation and Police Practices*, Clarendon Press.

Edwards, C, 1999, *Changing Policing Theories for 21st Century Societies*, Federation Press.

FCLC, 1994, Letter to Attorney-General Jan Wade, Federation of Community Legal Centres, Victoria.

Freckelton, I, 1996, 'Suing the Police: The Moral of the Disappointing Morsel', *Alternative Law Journal* 21(4) 173-77 190.

Freckelton, I, 2000, 'Legal Regulation of the Police Culture of Violence: Rhetoric, Remedies and Redress', in T Coady, S James, S Miller and M O'Keefe (eds), *Violence and Police Culture*, Melbourne University Press.

George, A, 1993, 'Sexual Assault by the State', *Alternative Law Journal* 18(1), 31-3.

Flemington/Kensington Legal Centre, 1992, *Police Shootings in Victoria 1987-1989: You Deserve to Know the Truth*, Fitzroy Legal Centre, Victoria.

Harding, R, 1975, 'Changing Patterns in the Use of Lethal Force in Australia', *Australian and New Zealand Journal of Criminology* 8(2) 125-36.

Jellett, S, Pope, N and Voges, K, 1994, 'The Stress of Litigation', *Australian Police* 48(4) 163-67.

Kappeler, V, 1993, *Critical Issues in Police Civil Liability*, Waveland.

Kappeler, V, Kappeler, S and del Carmen, R 1993, 'A Content Analysis of Police Civil Liability Cases: Decisions of the Federal District Courts 1978-1990', *Journal of Criminal Justice* 21(4), 325-37.

Lawson, I,1998, 'No Win – No Fee', *Alternative Law Journal* 23(6) 280-83 294.

McCulloch, J, 1996, 'Blue Murder: Press Coverage of Fatal Shootings in Victoria', *Australian and New Zealand Journal of Criminology* 29(2) 102-120.

McCulloch, J, 2001, *Blue Army: Paramilitary Policing in Australia*, Melbourne University Press.

McKenzie, I 1994, 'Get Yourselves Ready for 2001', *Policing* 10(2), 99-110.

Roberts, B 1992, 'Legal Issues in Use of Force Claims', *The Police Chief* LIX(2) 16-29.

Skolnick, J and Fyfe, J, 1993, *Above the Law: Police and the Excessive Use of Force*, Free Press.

Victoria Police, Freedom of Information Unit (2001), Letter to Jude McCulloch, 8 May.

Victoria State Coroner, 1994, *Investigation into the Death of Edward Hulsman: Inquest Findings*, Melbourne.

Victoria State Coroner, 1995, *Investigation into the Death of Anthony Drennan: Inquest Findings*, Melbourne.

Victorian Hansard, 2001, <http://tex2.parliament.vic.gov.au/ bin/texhtmlt? form=VicHansard> accessed 1 March.

Worrall, J and Marenin, O, 1998, 'Emerging Liability Issues in the Implementation and Adoption of Community Oriented Policing', *Policing: An International Journal of Police Strategies and Management* 21(1) 121-136.

Wootten, H, 1991, 'Report of the Inquiry into the Death of David John Gundy', in E Johnson, *Royal Commission into Aboriginal Deaths in Custody: National Report*, Australian Government Publishing Service.

York, S, 1996, *Critical Analysis of How the New South Wales Police Service Deals with High Risk Policing Incidents*, MA thesis, University of Technology, Sydney.

Cases

Adams v Kennedy (2000) 49 *NSWLR* 78 at 87.

Frazer v Obeid, , unreported, Victorian County Court 24 November 2000.

Gray v Hatch, unreported, Victorian County Court, 30 March 2001.

Horvath v Christensen, unreported, Victorian County Court, 23 February 2001.

Montoya v Victoria and Kelly, unreported, Victorian County Court, 6 October 1998.

Plater v Habel, unreported, Victorian County Court; Devine, County Court, 26 June 1998.

Shaw v Kyte, unreported, Victorian Country Court, 15 April 1997.

Witney v Victoria, unreported, Victorian Country Court, 2 December 1998.

Zalewski v Turcarolo (1994) *Aust Torts Rep* ¶ 81-280.

13

Independent Investigation of Complaints

Tim Prenzler

In 1991 *Complaints Against the Police: The Trend to External Review* was published. Andrew Goldsmith's edited volume described a movement away from police having control of disciplinary processes towards greater input from civilian oversight agencies. Now, a decade later, there is an emerging trend for civilian agencies to go beyond 'review' to engage directly in investigations and disciplinary decisions. This chapter reports on the experiences and principles driving this trend. The chapter focuses on the views of the three primary stakeholders involved in the discipline process:

1. complainants,

2. oversight agencies, and

3. police.

In each case, the perspective of the stakeholder group is explained in terms of their specific interests, the problems they experience with internal police control and how they see external control as a remedy. There are other sources of opinion not considered in this chapter. They include inquiries into police conduct (for example MacPherson 1999; Wood 1997), public opinion surveys (CJC 2000; Tarling and Dowds 1997), government reviews (ALRC 1995; KPMG 2000) and reports from civil liberties groups (Harrison and Cunneen 2000; Human Rights Watch 1998).

Background

Because policing entails conflict, police work typically generates large numbers of complaints. Complaints normally involve at least one allegation of a breach of duty by a police officer. To ensure accountability, an obvious response is to conduct a formal investigation, determine guilt or innocence, and punish the guilty. This has been a traditional task of police supervisors and internal affairs departments. But wherever police corruption and abuses of power have been exposed it is almost inevitable that the report will castigate the quality of these internal investigations (ALRC 1995). Sometimes the problem is one of lack of sophistication or effort on the part of investigating officers. In other cases, the problem is one of complicity with corruption and deliberate protection of corrupt colleagues. The following statement from the Fitzgerald Inquiry in Queensland, Australia, combines these criticisms in a commonly heard critique:

> The Internal Investigations Section has been woefully ineffective, hampered by a lack of staff and resources and crude techniques. It has lacked commitment and will, and demonstrated no initiative to detect serious crime. Corrupt police have effectively neutralised whatever prospect there might have been that allegations against police would have been properly investigated... The ... Section has provided warm comfort to corrupt police. It has been a friendly sympathetic, protective and inept overseer. It must be abolished (Fitzgerald 1989: 289).

A major task of *Complaints Against the Police: The Trend to External Review* was to use case studies, such as the Fitzgerald Inquiry, to explain and justify the need for civilian review as a means of checking this form of corrupt process. That task should no longer be necessary. As the police scholar David Bayley has stated, the first principle of modern police accountability is that 'Police cannot be trusted to police themselves. Exclusive reliance on internal investigations and discipline is foolhardy. Civilian review is essential' (1991: iv).

What is civilian review? A civilian review agency looks very much like a permanent or 'standing' royal commission or judicial inquiry. It has a name, such as Police Complaints Authority, Civilian Review Board, Anti-Corruption Commission or Ombudsman. It occupies offices separate to the police department and is staffed primarily by people who have never worked as police and have no ties to police. It is normally headed by a person with experience as a judge, magistrate or senior prosecutor. Some senior staff will have experience in criminal law, usually as prosecutors. There would normally be complaints officers, who receive and assess complaints, and there may be some investigators.

The powers and procedures of these agencies can vary significantly. Staff will usually audit files on investigations and disciplinary decisions made by police, and recommend changes to procedures or decisions. This is the minimal function, but experience has shown that such agencies are usually too weak to be effective (Goldsmith 1991). The more advanced agencies will have the power to challenge disciplinary decisions; and may be able to conduct their own investigations or supervise the police investigations, and make judgements on serious matters. The latter model is now what could be considered the proper embodiment of the idea of civilian oversight. Thus, the core profile of a civilian oversight agency is as follows:

1. police internal affairs do most of the work of investigating complaints and other intelligence of police misconduct and make disciplinary decisions.

2. This work is scrutinised by the external agency by auditing case files and responding to appeals from dissatisfied complainants.

3. The agency has power to criticise police procedures and might be able to appeal against disciplinary decisions to a judge or magistrate, and

4. The agency may be required to investigate very serious complaints or incidents (such as police shootings or deaths in police custody).

There is a growing number of voices asserting that this approach is insufficient to properly detect and prevent police misconduct, and insufficient to ensure confidence in the integrity of the complaints process. A better system is one in which all formal investigations of complaints and all decisions on disciplinary outcomes are carried out by the independent authority. Before developing the arguments supporting this position, a number of qualifications need to be made to place this alternative model in a proper context:

1. The decision to conduct a formal investigation needs to be considered in the context of alternative responses that may provide a better all round outcome (see Chapter 9 on informal resolution, mediation and managerial resolution of complaints).

2. Findings of misconduct following from investigations need not always entail punishment (fine, demotion, dismissal). They can also result in orders for apology, counselling, retraining or enhanced management supervision.

3. Findings from investigations and the criteria for assigning complaints to formal investigation need to be integrated within a

larger research-based risk management approach to police integrity (see Chapter 10).

4. Independent investigation and adjudication need not exclude police input into the preliminary assessment about how to proceed with a complaint nor the final decision about how to respond to a finding of misconduct.

5. Nor does it exclude police from responding to complaints. Police supervisors and internal affairs can play a large role in alternatives to formal investigation, such as informal resolution (see Point 1 above).

6. Nor does independent investigation and adjudication absolve police of responsibility for misconduct prevention. Police will still have a large role to play in building integrity through human resource management and other strategies (see Chapter 1).

Complainants

Complainants are important stakeholders as ultimate consumers of the complaints system. One of the earliest studies of complainant satisfaction was done as part of an evaluation of the complaints system for England and Wales. This system was relatively advanced, with the Police Complaints Authority (PCA) supervising police investigations of more serious cases. As a first step, Maguire and Corbett (1991) considered the extent to which complaints were trivial or vexatious. They concluded that the very large majority of complainants were honest in feeling genuinely aggrieved – even if in some cases they misunderstood what had happened in their unhappy encounter with police. From surveys of complainants, the researchers found that 96 per cent were dissatisfied with the outcome and 83 per cent were dissatisfied with the way the police conducted the investigation (1991: 164 148). Almost 90 per cent supported the view that 'the whole investigation should be carried out by someone other than the police' (p 180). Typical comments from respondents were as follows (1991: 168 177):

- I achieved the knowledge that police investigating police is a farce.

- I can't help but think the PCA is connected to the police.

- I feel that the PCA try to be unbiased, but because much of their information comes through the police they are prone to deception.

- They sit in their office in London and let the police investigate themselves.

A follow up study (Waters and Brown 2000: 631-2) found similar sentiments: 80 per cent of complainants surveyed felt their complaint had not received fair treatment and 67 per cent strongly agreed that 'complaints should be investigated by an independent body' (see also Brown 1988).

In Canada, interviews with complainants concerning their experiences with the Ontario Police Complaints Commissioner (PCC) showed that the presence of the PCC created a false impression of a thoroughly independent process (Landau 1996). Many complainants were not initially aware of the existence of the PCC, but were then shocked to discover that the complaint lodged with the Commissioner was referred to police and investigated by police. About 75 per cent of interviewees felt the Commissioner was 'not at all, or not very involved in their case' (1996: 307). Landau noted that PCC auditing was overly reliant on paper reviews of the existing investigation. There was a high level of disillusionment and cynicism on the part of complainants about the whole process. It was felt that police continued to operate largely as a law unto themselves, and that police investigators were protective of their colleagues. Landau concluded:

> Perhaps the most salient feature in the minds of complainants remains the fact that the police investigate the police. While this is itself a great source of concern, complainants are additionally dissatisfied with particular aspects of the investigations which could, at least to some extent, over-ride their lack of confidence in the investigation. [These include] concerns over not listening to their side of the story, narrowly focusing on documentary and physical evidence, giving too much weight to the subject officers' version of events and not enough to the complainant or complainants' witnesses (1996: 310).

It is important to note that the dissatisfaction of many complainants does not follow automatically from the fact that no police officer was punished. Most complainants will be satisfied with an apology or official acknowledgment that 'their complaint had substance' (Maguire and Corbett 1991: 168). Their primary criticism is of the investigation *process*, which they see as biased in favour of police, starting with the fact that investigations are done by police.

Oversight agencies

Most civilian oversight agencies prefer that police deal with the bulk of complaints, and they adopt a policy that police should have primary responsibility for discipline (ALRC 1995). However, their experience in oversighting police discipline is often exasperating, adding to the case for the agency to assume control over the whole process. Agency reports are frequently marked by repeated criticisms of the failure of police to conduct proper investigations or act on the agency's recommendations (eg, NSW Ombudsman 1995). One of the most recent examples concerns the New South Wales Police Integrity Commission (PIC), established in 1996. Following its first review of police Internal Affairs, it felt compelled to make a special report to parliament, cataloguing the 'inherent bias' of police investigations and the failure of investigators to engage in proper investigative rigour and sophistication (PIC 2000: i-ii).

The Queensland Criminal Justice Commission conducts routine monitoring of police disciplinary actions, but it has also initiated two in-depth studies of police case files following frustration with police actions. The first review was undertaken by a former Magistrate. His assessment was summarised as follows (CJC 1996: 15):

> Mr Frankcom reviewed 15 matters involving 30 disciplinary charges against 19 officers. Mr Frankcom concluded that there was sufficient evidence to substantiate 23 of the 30 charges. However, only four of the charges were proved against the officers of the Queensland Police Service.
>
> In relation to four matters that the Service found sufficient evidence existed, Mr Frankcom considered that in two of those matters the penalty imposed was manifestly inadequate.
>
> Mr Frankcom concluded that there were 12 charges against eight police officers where he considered that justice had not been done.

The second review was conducted by a retired Supreme Court Judge, using a sample of 180 cases. Of these, 30 were deemed to have been 'inadequately investigated' (23). A protective style of questioning by police investigators was identified, along with failure to follow all potential leads or properly secure physical exhibits. These findings, and public disquiet over prominent cases in which police received light sentences for serious misconduct, compelled the CJC to request the government give it authority to appeal to a Misconduct Tribunal against disciplinary decisions by police (obtained in 1997).

Another frustration for review agencies is that police internal affairs departments are often content to treat complaints on a case-by-case basis. Where a complaint is investigated the process terminates with a finding and, sometimes, a penalty; but there is no analysis of complaints to find patterns that may be amenable to targeted prevention initiatives (CJC 1996). For example, the PIC review of NSW Police Internal Affairs was highly critical of the 'reactive focus of the complaints system on single instances of misconduct', with a consequent failure to identify organised corruption or develop management responsibility for prevention (PIC 2000: i).

These frustrations have driven the evolution of police oversight agencies in lobbying for, and obtaining, more power to supervise investigations, conduct their own investigations of serious matters, overturn police disciplinary decisions, and make independent disciplinary decisions. Surprisingly perhaps, there have been few attempts to assess the impact of these changes by comparing the effectiveness of internal affairs with civilian review. This is in fact a difficult task because of the number of variables involved including powers, resources and the skill levels of investigators. There is also difficulty in developing objective performance indicators. Nonetheless, some research has been attempted, using measures such as police officer perceptions of the rigour and deterrent impact of the different systems, as well as substantiation rates, 'actions taken', and public confidence. The limited evidence available suggests that the more assertive an oversight body is, and the more it engages in direct supervision of police investigators, the more likely it is to produce improvements (CJC 1997; Maguire and Corbett 1991). It would seem to make sense then to push the process further, to have independent agencies be truly independent by doing the more sensitive tasks of investigation and adjudication themselves.

Police

In many jurisdictions police have been stridently opposed to civilian oversight and have often mobilised successfully to block the introduction of external review or to curtail agency powers. However, Bayley (1991) observed a change during the 1980s, mainly amongst police managers. 'Senior officers', he remarked,

> have begun to recognise that civilian participation in the complaints-handling process is essential to their image of being community conscious. 'Community policing', which became the most popular slogan of the police during the 1980s, requires sympathetic and generous treatment of community input (vii).

Bayley cautioned that to some extent police managers were accepting civilian review for their own publicity purposes. But he emphasised that gaining this support was essential to the success of external review. Interviews by Reiner (1991) with chief constables in England and Wales revealed that opinions were divided on the issue. While 52 per cent rejected the proposition of a fully independent system, 30 per cent were supportive, and 18 per cent felt there were strong arguments for both systems. Interestingly, the 30 per cent in favour did not believe that a more independent system would be more effective in identifying and preventing misconduct. They tended to agree with the majority that police investigators were in the best position to penetrate the police culture of solidarity and use their inside knowledge to advantage. Nonetheless, they felt an independent system was essential to ensure public confidence. Many in this group also supported an external system in order to reduce the costs to police of dealing with complaints, and to address police morale over delays with investigations and excessive bureaucracy.

In their study of the PCA, Maguire and Corbett examined the views of police officers who had been the subject of a complaint. Just over half the interviewees were concerned that outside investigators lacked the necessary insight into police practices to conduct a fair investigation and could not understand the pressures on police. However, just under half expressed 'some positive comments about the idea of outside investigators replacing senior police officers' (1991: 70). They felt civilian investigators would improve the credibility of the complaints process, and could also "weed out' trivial or malicious complaints at an early stage without being suspected of doing so unfairly' (1991: 70). The views of investigating police officers canvassed by Maguire and Corbett were also very mixed. A majority insisted they were more effective than outsiders. However, one-third favoured an independent system because of its perceived benefit for public confidence and because it would reduce the 'ill-feeling and divided loyalties' that existed under a predominantly internal system (1991: 71).

Police unions have been in the forefront of the struggle against externalisation of complaints management. However, in England and Wales the Police Federation has campaigned since 1981 for a system of fully independent investigation and, in more recent years, for independent adjudication. According to the Federation, the primary impetus for reform is ensuring public confidence in the complaints system:

The Police Federation believes that the system needs to be changed so that it becomes, and is seen by the public to be, wholly independent of the police service. Although we believe that all investigations are conducted in a thoroughly scrupulous fashion, the fact that police officers undertake the investigations, albeit under the direct supervision of PCA members, lays the system open to allegations of partiality and cover-up (Police Federation 1997: 5).

In New South Wales, during the Royal Commission (1994-1997), the Police Association (1995) developed a policy of complete externalisation of investigations as a way of removing any doubt about bias. Within a two-tiered scheme of complaints, the Association recommended that lower level 'internal disciplinary matters' be returned to police once the credibility of the complaints system was re-established. However, in light of the PIC's review of Internal Affairs (above) this is taking longer than expected!

Discussion

The above arguments do not make for a watertight case in favour of the complete externalisation of police discipline. In fact, it would be naïve to think that simply replacing police investigators with civilians, and leaving disciplinary decisions to civilians, would solve all the problems of complainant and police dissatisfaction, lack of investigative rigour and lenient sanctions. There does, however, appear to be a growing convergence of opinion that external control is essential for 'serious matters'. And some stakeholders believe that minor complaints, which may be of great personal significance to the complainant, might also be amenable to independent processing. Given that minor matters often make up the bulk of complaints, and often occur in large numbers, police-public relations might be better served this way – given also that investigations by police merely compound complainants' grievances. Where does this leave minor 'internal' police conduct issues that do not necessarily involve a complaint by an aggrieved party? The United Kingdom Police Federation has suggested what seems to be a reasonable position on this issue. It has argued that police supervisors should have primary responsibility for 'administrative matters', such as 'lateness for duty, impertinence or insubordination, failure to carry out administrative orders and so forth', while all other matters should be controlled primarily by an external body (Working Party 1981: 4).

It is debatable whether the arguments advanced here would simply entail strengthening the civilian review model (as described at the beginning of this chapter) or adopting a distinctly different model of external control. Nonetheless, there is a strong case for jurisdictions to consider reducing their reliance on police by moving further along the continuum towards more direct civilian involvement. Whatever specific form such as agency would take (and it could be a larger public-sector wide commission), there would need to be firm quality control measures in place – including satisfaction surveys of stake-holders, auditing of investigations and disciplinary decisions, and thorough training and careful selection of civilian investigators.

Conclusion

The issue of control of police conduct is complex and difficult. Each approach has pros and cons. Finding the best system will require experimentation and the application of reliable performance measures. Experience with police-based systems shows that civilian input is essential for accountability. However, there are increasing calls and some strong arguments for going beyond 'review' to give civilians greater direct input and control over complaints processing. 'Independent control' does not exclude police management from input into disciplinary decisions, and police can retain a large role with alternatives to formal investigations and in preventing corruption through a wide range of strategies. Additionally, in considering this model, it should be kept in mind that the principle that 'police should not investigate police' extends to many occupations at risk from misconduct. As one Australian Chief Justice recently stated with reference to complaints against lawyers: 'Where ever the control mechanism is seen as an emanation of the profession, however conscientiously responsible it is, there will be public disquiet' (de Jersey 1999: 5).

References

ALRC, 1995, *Under the Spotlight: Complaints against the AFP and NCA*, Australian Law Reform Commission.

Bayley, D, 1991, 'Preface', in A Goldsmith (ed), *Complaints Against the Police: The Trend to External Review*, Clarendon.

Brown, D, 1988, 'The Police Complaints Procedure: A 'Consumer' View', *The Howard Journal* 27(3) 161-171.

CJC, 1996, *Submission to the Queensland Police Service Review Committee*, Criminal Justice Commission.

CJC, 1997, *Integrity in the Queensland Police Service: Implementation and Impact of the Fitzgerald Inquiry Reforms*, Criminal Justice Commission.

CJC, 2000, *Public Attitudes Toward the CJC*, Criminal Justice Commission.

de Jersey, P 1999 'Legal Reform and the Green Paper', *Proctor On-line* 19(10) 12-15.

Fitzgerald, G, 1989, *Report of a Commission of Inquiry Pursuant to Orders in Council*, Goprint.

Goldsmith, A, (ed) 1991, *Complaints Against the Police: The Trend to External Review*, Clarendon.

Harrison, J and Cunneen, M, 2000, *An Independent Police Complaints Commission*, Liberty: The National Council for Civil Liberties.

Human Rights Watch, 1998, *Shielded from Justice: Police Brutality and Accountability in the United States*.

KPMG, 2000, *Feasibility of an Independent System for Investigating Complaints Against the Police*, KPMG/Home Office.

Landau, T, 1996, 'When Police Investigate Police: A View from Complainants', *Canadian Journal of Criminology*, July 291-315.

MacPherson, W, 1999, *The Stephen Lawrence Inquiry*, Her Majesty's Stationary Office.

Maguire, M, and Corbett, C, 1991, *A Study of the Police Complaints System*, Her Majesty's Stationary Office.

NSW Ombudsman, 1995, *Police Internal Investigations: Poor Quality Police Investigations into Complaints of Police Misconduct*, New South Wales.

PIC, 2000, *Special Report to Parliament: Project Dresden, An Audit of the Quality of NSW Police Service Internal Investigations*, New South Wales Police Integrity Commission.

Police Association, 1997, *Submission to the Royal Commission into the NSW Police Service*, Police Association of New South Wales.

Police Federation, 1997 *Where We Stand: Police Accountability*, Police Federation of England and Wales, www.polfed.org.uk/wherewes.html accessed 7 January 2002.

Reiner, R, 1991, 'Multiple Realities, Divided Worlds: Chief Constables' Perspectives on the Police Complaints System', in A Goldsmith (ed), *Complaints Against the Police: The Trend to External Review*, Clarendon.

Tarling, R and Dowds, L 1997, 'Crime and Punishment', in R Jowell et al, (eds), *British Social Attitudes*, Ashgate.

Waters, I and Brown, K, 2000 'Police Complaints and the Complainants' Experience', *British Journal of Criminology*, 40(4), 617-638.

Wood, J, 1997, *Royal Commission into the New South Wales Police Service: Final Report*, Government Printer.

Working Party, 1981, *The Establishment of an Independent Element in the Investigation of Complaints Against the Police, Report of a Working Party Appointed by the Home Secretary*, Her Majesty's Stationary Office.

14

Predicting Misconduct Before Hiring Police

Michelle Karas

The ability to make accurate predictions of misconduct is crucial in the area of corruption prevention and police officer recruitment. Police misconduct is nevertheless a complex behaviour and theories of police integrity reflect many factors and processes. Given this complexity, it is hardly surprising that the prediction of police performance from information collected at the time of recruitment is fraught with difficulties. Clearly, prediction of future work performance is challenging because of the long time periods between recruitment and the emergence of the behaviour. In police organisations, two processes further complicate such prediction. First, the police environment exerts strong influence on behaviour. Second, experiences occurring throughout the career of the police officer may change his or her values, attitudes or personality in ways that increase the propensity for misconduct. In both cases, the situation exerts a potentially strong, causal influence on the police officer's behaviour.

This chapter focuses on the potential benefits of screening out individuals predisposed to misconduct by incorporating the influence of the situation into police recruitment procedures. By doing so, theories of police selection can go beyond the polemic of bad apple versus bad barrel to inform procedures that have the potential to predict the longer term integrity outcomes of new recruits. This chapter also describes some of the techniques developed within psychology that may assist police practitioners to achieve their recruitment objectives. Specifically, the prediction of behaviour outcomes through the use of biographical information about the individual prior to their employment is examined.

Role of the situation

The long debate within psychology over the relative significance of the situation *versus* the person in determining individual action has largely given way to an acceptance of interactionist theory (Kendrick and Funder 1988). According to interactionist theory, equivalent roles are given to both the person and the situation. Behaviour can be determined by either the person, the environment (situation), or by an interaction between the person and the situation. When situations are weak, such as within the family home, stable, personal attributes play a relatively larger role in determining behaviour. In contrast, when situations are strong, such as in certain organisational cultures, the situation overrides characteristic tendencies and plays the relatively stronger, causal role.

The powerful effect of situations involving demands from authority in causing individuals to perpetrate destructive acts was demonstrated in the well-known Milgram (1974) experiments. In these studies, 64 per cent of individuals obeyed instructions given by authority figures (university scientists) to cause apparent harm to another human being. Trevino and Youngblood (1990) found that in an assessment centre, individuals completing an in-basket management task were more likely to report sexual harassment or whistle blowing if they expected to be rewarded for doing so. Individuals who expected to be punished were less likely to report such behaviour. By extrapolating to police organisations, one might expect a strict command and control structure that actively discourages the questioning of authority creates a situation that can facilitate the condoning and spread of low integrity behaviour, particularly where such behaviour is systemically entrenched in many areas of the organisation.

A second challenging situation arises when personal gain (monetary or otherwise) can be obtained in exchange for destructive behaviour. Forsyth and Nye (1990) found that personal gain can lead an individual to give damaging feedback to their peers. In police work the opportunity for ill-gotten, personal gain is prevalent.

Situations causing psychological distancing can also generate negative behaviour. Psychological distancing can result from conditions leading to alienation (Fromm 1973), exposure to a harsh environment (Staub 1989) and bureaucratic depersonalising structures (Diener, Dineen, Endresen, Beaman and Fraser 1975). Each of these situations has the potential to arise in a policing context. For example, constantly dealing with injury, violence, and hostile offenders can lead to alienation. Harsh environments can be encountered in many of the outdoor activities and shiftwork conditions of police work, and bureaucratic structures are potentially a feature of large public sector organisations.

Events that lead to a temporary decrease in self-efficacy can also lead to damaging behaviour. Negative feedback or performance failure can lead to such destructive behaviour if the individual uses negative ego defences in order to restore a sense of self-efficacy, particularly if such defences involve projection of flaws onto others. A deflated sense of self-efficacy can also result in individuals following the path of least resistance or even hampering self-regulation (Bandura 1989). In the often thankless and negative environment of police work, the demands of management and stakeholders have the potential to elicit both temporary and ongoing decreases in self-efficacy.

The police organisation therefore contains many situations that have the potential to elicit inappropriate behaviour. The challenge in selecting police officers therefore is to assess those factors that are central to interaction theory: the person, the situation and the interaction between the person and the situation. In order to perform this task effectively a number or tools and techniques are required.

Selection systems for police recruitment based on interactionist theory

If a police organisation wishes to screen out pre-existing 'bad apples' or those who may easily succumb to pressures to engage in misconduct then it must identify and assess those personal attributes that have been shown to predict low integrity behaviour across a range of contexts. This is the person component of interactionist theory, and it acknowledges that in a small number of cases, individuals enter the police organisation with personal attributes that predispose towards misconduct. Such individuals are likely to behave inappropriately in any organisation they join, although where the opportunities for corruption or misconduct are low such individuals may inflict relatively little damage. Examples of such dispositions might be a tendency to betray trust or abuse power. These attributes capture the themes of many specific examples of police misconduct and corruption described in Chapter 1.

A comprehensive selection system also includes an assessment of the situations to which an applicant has been exposed. Such an assessment should focus on those situations that are conceptually similar to the potentially negative situations that exist within the police environment. The rationale for this assessment is that if it is accepted that the police environment influences behaviour, then it is reasonable to expect that other, similar environments can also affect behaviour. An example of such an environment would be past membership of groups that had strong expectations of individual group member's behaviour and which applied sanctions to behaviour outside the norm. The greater the exposure to such environments, the greater the likelihood that semi-permanent behaviour change has occurred. Such changes may be latent and may not manifest until the individual enters a situation similar to the original one. It must be stressed, however, that exposure to situations alone, no matter how conceptually similar to the police culture, should not be the sole criterion for selecting police officers.

The third component of interactionist theory is the role of the person-situation interaction. Accordingly, attention should be directed at those attributes, which, in themselves do not directly cause misconduct, but that place the officer at risk when placed in a negative police environment. Although such attributes may result in benign person-situation interactions in other occupational settings, they make the individual vulnerable to the potentially negative aspects of the police occupational context. Thus a high susceptibility to being influenced may not place a clerk in an insurance office at significant risk because the organisational culture and subcultures of the insurance company do not contain the same potentially negative elements as police organisations. The likelihood of misconduct is increased when the individual's vulnerabilities match the negative elements of the environment.

The following sections describe some of the traditional attempts to assess person related factors in police recruitment. These two related techniques - testing for psychological problems and personality testing - have been used by numerous police organisations for some time.

Screening for mental illness and psychological disorder

Because the consequences of police misconduct can be significant, many police organisations have implemented psychological testing to identify applicants with significant emotional instability or psychological disorders with a view to screening them out of the recruitment process. Mental illness and psychological disorders refer to a spectrum of conditions that are experienced as highly distressing and produce significant incapacity in one or more life domains. One of the better known forms of mental illness is schizophrenia, a condition characterised by having thoughts and beliefs divorced from reality, delusions and/or hallucinations and social withdrawal. A much more common disorder is clinical depression in which individuals experience profound sadness, hopelessness, withdrawal from activities and a heightened negativity towards themselves and the world. The assumption underlying the use of screening for psychological disorders is that individuals with a mental illness or significant psychological problem may lack the capacity to effectively perform the more demanding and potentially dangerous aspects of the police role. In particular, many practitioners hold the implicit view that individuals lacking in firm reality testing capacity should not be issued with a firearm or other device capable of inflicting harm to themselves or others.

The principal limitation of psychological screening is that the majority of individuals with psychological disorders are not inherently predisposed to police misconduct or corruption but suffer from feelings and thoughts that are distressing. For example depressed individuals suffer from severe sadness and a sense of worthlessness self-blame and guilt. Indeed such a state is quite in contrast to the anecdotal reports of over-confidence observed in some integrity violators.

More likely then, psychological conditions will cause general performance problems because the individual manifests deficits across a wide range of behaviour domains, including work. Psychological impairment may also make an individual more prone to experiencing stress in the workplace. Policing has been recognised as an inherently high stress occupation (Farmer 1990; Langworthy, Hughes and Saunders 1994) and this high stress environment may exceed the self-monitoring and self-control capabilities of stress prone individuals. The high levels of stress that such individuals experience may produce performance problems that, although manifesting as low integrity, may be more appropriately framed as performance or occupational health issues.

Psychological screening also has a limited 'shelf life'. This is a shortcoming that it shares with numerous selection techniques and it is an issue that is rarely acknowledged by those involved in selection and recruitment. With regard specifically to psychological screening, significant emotional or psychological disorders represent short to medium term impairments and therefore a number of applicants who are free of problems at the time of recruitment may develop problems in the future. Clearly, some form of ongoing psychological testing may be required to ascertain the emotional and mental stability of officers or to screen internal applicants for highly demanding or sensitive positions.

Personality testing

Personality testing is a special category of psychological testing that aims to assess attitudes, feelings, values and preferences that are stable across time and contexts. These tests differ from assessments of psychological disorders in that their focus is on enduring and defining aspects of the person's disposition rather than temporary sets of illness-related symptoms. In addition, personality tests describe a person's characteristic way of behaving on various dimensions of interest. Often, these dimensions do not encompass notions of problem behaviour. That is, they are descriptive, not implicitly evaluative. Examples of personality traits that may have relevance to policing and that are assessed through commercially available tests are dominance, risk-taking and conformity. Thus, an individual may be high or low in dominance and whether this fact is a shortcoming or a strength depends on the performance demands of the job. Furthermore, personality traits coexist with the individual's psychological problems and mental health status. Thus an individual suffering from clinical depression may also be extroverted, although he or she may not display extroverted behaviour during periods of depression.

Despite the broader focus of personality tests, their success in predicting police misconduct has been modest (O'Connor Boes, Chandler and Timm 1998). In a review of the practice and research on personality testing in police selection, the National Police Research Unit (NPRU 1995) pointed out that research has failed to consistently identify a distinct personality profile associated with higher *vs.* lower performing officers. Nor has research identified a distinct profile of officers who engage in misconduct compared to those who do not. This difficulty is not unique to policing and is found in other occupations, such as management where incumbents must perform a range of diverse tasks and where desirable performance outcomes are not rigidly defined. In such occupations, desirable outcomes can be achieved through a range of possible personality profiles.

Furthermore, the presence of a potentially negative attribute can be compensated for by the presence of a positive attribute. For example, police applicants often demonstrate high levels of risk taking and sensation seeking behaviour. Whereas such tendencies enable police officers to enter situations that threaten safety, they may also result in reckless behaviour that unnecessarily compromises the safety of the officer or of others. Therefore, such police applicants are also expected to display high levels of self-discipline that inhibit inappropriate behaviour in high-risk situations.

Despite the absence of a clear profile of the 'flawed' police officer, certain personal attributes, when considered on their own, have been found to be related to police misconduct in the workplace. The Psychopathic Deviate and Hypomania scales of the Minnesota Multiphasic Personality Inventory – Version 2 (MMPI-2) have been found to predict police misconduct in a number of studies (Azen, Snibbe and Montgomery 1973; Bernstein, Schoenfeld and Costello 1982; Hiatt and Hargrave 1988; O'Connor, et al 1998). In the MMPI-2, the Psychopathic Deviate scale assesses problems with accepting authority, and a tendency towards antisocial and unreliable behaviour. The Hypomania scale assesses poor impulse control, sensation seeking and heightened activity levels. Recent internal research conducted in the AFP has also shown that the Agitation scale of the Clinical Analysis Questionnaire (CAQ), which is very similar to the MMPI-2 Hypomania scale, predicts the number of substantiated complaints in police officers with two or less years of service. Officers obtaining higher scores on the Agitation scale at the time of recruitment obtained a higher number of substantiated complaints.

Recent research has also shown however that when personality tests are used to predict police misconduct, prediction is maximised when more specific attributes are employed, compared to the more general attributes commonly used by both researchers and practitioners (Cullen and Ones 2001; Sarchione, Cuttler, Muchinsky and Nelson-Grey 1998). These more specific personality attributes include delinquency, low responsibility, high conformity, inflexibility, conflict proneness, intolerance, pessimism and impulsivity. The relatively higher predictive power of these more specific behavioural tendencies may be due to the fact that they more readily interact with those features of the police environment thought to influence misconduct. For example, conflict proneness or intolerance may place officers at risk when dealing with a hostile public or offender group. Inflexible officers may experience difficulties performing the diverse nature of policing functions, the contradictory nature of these roles, and the speed at which the roles must be adopted. High conformity officers may be susceptible to strong interpersonal pressures to engage in or condone inappropriate behaviour. Clearly it is not just the existence of such attributes that are problematic; it is the potential of the police environment to engage with and activate the individual police officer's specific vulnerabilities to produce poor integrity outcomes. Where an officer is high on one or more of these above attributes, good supervision is required to counteract the effect of the environment. Similarly, ongoing training may help in developing attributes that serve to 'inoculate' the officer from the potentially negative effects of the police environment.

Increasing the prediction of police performance

Most of the problems with psychological testing (both personality testing and screening for psychological disorders) do not involve an inherent problem of the tests themselves, but in their application. These tests have undergone a rigorous research and development process and assess a particular set of personal attributes. It is the responsibility of test users to decide whether the attributes assessed by these tests are related to the job in question, and if so, at what levels. For example, the job of police officer may require moderate levels of risk-taking whereas a trader of derivatives may require high levels of this attribute.

Recruiters also need to distinguish between the role of screening and selection. In screening, individuals who are deemed to be unsuitable to perform the job are excluded from subsequent stages of the selection process. This may be on integrity grounds or for another reason. Applicants remaining following the screen are indistinguishable in their predicted potential to perform the job well. In order to distinguish between remaining applicants in terms of their relative potential to perform the job, the recruitment process needs to employ a selection method. In this way, remaining applicants can be rank ordered and selected from the top or the order of merit.

In addition to the issue of screening and selection, police practitioners need to be clear about a related issue concerning distinctions between different types of performance. Most selection systems implicitly target work performance; that is, they are looking for applicants who will be successful in the job. Recruiters need to be aware that the prediction of who will succeed (the positive aspect of performance) is a different process compared to predicting who will do harm to the organisation (the negative aspect of performance). Police selection systems need to target both sets of factors, as the positive and negative aspects of performance may be predicted by different factors.

According to the NPRU, many police selection procedures have been 'based on intuition rather than comprehensive analysis of job requirements' (NPRU 1995: 8). Job analysis is a method for collecting targeted job information such as tasks performed, task difficulty and importance, context and tools used that assists in the specification of the knowledge, skills and personal attributes that determine job performance. The NPRU has conducted such an analysis with regard to the positive aspects of police performance; in other words, what does it take to do this job well? The prediction of police misconduct could be enhanced if job analysis techniques were applied to the darker side of police performance.

To date, the contribution of psychological testing to corruption prevention has been modest. What these procedures can do is to provide a tool for researchers to identify those attributes that specifically predispose an individual towards misconduct. Police officers can then be periodically assessed against these attributes as a way of monitoring the effect of the police environment on the individual as manifested through personality change.

Selection of new recruits in the Australian Federal Police

Assessment of integrity is a key component of the recruitment and selection procedures of the Australian Federal Police (AFP). Applicants for the position of new recruit undergo a range of assessment procedures aimed at determining their suitability for employment as a police officer. Employment suitability assessment consists of screening for the presence of psychological problems, and an interview based assessment against a range of competency-related and attitudinal factors. A security evaluation process – consisting of background checks, financial declaration, associations, applicant and referee interviews – determines whether or not an individual constitutes a security risk. Finally, urinanalysis is used to detect recent illicit drug use.

Although comprehensive, the AFP selection processes places considerable emphasis on psychological well being, maturity (as assessed through the selection interview), absence of security risks and recent drug use as being indicative of the applicant's present and potential integrity status. These procedures, although valid and laudable, have limitations on the medium to long-term prediction of counterproductive behaviour. The limitations of psychological and personality testing have been described above. Security assessment, with its emphasis on overt and significant events and lifestyles, does not adequately address the more subtle personal characteristics that can be masked by outward social conformity and stable lifestyle. Drug testing, in particular, is focussed on very recent behaviour in a specific behavioural domain, and the predictive links between recent illicit drug use and longer term counterproductive behaviour are uncertain. Finally, none of these procedures target attributes that render the individual vulnerable to the potentially negative influence of the police environment.

Biodata

Because of the limitations of psychological testing and security screening, the AFP decided to consider use of alternative procedures for identifying applicants who might be at risk for engaging in misconduct following recruitment. In 1998, the AFP commenced an ongoing research program to develop a method of predicting police integrity. As part of this research, the AFP elected to trial a general technique known in the psychology literature as biodata. Biodata is a selection method relatively unknown in Australia that has been used overseas in its most basic form since the early 1900s. Literally, biodata means 'biographical data'. A biodata inquiry is typically made via a questionnaire that asks individuals about their past experience and behaviour in situations. Such questionnaires are composed of items that describe the individual's view of his of her own history and canvass past behaviour across a wide variety of situations and life domains. Unlike typical questions on psychological tests, biodata items are usually specific to behaviour and experiences from a person's past and are potentially verifiable through background checks (Mastrangelo, Jankiewicz, Arble, Melanson and Greenamyer 2000).

A fundamental premise of the biodata technique is that the best predictor of future behaviour is past behaviour. This premise is linked to two measurement principles associated with biodata. The first principle is that past experiences lead to the *development* of personal attributes. According to this principle, an individual's attributes and present behaviour are a product, in part, of his or her life history. The capture of information about the situations a person has experienced helps us understand how that individual has developed, and therefore facilitates the prediction of his or her subsequent behaviour. This principle incorporates the substance of interactionist theory: that experience in situations not only determines behaviour in that situation but has a longer term effect on the individual's behaviour, in particular when he or she enters the same or similar situation in the future.

The second measurement principle of biodata concerns the *sign* value of behaviour. Where a person shows signs of similar behaviour over time and across situations, this is regarded as evidence that he or she has acquired certain attributes. Where there is evidence of behavioural consistency, one may expect such consistency to generalise to future situations. The assessment of stable personal attributes through the collection of behavioural information provides information on the likelihood that an individual has 'bad apple' tendencies or possesses vulnerabilities that may interact with the negative aspects of the police environment to produce misconduct.

Biodata has proven itself to be a powerful technique for predicting a wide range of outcomes including work performance, honesty, theft and disloyalty (Stokes, Mumford and Owens 1989). Biodata is suited for application to police selection because it involves measurement of an individual's past experience of situations and their behavioural responses to situations. In particular the verifiable accounts of past behaviour make them open to verification through background vetting procedures.

The AFP has developed a biodata questionnaire, in collaboration with the University of Baltimore. The Survey of Life Experiences (SLE) asks police applicants 207 questions pertaining to past behaviour and experience that are specifically related to negative behaviour themes observed in police misconduct, the situations that are conceptually related to potentially negative situations encountered in the police environment, and to situations that have been empirically demonstrated to lead to misconduct. Intellectual property considerations prevent the AFP from disclosing SLE content or the hypotheses that underlie groups of questions. Nevertheless, it is possible to discuss a trial question as an example to give the reader a better idea of the application of biodata. This example also demonstrates how the same behaviour can have different implications when making predictions to different situations. The SLE contains a question that asks about the number of hours the individual usually sleeps each night. In a military selection context, individuals who require less sleep are regarded as potentially more resilient and vigorous and therefore better equipped to withstand the rigours of military demands (Mael and Hirsch 1993). In the context of selection to the AFP, where substance abuse, particularly illegal substance abuse concerns are considerable, reports of less sleep are considered a risk factor for substance abuse because of the association between nocturnal lifestyle and substance abuse. Ongoing empirical research will determine the utility of this hypothesis for predicting substance abuse outcomes in police officers.

All applicants for AFP police recruit positions between 1998 and 2000 completed the trial version of the SLE and each one of these applicants was allowed to proceed in the recruitment process, regardless of their SLE responses (although some applicants were screened out on other grounds). In 2001 the integrity outcomes of applicants who joined the organisation were examined. A number of SLE past behaviours were found to predict various outcomes including dishonesty in the recruitment process, undesirable training conduct, and number of complaints and allegations. Examples of these behaviours include applicants lying about past recreational drug use (the facts of which were later discovered), incidents of harassment and plagiarism during new recruit training. As the length of time in the organisation examined in this research was between three and 22 months, conclusions can only be drawn about the ability of the SLE to predict undesirable outcomes during the initial career stage. Ongoing research is aimed at determining whether the SLE predicts medium term complaint outcomes.

The biodata method also offers potentially more to police organisations than a selection method. For example, past experiences that demonstrate a capacity to protect officers against engaging in misconduct could be incorporated into training programs. Furthermore, if a set of pre-employment behaviours and experiences can be found that predict post-hire misconduct, a taxonomy of risk indicators can be constructed to guide practitioners working in the development early warning systems. Such a taxonomy could apply to general work and non-work behaviour and would supplement information on more obvious integrity flags such as complaints, and traditional risk factors such as financial stressors.

Conclusion

Psychological testing is a useful part of the police selection process because it assists in the identification of individuals whose emotional and cognitive impairments interfere with the competent execution of police duties. Personality testing that is targeted at assessing attributes that are specifically related to integrity outcomes, as opposed to broad and general characteristics available in many commercial personality tests, provides modest success in the prediction of integrity outcomes. The choice of these attributes should be based on a sound job analysis of the problem behaviour and the context in which it occurs. Alternative selection methods, of which biodata is an example, not only have the potential to improve prediction accuracy, they also provide organisations with vehicles for assessing hypotheses about the types of experiences and environments that lead to changes in individuals that predispose them to misconduct. By doing so, they highlight frameworks for early identification following employment and for intervention through training and environmental change.

Disclaimer

The views expressed here are those of the author and do not necessarily represent the views of the Australian Federal Police.

References

Azen, S, Snibbe, H and Montgomery, H, 1973, 'A Longitudinal Predictive Study of Success and Performance of Law Enforcement Officers', *Journal of Applied Psychology* 57(2) 190-192.

Bandura, A, 1989, 'Self-regulation of Motivation and Action through Internal Standards and Goal Systems', in L Pervin (ed), *Goal Concepts in Personality and Social Psychology*, Erlbaum.

Bernstein, I, Schoenfeld, L and Costello, R, 1982, 'Truncated Component Regression, Multicollinearity and the MMPI's Use in a Police Officer Selection Setting', *Multivariate Behavioral Research* 17(1), 99-116.

Cullen, M and Ones, D, 2001, 'The Role of Conscientiousness and Neuroticism in Predicting Police Corruption', paper presented at the *16th Annual Conference of the Society for Industrial and Organizational Psychology*, San Diego, 26-29 April.

Diener, E, Dineen, J, Endresen, K, Beaman, A and Fraser, S, 1975, 'Effects of Altered Responsibility, Cognitive Set, and Modelling of Physical Aggression and Deindividuation', *Journal of Personality and Social Psychology* 31(2), 328-337.

Farmer, R, 1990, 'Clinical and Managerial Implications of Stress Research on the Police', *Journal of Police Science and Administration* 17(3) 205-218.

Forsyth, D and Nye, J, 1990, 'Personal Moral Philosophies and Moral Choice', *Journal of Research in Personality* 24(4), 398-414.

Fromm, E, 1973, *The Anatomy of Human Destructiveness*, Holt, Rhinehart and Winston.

Hiatt, D and Hargrave, G, 1988, 'Predicting Job Performance Problems with Psychological Screening', *Journal of Police Science and Administration* 16(2) 122-125.

Kendrick, D and Funder, D, 1988, 'Profiting from Controversy: Lessons from the Person-situation Debate', *American Psychologist* 43(1) 23-34.

Langworthy, R, Hughes, T and Sanders, B, 1994, *Law Enforcement Recruitment, Selection and Training: A Survey of Major Departments in the US*, University of Cincinnati, Academy of Criminal Justice Sciences.

Mael, F, and Hirsch, A, 1993, 'Rainforest Empiricism and Quasi-rationality: Two Approaches to Objective Biodata', *Personnel Psychology* 46(4), 719-738.

Mastrangelo, P, Jankiewicz, M, Arble, R, Melanson K and Greenamyer, C, 2000, 'Developing a Transportable Biodata Instrument to Predict Employee Drug Abuse', paper presented at the *24th Annual IPMAAC Conference on Professional Personnel Assessment*, Washington DC, 3-7 June, San Diego, 26-29 April, <http://www.ipmaac.org/conf00/>.

Milgram, S, 1974, *Obedience to Authority: An Experimental View*, Harper and Row.

NPRU, 1995, *Is the Psychological Screening of Police Applicants a Realistic Goal? – The Successes and Failures of Psychological Screening*, National Police Research Unit.

O'Connor Boes, J, Chandler, C and Timm, H, 1998, *Police Integrity: Use of Personality Measures to Identify Corruption-prone Officers*, Defense Personnel Security Research Center, Monterey.

Stokes, G, Mumford, M and Owens, W 1994, *The Biodata Handbook: Theory, Research and Use of Biographical Information in Selection and Performance Prediction*, CPP Books.

Sarchione, C, Cuttler, M, Muchinsky, P and Nelson-Gray, R, 1998, 'Prediction of Dysfunctional Job Behaviors Among Law Enforcement Officers', *Journal of Applied Psychology* 83(6), 904-912.

Staub, E, 1989, *The Roots of Evil: The Origins of Genocide and Other Group Violence*, Cambridge University Press.

Trevino, L and Youngblood, S, 1990, 'Bad Apples in Bad Barrels: A Causal Analysis of Ethical Decision-Making Behavior', *Journal of Applied Psychology* 75(4), 378-385.

15

Situational Corruption Prevention

Andrew Ede, Ross Homel and Tim Prenzler

This chapter tests the hypothesis that situational crime prevention techniques can be useful in preventing police corruption. A situational analysis was made of police complaints files as an example of how this could be initiated. Using three years of complaints data, productive analysis was made of four categories of corruption involving misuse of authority for a reward or a breach of criminal law. The categories were opportunistic thefts, driving under the influence of alcohol, assault (while off-duty) and theft from employer. The analysis identified opportunity factors that could be addressed with situational techniques including forms of target hardening, access control, rule setting and compliance facilitation. The findings indicated that with a larger data set more categories of police corruption and misconduct would be amenable to this type of analysis.

Situational crime prevention and police corruption

Police deviance, like other forms of crime, is sometimes explained in terms of 'propensity to crime' or 'criminality' (Gottfredson and Hirschi 1990: 4). This perspective emphasises predisposing elements of the collective 'police personality', such as an action orientation that can lead to frustration with legal constraints. It also takes into account factors such as poor education and camaraderie that can contribute to cynicism about compliance with departmental standards and to group pressures toward participation in corruption (Crank 1998). Hence the strong emphasis that is placed on changing the organisational culture of the police. However, the existence of 'motivated offenders' is only one component in the occurrence of corruption. Attention also needs to be given to 'situational factors' (Clarke 1992) that create opportunities in the physical and social environment in which the corruption event occurs. Opportunity-reducing techniques include such well-known measures as 'entry screening' and 'target hardening', and have recently been extended to 16 main techniques by Clarke and Homel (1997). In the latter model, the techniques are divided into four areas: 'Increasing Perceived Effort', 'Increasing Perceived Risks', 'Reducing Anticipated Rewards' and 'Inducing Guilt or Shame'.

An approach to prevention that combines both dispositional and situational strategies is essential because there are limits on the extent to which any agency with a mission for crime prevention can control offender motivations (Pease 1994). The immediate circumstances of offending should be addressed because, except in the most extreme cases of mental illness or passion, motivated offenders will always engage in some degree of calculation about the risks and potential benefits of illicit behaviour. And low risk opportunities may in fact generate motivation where it was not prominent before (Clarke 1992). Although the literature on successful situational prevention tends to focus on 'street crimes', such as burglary (Pease 1994), workplace crime can present a textbook case for situational interventions because the workplace is often a highly controllable environment. Employees also frequently have a high stake in conformity, in maintaining income and status, and are therefore susceptible to deterrence measures. Thus, policing may present as a suitable environment for situational corruption prevention. The problem, however, is that most police work is done away from a controllable location. Police generally work singly or in pairs in a highly unstructured context in which supervision is extremely difficult (Cordner 1978). While management collusion is often a factor in police corruption, the lack of surveillance of operational policing is a major factor in the low risk of detection. Nonetheless, given the significant problem of police corruption and the reported successes of situational crime prevention, it seems reasonable to explore the possibility of situational corruption prevention for police.

There is some research that affirms the effects of situational factors on police behaviour. For example, using an observational method, Worden concluded that a police officer's decision to arrest is 'based to a significant degree on situational cues that officers interpret in similar ways' (1989: 702). These cues included the gravity of the violation, the presence of bystanders and other officers, and the suspects' attributes (race, sex, alcohol consumption) (see also Uildriks and van Mastrigt 1991). Another study, of complaints of excessive force, identified some basic situational factors that were often present in police-citizen encounters involving conflict (CJC 1997b). Conflicts occurred mostly late in the evening (and most often on weekends) in a police-controlled space (such as police vehicles, interview rooms and watch-houses) where no other people were present and the civilians involved had used alcohol or drugs. The study recommended changes to procedures to reduce the likelihood of conflict, including making greater use of summonses instead of arrests, better training in communication, teaming 'rookie' officers with experienced officers, and making more use of electronic recording devices in watchhouses and interview rooms.

Some inquiries into police have recommended reforms consistent with situational crime prevention methods. For example, the Knapp Report recommended eliminating as many situations as possible that expose police to corruption opportunities; and imposing strict controls over those situations where 'corruption hazards' are unavoidable, such as dealing with expense money and contacts with informants (Sherman 1978). Table 15.1 groups commonly recommended strategies to prevent police corruption that have a situational basis. The table shows there is a considerable implicit situational framework in many strategies.

Method

The purpose of this study was to test the hypothesis that situational crime prevention techniques are applicable in the prevention of police corruption. The experiment was conducted with a selection of complaints files held by the Queensland Criminal Justice Commission (CJC). The CJC reviews investigations of police conducted by the Queensland Police Service (QPS) and also conducts its own investigations of more serious matters. The QPS has approximately 7,000 officers and the CJC oversees the assessment of more than 3,000 allegations made against police per year (CJC 1997a). ('Allegations' are elements of 'complaints'.) Complaints can be made by anyone, including members of the public, public servants, politicians or lawyers. Police are under a statutory obligation to report all suspected misconduct. Complaints made to the QPS must be referred to the CJC. These factors add considerably to the strength of complaints data in providing information about the nature and causes of police corruption. Complaints against police are assessed by the CJC in terms of the following three categories:

1. Official Misconduct

2. Misconduct, or

3. Breach of Discipline.

Table 15.1: Police anti-corruption strategies containing a situational component

Technique	Description
Target Hardening	Strategies designed to increase the security of drugs, cash or other property seized by police.
Deflecting Offenders	The removal of arrest quotas which place a priority on quantity over quality and pressure police to fabricate evidence. Compulsory rotation, based upon the assumption that it takes time to develop the ties necessary for most corruption.
Controlling Facilitators	Computer audit trails to reduce the incidence of the misuse of police computer information facilities.
Entry Screening	Recruitment procedures such as the inclusion of background investigations, tests of emotional and psychological fitness, probationary periods for recruits.
Formal Surveillance	Strategies to increase effective supervision of personnel, such as management accountability, which makes it part of the commander's role to seek out and eliminate any corrupt activities that exist among the commander's personnel. Integrity testing which purposely places officers in potentially compromising positions and then monitors their resulting behaviour. The establishment of an external oversight body with capacity to investigate police and carry out physical surveillance to increase perceived risks of detection.
Surveillance by Employees	Protections and rewards for whistle-blowers and informers. Field Associates who are police officers (usually recently graduated recruits) recruited to secretly report any corruption they observe during the course of their regular duties.
Natural Surveillance by the Public	Strategies to encourage complaints, such as easy to access complaints systems.
Reducing Temptation	Eliminate police policies of discretionary enforcement for minor offences likely to give rise to corruption problems (for example, speeding, drink driving, prostitution).
Rule Setting	Strategies that centre on instilling professionalism via a detailed explicit code of ethics. The tightening of regulations governing situations that are most likely to give rise to allegations of corruption; such as strict procedures for dealing with seized money and drugs; systems for the registration of informants; and policies of requiring two people to be present during meetings with informants, counting money, and male-female encounters.
Identifying Property	Marking or tracing of drugs, cash or other property seized by police.
Denying Benefits	The use of the 'exclusionary rule' (where judges disallow evidence which is obtained illegally by police).

Official Misconduct and Misconduct cover degrees of more serious allegations and fall within the jurisdiction of the CJC. Discipline matters are dealt with by the QPS with review by the CJC.

The research plan entailed analysing CJC complaints files that were readily accessible to the authors. The plan was to analyse the files from the perspective of the opportunity-reducing techniques described by Clarke and Homel (1997). It must be emphasised that this was exploratory research. Proper implementation of situational prevention entails pre-test measures of offences, application of an intervention, and post-test measures of impact – with controls on other variables. This was not immediately possible in the setting within which the study was undertaken. Nonetheless, the approach was consistent with the first key step in situational prevention – analysis of situational variables – in order to test the hypothesis at that level.

A number of preliminary steps were taken to develop a workable sample. The first decision was to confine the sample to substantiated cases because these would be less contentious as valid cases of malpractice and because these files tended to contain more information. The second step involved creating a typology of complaints. This was done by synthesising CJC categories with Barker's (1983) typology (see Chapter 1), as follows:

1. 'Corruption' is any act involving the misuse of authority when a police officer receives or is promised a material reward or when a police officer violates criminal law.

2. 'Misconduct' is any violation of departmental rules or regulations that does not involve receipt of a material reward or gain.

A preliminary scan of files in both categories resulted in a decision to restrict the analysis to 'corruption' cases. The primary reason for this was that files involving more serious allegations tended to contain more specific information. Additionally, it was not envisaged that including misconduct complaints would add to the study as an example of how situational analysis could be used to develop preventive strategies. (For a more detailed description of these steps, and for the misconduct categories, see Ede 2000). Finally, a listing was compiled of all substantiated corruption files from 1993 to 1995. These provided the most consistent data when the study commenced, and resulted in 174 complaint files involving 213 allegations. The final sample is shown in Table 152. The next step was to construct a summary description for each of the corruption files using all the information in the file relevant to a situational analysis. This process was

Table 15.2: Final typology, police corruption

Corruption (Involves a material reward or criminal activity)		
Allegations (n=213)	**Code**	**Description**
	C1	Corruption of Authority
	C2	Kickbacks
	C3	Opportunistic Thefts (of A=drugs; B=money; C=other) from
9(B) 2(C)		-1 arrestees
2(B)		-2 victims
		-3 crime scenes
1, 3(B), 5(C)		-4 unprotected property
7(A), 5(B), 9(C)		-5 police possession
		-6 during searches
3	C4	Shakedowns
4	C5	Protection of Illegal Activities
	C6	Fixes
2		-1 traffic/regulatory offences
1		-2 misdemeanour/simple offences
		-3 crime
4	C7	Flaking/Padding
1	C8	Internal Payoffs
	C9	Direct Criminal Activities
4		-1 drug dealing
6		-2 drug use
2		-3 public exposure
4		-4 insurance fraud
5		-5 other fraud
1		-6 credit or SP gambling
1		-7 fare evasion
2		-8 other bill evasion
12		-9 dangerous driving/failing to stop
14		-10 driving under the influence
7		-11 unregistered vehicle/false number plates/ unlicensed driving
3		-12 stalking
2		-13 breaking domestic violence order
21		-14 assault
10		-15 sexual assault
1		-16 wilful damage
3		-17 shop-lifting
1		-18 murder

2		-19 unlicensed possession of concealable firearm
1		-20 sale of firearm without licence to possess
2		-21 receipt of stolen goods
1		-22 non-payment of fines
1		-23 failing to comply with national park regulations
1		-24 auto theft
6	C10	*Outside Employment Conflict of Interest*
	C11	*Theft from Employer*
5		-1 money
6		-2 property
4		-3 fraudulent time claim
9		-4 fraudulent expenditure, allowance, or leave claims
1		-5 legal advice
5	C12	*Sale of Confidential Information*
1	C13	*Sale of Licences*

was derived from the 'procedural analysis of offending', described by Cornish (1994). 'Crime scripts', that place elements of a crime in a time sequence, can provide a more comprehensive and explicit set of variables, 'drawing attention to a fuller range of possible intervention points' (1994: 151). Also noted beneath the descriptions were any situational techniques that may have been helpful in preventing the offending behaviour. Examples are given in Boxes 15.1 and 15.2.

Tables summarising common features of the cases were then constructed for each category in which there were sufficient files to make the exercise worthwhile. As many situational factors as possible were identified for each case. The table format was adapted from Poyner's (1986) use of 'crime sets', which position situational elements diagrammatically to allow for easier recognition of patterns. This allowed for a schematic version of the crime scripts.

Box 15.1

Typology Classification:
C3-5 Opportunistic Thefts – police possession (C=other)

File Number X

Younger brother of Officer S had his bicycle stolen. The officer admitted that on the way to the station to look at lost property he said to his brother something like, 'We will go and have a look for a ̄bike and if there is something similar to yours we will grab that one'. ̄nce at the station they were shown property by Officer R who ̄ ̄rned the bicycle and issued a receipt but failed to check the ̄ ̄al Criminal Offence Report (of when bicycle reported stolen).

216

Another officer did check this and discovered they were not the same bicycles and this investigation resulted.

Officer R was corrected for not checking with original paperwork and Officer S resigned pleading guilty of stealing in court.

Possible situational techniques

Rule Setting: returned property must be checked against original Criminal Offence Report.

Strengthening moral condemnation: 'stealing from the property room is stealing from the victim'.

Facilitating compliance: What happens to unclaimed recovered property? Could it be offered to those whose property was not found?

Box 15.2

Typology Classification:
C9-10 Direct Criminal Activities – driving under the influence

File Number X

Off-duty officer driving departmental vehicle at 1.30am involved in two accidents had blood alcohol concentration of 0.14 per cent. The first accident involved some limited damage to parked car and the second accident resulted in the police vehicle leaving road, overturning and being written off (total damages bill $21,600, no one injured). The officer was entitled to use vehicle for travel to and from work and he stated as the reason for use of departmental vehicle that while he was off-duty he was still on-call. In addition, he had gone straight from work to his birthday celebrations and had not yet returned home. The CJC's view was he used the vehicle for private purposes to drive to the birthday function (as he had even changed into civilian clothes). He left the vehicle for 7.5 hours while drinking with friends, and then drove the vehicle to another position in the same street for the private reason of obtaining a hotdog (at which time the parked car was damaged). Police were called to the scene at the time of the first accident as there were several witnesses, but upon seeing the officer sitting in the police vehicle eating, called to the station for further instructions from the Officer-in-Charge. They were instructed to return to the station.

The officer was fined $600, disqualified from driving for 7 months, reduced in rank pending completion of 250 hours community service, and made to pay the damages bill. The Officer-in-Charge was reprimanded.

> ### *Possible situational techniques*
>
> *Formal surveillance*: better supervision by Officer-in-Charge would have prevented second accident; better supervision by managers in general would help prevent police vehicles being used for non-work purposes.
>
> *Rule setting*: police must not be in charge of a police vehicle if they have consumed any alcohol.
>
> *Strengthening moral condemnation*: 'When those who enforce the law, break the law, there is no law'. 'Don't be a bloody blue idiot'. (The word 'blue' refers to the colour of QPS uniforms.)

Results

The most productive findings were in the four categories of 'Opportunistic Thefts' (C3), 'Direct Criminal Activities – driving under the influence' (C9-10), 'Direct Criminal Activities – assault' (C9-14) (the assaults were off-duty) and 'Theft from Employer' (C11). In the remaining categories there were either insufficient cases or a situational analysis did not appear to be applicable. Two examples of summary tables are provided below, for 'Opportunistic Theft' (Table 15.3) and 'Theft from Employer' (Table 15.4).

Notes for Table 15.3: Opportunistic Thefts (C3) ⟶

Notes: 1. **C3-1** from arrestees (cases 1-6), **-2** from victims (case 7), **-3** from crime scenes (cases 8-9), **-4** unprotected property (case 10), **-5** from police possession (cases 11-31), **-6** during searches (none). 2. 'Failure to Comply Fully With Standing Procedures' includes not providing full details in paper work, not checking properly against inventories or criminal reports, and property not verified/counted in prisoner's or other officer's presence. 3. Case 7 involved an officer who was illegally charging the owners of stolen cars for the return of the cars. The money was paid back into QPS accounts and then used to continue the undercover operation against car thieves. 4. The number of 'cases' presented in the summary tables do not correspond to the number of allegations as presented in Table 15.2. This is because of four main reasons. One 'case' can involve several allegations or even several files where the same or similar allegations may have been repeated. Allegations included in the typology show some level of substantiation but sometimes this substantiation may not be against an officer but a member of the public also involved in the case or even the complainant in the event of a false complaint. The review of the file uncovered more specific information than was contained in the file summary revealing that the allegation was more appropriately classified under another category. Most often when this situation occurred, one of the misconduct categories was more appropriate than the corruption category. Some files were unavailable at the time of analysis.

Table 15.3: Opportunistic Thefts (C3)

Analysis number	Failure to comply fully with standing procedures	Property not put in property room – paper work completed	Property not put in property room – paper work not completed	Poor management practices	Lack of training and experience of officers	Property taken from exhibit room	Paper work contained clerical errors	Property missing
1					Y	Y		$100
2		Y						Gold jewellery
3	Y							$93.40
4	Y							$250
5					Y		Y	$203
6	Y							$69.05
7				Y				See note below
8			Y					Tool box (value $5,000)
9			Y					$9,160
10			Y					$100
11						Y		Bicycle
12			Y	Y				2-way radio
13						Y		Gun case
14	Y						Y	Small envelope of green leaf material
15	Y			Y	Y			Camera
16	Y			Y	Y		Y	Cannabis plant, seeds, smoking paraphernalia
17			Y	Y	Y			Sports bag, 6 gold-plated spoons 2 CDs 20 cents
18	Y	Y						3 packets of cigarettes
19	Y							Jacket
20	Y	Y						3 City Counc' warning ligh'
21	Y		Y		Y			Mobile tele'

No.								Item
22	Y				Y		Y	(extra cannabis plants found)
23						Y		Firearm
24	Y				Y	Y		Set of green satin sheets
25							Y	500 cannabis seeds
26	Y		Y					Sleeping bag (borrowed, used, returned)
27	Y				Y	Y		400 grams of cannabis
28	Y		Y					1 head of cattle
29	Y		Y	Y	Y			Wallet
30	Y				Y	Y		4 casks wine, cask port, carton beer
31				Y		Y	Y	$376.40

The summary table for 'Opportunistic Theft' (Table 15.3) revealed deficiencies in the following areas of police responsibility.

1. poor management practices (11 cases, 35%),

2. the performance of duties by inexperienced or untrained officers (10 cases, 32%),

3. inadequate security of exhibit rooms (6 cases 19%).

It also showed that the following features were common from an offender point of view:

1. failure to store property in the property rooms (10 cases, 32%),

2. clerical errors (7 cases 23%),

3. failure to fully comply with standing procedures (17 cases, 55%).

The summary table for 'Theft from Employer' (Table 15.4) revealed deficiencies in the following areas:

1. poor supervision of accounts, property, over-time claims or extra expense claims (12 cases, 75%),

2. inexperienced/untrained officers assigned to handle accounting or their own extra expense claims (5 cases, 31%),

3. lack of, or poor, procedures for officers to follow (5 cases, 31%),

   storage facility not secure or too many staff with access (4 cases 25%).

Table 15.4: Theft from Employer (C11)

Analysis number	Failure to comply fully with standing	Poor or lack of standing procedures	Poor book keeping	Poor supervision	Lack of training	Safe/strongbox/ Storage not secure/ Too many with access	Property missing
1	Y		Y	Y	Y	Y	$40
2		Y	Y				$1421 (from Police Club)
3		Y	Y			Y	$235 (from gift collection)
4		Y	Y	Y	Y		$416.35
5			Y		Y	Y	$89.50
6	Y			Y			Bench
7	Y			Y		Y	Firearms
8		Y		Y*			Tape measure and torch
9		Y		Y *			2 sets of police overalls
10	Y			Y			Hand-held radio and claims for unnecessary overtime.
11	Y		Y	Y			One day's overtime
12	Y		Y	Y			False claim for escort duty
13	Y		Y	Y	Y		Extra travelling allowance
14	Y			Y			$13,000 in Workers' Compensation Payments
15			Y	Y			$57.05
16	Y		Y		Y		Extra mileage claim

Notes: 1. **C11-1** money (cases 1-5), **-2** property (cases 6-10), **-3** fraudulent time claim (cases 10-12), **-4** fraudulent expenditure, allowance or leave claims (cases 13-16). Ca[se] 10 involves both property and fraudulent time claims. 2. Note 4 from Table 3 also applies here. * Of items.

The following deficiencies were common from an offender point of view:
1. poor book keeping (10 cases, 63%),
2. failure to fully comply with standing procedures (9 cases, 56%).

In several instances – mainly involving overtime, allowance or claim discrepancies – officers mentioned they felt owed the money for unpaid overtime.

Table 15.5: Opportunity Reducing Techniques Derived from Theft Findings

Target Hardening	Establish minimum standards throughout the Police Service for the storage of money (even social funds) and other valuables (including firearms, see case 7).
Access Control	Reduce number of officers with access to money storage.
Strengthening Moral Condemnation	Cashbox stickers: 'Only a dog steals from mates' On forms: 'Claiming for time you did not work is stealing', 'Check dates as false claims will result in departmental action' On pay-slips: 'Paid work while on sick leave is stealing' Similar warning on Workers' Compensation Board payments.
Surveillance by Employees	Rotation of treasurers would prevent long periods where one person sees the books. Policies ensuring dual responsibility (two signatures) for monies paid out and requiring the presence of another officer when counting or moving money or valuables.
Formal Surveillance	More regular checks on books, claim forms and QPS property in the possession of officers. More stock-takes of goods and property storage facilities. Placing the onus for loss upon managers to ensure that checks and stocktakes are conducted thoroughly.
Target Removal	More frequent banking would have prevented the large loss suffered by the Police Club (case 2).
Identifying Property	QPS property was stolen in five cases. The marking of property clearly and permanently with the 'QPS' initials may deter theft of property for private use.
Rule Setting	Education of officers in the rules for claiming travelling allowances and the training of officers acting in positions with book keeping responsibility. More onus to comply with existing rules via the use of sanctions for failing to comply and rewards (such as supervisor recognition) for following procedures. Establish rules where none or poor ones exist (for example, in many book keeping areas and in regard to the use of QPS property by officers over long time periods).
Facilitating Compliance	The provision of an in-house financial consultant available for appointments or telephone advice. Paying officers for overtime rather than fostering the expectation that officers should not be compensated for this overtime, which can result in an officer's rationale to recover such payment from the QPS via corrupt means. Making forms easier to complete via such methods as redesign and printing calculation rates on the forms.

From the summary tables situational interventions were devised which could be useful in preventing such corruption. The 'Opportunistic Theft' cases suggested some obvious interventions involving rule setting and improved procedures. To illustrate the situational formulation in more detail, techniques derived from summary Table 15.4 – Theft from Employer – are listed in Table 15.5.

Results in the categories 'Direct Criminal Activities – driving under the influence' and 'Direct Criminal Activities – assault' are not shown here (for details see Ede 2001). However, poor supervision of police vehicle usage figured in the DUI cases (see Text Box 2), as did officer relationship and work stress problems that may have been amenable to management interventions. Five of the 16 assault cases were domestic incidents, and it is possible that police management could provide better access to welfare support or relationship assistance. The remaining cases involved situational elements such as drinking and escalating disputes between males in licensed premises, but these appeared resistant to direct situational interventions by police management.

Discussion

The findings of this study provide support, albeit limited, for the hypothesis that situational crime prevention methods are applicable to police corruption. Sufficient homogenous cases were gathered from three years of complaints data to construct crime scripts and summary tables, and to allow situational analysis in four categories of corruption. This resulted in some potentially very useful recommendations for closing off opportunities. None of the corruption categories involved what would be regarded as classic corruption in the form of bribery or shakedowns. Nonetheless, the categories covered conduct officially deemed corruption – largely by virtue of being crimes. The most likely explanation for the absence of more extensive positive findings lies in the very small numbers of cases in the numerous corruption categories. The inference that situational analysis is not appropriate should only be made if more homogenous data were added to these smaller categories and summary tables still did not produce fruitful results. It should be noted that the types of deviance covered by the four categories were diverse, suggesting that, with sufficient data, many categories of police corruption and misconduct would be amenable to situational analysis.

The lack of relevant information recorded in complaints files raises a crucial question. Are investigators recording information relevant to prevention efforts or are they simply focused on facts that are needed to prove or disprove an allegation? Poyner (1986: 27) has outlined the essential elements that need to be addressed in detail to maximise the diagnostic capacity of information about crime. These are: 'what happened, where it happened, when it happened, who was involved, physical environment and social environment'. The frequently cryptic nature of the recorded information in the CJC complaints files suggests that more specific information is known but not recorded. This may be because the investigator did not realise the information could be useful or because there was no designated place for recording it. It is also essential that the information is entered onto an electronic database to allow for more efficient analysis than is possible with hardcopy files.

Conclusion

This study has demonstrated how opportunity factors are relevant to understanding some forms of police corruption, and how these factors are potentially useful in designing anti-corruption strategies. Complaints against police, especially substantiated cases, are a key source for this purpose. It follows that data derived from complaints against police have been under-utilised in corruption prevention. More useful findings would require a much more systematic process for recording situationally relevant information, with case file formats designed to require the inclusion of as much situationally-specific information as possible.

Acknowledgement

The authors would like to thank the Queensland Criminal Justice Commission for assistance with this project and for permission to use the data.

References

Barker, T, 1983, 'Rookie Police Officers' Perceptions of Police Occupational Deviance', *Police Studies* 6(2), 30-38.

CJC, 1997a, *Integrity in the Queensland Police Service: Implementation and Impact of the Fitzgerald Inquiry Reforms*, Criminal Justice Commission.

CJC, 1997b, *Reducing Police-Civilian Conflict: An Analysis of Assault Complaints Against Queensland Police*, Criminal Justice Commission.

Clarke, R, 1992, *Situational Crime Prevention: Successful Case Studies*, Harrow and Heston.

Clarke, R and Homel, R, 1997, 'A Revised Classification of Situational Crime Prevention Techniques', in S Lab (ed), *Crime Prevention at a Crossroads*, Anderson.

Cordner, G, 1978, 'Open and Closed Models of Police Organisations: Traditions, Dilemmas and Practical Considerations', *Journal of Police Science and Administration* 6(1) 22-34.

Cornish, D, 1994, 'The Procedural Analysis of Offending and its Relevance to Situational Prevention', *Crime Prevention Studies* 3 151-96

Crank, J, 1998, *Understanding Police Culture*, Anderson.

Ede, A, 2000, *The Prevention of Police Corruption and Misconduct: A Criminological Analysis of Complaints Against Police*, PhD Thesis, Griffith University.

Gottfredson, M and Hirschi, T, 1990, *A General Theory of Crime*, Stanford University Press.

Pease, K, 1994, 'Crime Prevention', in M Maguire, R Morgan and R Reiner (eds), *The Oxford Handbook of Criminology*, Clarendon.

Poyner, B, 1986, 'A Model for Action', in K Heal and G Laycock (eds) *Situational Crime Prevention: From Theory into Practice*, Home Office Research and Planning Unit.

Sherman, L, 1978, *Scandal and Reform – Controlling Police Corruption*, University of California Press.

Uildriks, N and van Mastrigt, H, 1991, *Policing Police Violence*, Kluwer.

Worden, R 1989, 'Situational and Attitudinal Explanations of Police Behaviour: A Theoretical Reappraisal and Empirical Assessment', *Law and Society Review* 23(4), 667-711.

Index